THE
CHALLENGER
CUSTOMER

THE
CHALLENGER
CUSTOMER

Selling to the Hidden Influencer
Who Can Multiply Your Results

Brent Adamson, Matthew Dixon,
Pat Spenner, and Nick Toman

PORTFOLIO / PENGUIN

PORTFOLIO / PENGUIN
An imprint of Penguin Random House LLC
375 Hudson Street
New York, New York 10014
penguin.com

ISBN 978-1-59184-815-8

Printed in the United States of America
1   3   5   7   9   10   8   6   4   2

Set in Minion Pro
Designed by Sabrina Bowers

To the members of CEB around the world, who challenge us every day to deliver insights worthy of their time and attention

CONTENTS

FOREWORD

The odd combination of where I live and what I do for a living have turned me into a bit of a walking punch line over the past decade or so.

Let me explain.

I live in the Greater Washington, D.C., metropolitan area—the seat of the U.S. government—and I run one of the world's most widely used sources of insight into corporate performance. So several hundred times a year in cities around the world, I introduce myself by saying "I'm here from Washington, D.C., to share some insights about best management practices."

Business cultures differ widely across regions and nations, so the response to this statement runs the gamut from "You've got to be sh*&%ng me" (Silicon Valley, Amsterdam) to "I'm sorry, I think I misheard you" (Singapore, Minneapolis) to "Ah, you'll feel at home here after a glass of wine. Try the Super Tuscan" (Rome). While the tone of responses varies, no one misses the irony at the heart of the statement. Like many national capitals, Washington has become a byword for organizational dysfunction. This is largely because citizens believe the U.S. Congress and similar deliberative legislative bodies that seem to take forever to act are useless, especially since when they *do* act they achieve only modest—if any—results.

All around the world, I routinely hear how much better off we'd be if only government would run itself like a business. The unfortunate truth is that—in many respects—it already does.

More specifically, business is increasingly running itself like a dysfunctional legislative body.

I THOUGHT THIS BOOK WAS ABOUT SALES AND MARKETING?

You're now thinking that you've picked up the wrong book, but the headline of our recent work on sales, marketing, and the buying process suggests that in most B2B commercial environments purchasing looks a lot like a bickering Congress or Parliament on a bad day.

That's why we've done a deep dive into the modern company's buying process. As we started comparing notes across companies and industries, we realized that the stories commercial leaders were sharing were eerily similar to our own experiences—particularly when we were working with leaders to engineer dramatic innovations or step-function improvements in outcomes.

As the research team's work continued, my own mind kept going back to a conversation I had with the controller of a German multinational who was using our work to radically simplify and accelerate information flow through his company. I visited on a day when the project's kickoff (and ultimate ROI) had been delayed by *three months* due to a last-minute review requested by something called the "excellence assurance center of excellence" (that is not a typo).

The controller was in what could (charitably) be called a foul mood. The project itself was slated to last only six months, and he had enthusiastic support from the CEO and partnership from the CIO and head of HR. In terms of large-scale change management, he had really done everything right. And yet—at the eleventh hour, out of nowhere—a new stakeholder arrived on the scene, slowing down and lowering the aspiration of this fast-moving and ambitious effort. Leaning back in his chair, the CFO moaned, "I didn't even know we had an excellence assurance COE."

He got up, walked toward the window, and said, "This is a total [long German word that definitely didn't mean "Really great day for our company: I just couldn't be prouder to work here!"].

And it wasn't a great day. Nor, by the end, was it a great project. By the time the COE review was complete, the project was rescoped twice, suffered three delays, and ultimately delivered a fourth of the original business value.

When I shared this story with an HR chief of a major conglomerate, she remarked, "That's ridiculous." I nodded, thinking she was going to share a story about how decisive she and her C-suite peers were relative to this poor controller's company. She continued, laughing. "I once lost two months to our firm's project-naming committee. He should be happy with that outcome."

THE NEW REALITY FOR SALES: BIG, COMPLEX PROCESSES AND BIG, GERMAN CURSE WORDS

If it's this difficult for a C-level executive to drive change through an organization, just imagine how hard it is for someone on the outside to galvanize support for a disruptive new solution. The data that we analyzed points to purchase processes characterized by an ever-expanding array of stakeholders with often competing agendas, changing purchase criteria, and—most troubling—a reversion to lowest-common-denominator behaviors.

Why?

We see this behavior as part of a broader trend in corporate operations. Several factors are reshaping how companies operate and make decisions, and all of them have implications for sales and marketing.

First, simply put, big companies are just *bigger*. The smallest Fortune 500 company is many times the size of the smallest one just twenty years ago. And with big size comes big complexity.

Information flows are multiplying quickly. While this means more educated buyers, it also means more people in the process—each with access to competing information and each empowered to form (and share) opinions. At its worst, information overflow can lead to *complete* decision paralysis—bad for companies and bad for the suppliers trying to engage with them.

Professional and control functions are strengthening within companies, with many having a say in virtually every decision. This is driven partly as a result of the need for scale and consistency across larger entities and partly because of concerns about risk and regulation. Obviously from a commercial perspective, the most important of these is procurement, but procurement is only one of the folks invited to the party—compliance, data privacy, IT security, EH&S, and quality often all weigh in on major buying decisions.

Emphasis on collaborative decision making is increasing in an attempt to reap the benefits of diverse perspectives on business issues.

None of these things are bad. In fact, all are undeniably good—bigger opportunities, more information, professional and analytic participants, and collaboration among different parties all ought to *strengthen* buying dynamics and make the process more likely to yield a successful purchase.

But all too often they don't. Different functions bring different agendas to the table. Excessive collaboration adds time (but not value) to the process. Information abundance buries the core issues; opportunities that initially combined strategic advantage for the buyer with strategic opportunity for the seller get watered down or abandoned altogether. In the end, if any deal is reached, it's for less scope and impact than what was initially proposed.

IF YOU CAN'T BEAT 'EM, MOBILIZE 'EM

By now, I've painted a pretty depressing picture of what lies ahead: slow processes, stalled deals, and customers unable to agree, settling for the lowest common denominator—or worse still, the status quo. But, thankfully, that's not what's in store. Beyond documenting and understanding the drivers of this tough new buying environment, we also found pioneering strategies for not only surviving, but also thriving in it.

Supported by an enormous amount of research, real-world sales experience, and practical lessons from leading sales and marketing teams, this book lays out a step-by-step path anyone can follow to dramatically improve commercial performance. It's a path few are on today, but any company can pursue by carefully identifying and equipping a few select customer stakeholders to far more effectively mobilize the colleagues around them.

Whether you're in sales, marketing, service, or support—from the front line to the corner office—each chapter of *The Challenger Customer* provides surprising findings for rewriting the rules for how the best companies connect with current customers, dramatically boosting sales performance as a result. All designed to drive decisive action among customer

organizations increasingly predisposed to systematically avoid it. I hope
you read it all the way through and consider its recommendations closely.
Not only will your organization thank you, but your customers will too.

Tom Monahan
Chairman and Chief Executive Officer
CEB

THE
CHALLENGER
CUSTOMER

THE HARDEST PART OF SELLING SOLUTIONS

This is a book of surprises.

Chief among them is the surprising decline of historically effective selling strategies that now fail to generate anything near hoped-for returns.

Despite suppliers' improved ability to convey their unique value, there's strong evidence that today's customers are less willing than ever before to actually *pay* for that value, even when they perceive it—at least not when they believe the next best, less expensive alternative is "good enough" to meet their needs. While today's suppliers may win the battle for awareness, consideration, recommendation, and even preference, they still lose when it comes to what matters most: getting paid. As exasperating as it seems, the very solutions most companies developed to escape commoditization have themselves become commoditized in the eyes of their customers.

It all leaves commercial leaders wondering, "What do we do now? What's left when the classic sales and marketing playbook we've relied on for so many years falls short?"

It was partly in response to these questions that CEB's sales and marketing practice conducted the research that led to the publication of *The Challenger Sale*—an in-depth examination of the sales rep behaviors most likely to succeed in today's commercial environment. But while the debate raged around us as to whether Challenger was right or wrong, new or old, too controversial or not controversial enough, we were focused on something else entirely: What else is there?

In fact, the more research we did, the more insights we uncovered and the more convinced we became that there was a second part to this story—one potentially more powerful than the first. It turns out, the far bigger story isn't about suppliers' struggle to *sell* solutions, it's the customer's struggle to *buy* them. While there are many reasons customers fail to buy, our data shows clearly that the primary culprit is the dramatic increase in both number and diversity of customer stakeholders typically involved in solutions purchases today—and, more damning, the severe dysfunction that is bred by the ever-expanding number of individuals who need to weigh in before a deal is signed.

In the end, what has long seemed to salespeople like a well-designed strategy to "stick it to suppliers" or beat them up on price is more often than not a function of a far less sinister but arguably infinitely more intractable problem: the inability of customer stakeholders *themselves* to achieve broad agreement on a common course of action in the first place. Much of the commoditization pressure suppliers face today isn't the result of customers' willingness to settle for "good enough," it's *their failure to agree on anything more.* And that's a challenge most sales and marketing strategies fail to solve as it's a problem they were never designed to address in the first place. In fact, current sales and marketing tactics *exacerbate* this problem rather than overcome it.

Of course, it's hard enough to *sell* effectively. How exactly are we supposed to help our customers to *buy* more effectively? Here, the research holds a final, delightful surprise: just as we learned in our previous work that it is critical to have *Challenger sellers*, our latest work shows that it is equally (if not more) critical to have *Challenger buyers.*

In a series of quantitative studies, we were able to isolate and study these individuals. These aren't your run-of-the-mill "coaches" or advocates doling out information to the sales rep and vocally championing a given supplier with colleagues. These are a special breed of customer stakeholder focused much more on marshaling the internal resources and buy-in necessary to compel their colleagues to collectively think and act beyond the status quo, *irrespective* of supplier. As we've studied these individuals in a great deal of depth, what we've found is: in a world of diverse and potentially dysfunctional customer stakeholders, it's not just *that* you challenge, but *who* you challenge that really matters. To win today, you need a Challenger *inside* the customer organization.

These customer Challengers exist and can be found—but only if suppliers are looking for them in the first place. Because everything we've learned in all of our research clearly suggests that finding these individuals, winning them over, and then equipping them to win takes a completely different kind of commercial strategy than what's worked so well in the past.

Who are these customer Challengers? We call them *Mobilizers*, and this is their story.

CHAPTER ONE

THE DARK SIDE OF CUSTOMER CONSENSUS

THE PROBLEM OF 1 OF 3

If there is one concern most top of mind among senior sales and marketing leaders around the world, it is the inexorable downward pressure on deal size, margins, and growth as they navigate continued uncertain times. While their CEOs mandate a "return to double-digit growth," commercial leaders find themselves more frequently than ever before competing on little else but price.

Perhaps most frustrating, however, is that traditionally proven strategies designed to drive that growth no longer work nearly as well as they used to—leaving senior executives to assume they've somehow lost their way, broadly calling for a return "back to basics" as they exhort their teams to "recommit to more disciplined execution." However, getting ever better at an approach already proven to fail does little more than demoralize everyone in the face of ever-deepening underperformance.

As the head of sales and marketing at a global industrial fragrances company recently put it, "I just don't understand. We're the leading supplier in our industry. Our products are world class, our brand second to none, and our salespeople are highly skilled. There's not a single deal in our industry where we're not invited to participate—we make it to the table every single time."

"But even when we do," he went on, "we're always one of three suppliers at the table. Despite all of our commercial strength, we end up competing on nothing but price every single time. It's killing our business. Our premium position simply can't sustain that kind of margin erosion."

It's an incredibly common but still maddeningly frustrating scenario.

Here's a company that excels across every commercial metric that might matter but still faces deep commoditization nonetheless.

Welcome to what we've come to call the "1 of 3 Problem," where a supplier commonly wins the battle for customer consideration—even preference—but ends up competing against two others on little but price nevertheless.

How to respond? Typically, heads of sales and marketing would tell you, "If customers fail to fully pay us for all the incremental value we provide, then clearly they must not appreciate all the incremental value we provide." So they direct their teams to "sharpen" the company's value proposition. They equip reps to "more crisply" articulate the many ways in which their company can not only meet customers' needs, but exceed them. They carefully redesign marketing campaigns and sales collateral to better communicate the broad range of their company's "best-in-class, cutting-edge solutions" and "unique ability to provide moments of deep customer delight."

And yet in today's world, even when delivered well, most customers' reaction to suppliers' costly efforts to better articulate their company's value isn't so much "Wow! We had no idea!" but rather something akin to "Yeah, we knew that already."

Today's customers will often concede the point right up front, responding, "We totally agree! We think you guys are great! Your solution is by far the best, and we'd love to partner with you!"

Which feels fantastic, until they add, "In fact, *that's why* you're one of the three companies we've invited to participate in this bidding process! But as much as we *love* your solution, this other company's solution is good enough, and they're a lot cheaper. So if we can get *your* solution at *their* price, then we're good to go!"

And that's painful.

Despite suppliers' best efforts to better convey their unique value, there's little evidence that today's customers are any more willing to *pay* for that value even when they perceive it. At least not when they believe the next best alternative to be sufficiently "good enough."

So a supplier wins in every way possible—raising awareness, consideration, preference, even recommendations—and still loses when it comes to what matters most: getting paid. This is the core dilemma of selling solutions today: most suppliers' single biggest competitor isn't so much the competition's ability to sell as their own customer's willingness to settle.

Across the last five years, the CEB team has dug into this challenge with a huge amount of research into both sales and marketing capability and customer buying behavior, seeking to understand what suppliers can do differently going forward to avoid the underperformance of past approaches. What we've learned is fascinating—if not more than a little bit troubling. Much of the problem lies less in a supplier organization's inability to *sell* effectively and far more in a customer organization's inability to *buy* effectively. And a very large part of that challenge lies squarely in customers' struggle to achieve common agreement across the wide range of stakeholders now typically involved in virtually any solutions purchase.

THE RISE (AND FALL) OF THE 5.4

One might argue that the challenge of customer consensus is nothing new. Indeed, we've been hearing of the problem for years. And, of course, the economic downturn in 2009 did nothing but exacerbate the problem as increasingly cost-conscious and risk-averse decision makers balked at making even the smallest decisions on their own.

And yet, if we fast-forward to today, the strange thing is, while the global economy has significantly rebounded across virtually every metric that might matter, in that same time, the customer consensus challenge has become far worse. In a recent survey of senior sales leaders, we found nearly 80 percent reported the number of customer stakeholders involved in a typical deal continues to rise.

Why? There are all sorts of reasons for the added number of individuals involved in a deal today, but chief among them would be:

1. A sustained and widespread aversion to risk among both individual customer stakeholders and organizations in the aftermath of the global economic crisis

2. The fact that most "solutions" today have both a technological component and a higher price tag necessitating not only the involvement of IT but additional scrutiny by operations and procurements executives

3. A greater concern among legal and compliance officers that all corporate initiatives meet tighter regulatory requirements and information protection protocols

4. Governmental regulatory reform (especially in health care) forcing
   industry-wide shifts in how customers operate and buy

5. Customers' efforts to expand operations globally, bringing new
   regional players to the table

6. The simple fact that most "solutions" offered by suppliers today are
   purposefully designed to integrate more customer functions and
   tasks than ever before in order to provide customers higher impact,
   better value, and improved ease of use

7. New management styles and organizational structures leading to
   flatter, more networked organizations that place a premium on more
   frequent cross-silo collaboration

Every one of these trends not only means more people involved in
a typical purchase than ever before, but more important, more people
across more roles who likely hadn't been involved in the past. Of course,
none of these trends is likely to reverse itself anytime soon. Bottom line,
it's nearly impossible today to get a deal done without accounting for a
seemingly vast array of budget owners, influencers, end users, third-party
consultants, you name it.

But as the consensus story continues to evolve, the thing we find most
troubling isn't the rise in number of people who have to "buy in" but the
equally dramatic increase in number of people who have to "sign off." So
unlike the consensus challenge of 2006, which largely centered around
winning over a single, senior decision maker and his or her team, today's
consensus challenge has evolved into something far more complex. Today,
whether suppliers are selling to a customer with 50 or 50,000 people, they
rarely find that almost mythical "senior decision maker" able to individually approve a complex deal on behalf of all of their colleagues.

Instead, more often than not, it's purchase by committee. It's collective
consensus across a formal or informal group of senior employees, each with
the ability to stop a deal if it fails to meet their particular needs, or speak to
their individual priorities. And that problem, we find, stretches well beyond
just larger customers or more strategic accounts. Consensus challenges are

just as likely to crop up in small and medium customers where suppliers have traditionally been able to conduct most business through a single point of contact. As one sales leader in the food and beverage industry jokingly observed, "Even when we sell to mom-and-pops, we've got a mom and a pop, and they don't always see eye to eye." Small business isn't exempt from the consensus challenge.

In fact, let's put some real numbers against this problem. In a survey of over 3,000 stakeholders involved in a typical B2B purchase, we found that customers themselves report an average of 5.4 different people formally involved in a typical purchase decision. That's 5.4 opportunities for someone to say "No." And that one simple number raises all sorts of questions for suppliers. Things like: Do we even know who those 5.4 people are? For that matter, does our *customer* even know who those 5.4 people are? Sometimes they're not sure either! What does each of these individuals care about? How does our solution meet their individual needs? How do we win them over?

The real trick in this new world of customer consensus is: this isn't just 5.4 different people, it's 5.4 different perspectives. *Three-quarters* of customer stakeholders we surveyed told us these 5.4 individuals span a wide variety of roles, teams, functions, and geographies. And really, this is the true challenge of consensus today. It's not so much that there are *more people* in a sale that makes things so hard, but that there are so many *new perspectives*.

Every supplier has a version of this exact same story. For example, if you sell an IT solution, almost certainly you've traditionally called on the customer's CIO and his or her team. But as most IT solutions today touch other parts of the business (or more business decisions than ever before now feature a strong technological component), now you're just as likely to *also* sell to CMOs, COOs, or heads of HR—depending on who's using your system. Additionally, the broader scope and bigger footprint of your solution probably means you're also speaking with the CFO, to procurement, and maybe to regional presidents. Not to mention a whole range of end users, influencers, third-party consultants, and even potential partners. And lest we forget, legal (aka the "Sales Prevention Department"). Indeed, one head of marketing in the health care industry recently told us, "For us it's not 5.4 people, but 5.4 *committees* of people!"

Bottom line, every supplier has their version of the same story, regardless of industry. We used to sell to X, and now we sell to X, Y, Z . . . as well as A, B, and sometimes C. And every one of them is different. Different priorities, different perspectives, different authority, even different levels of knowledge of what the supplier's solution actually does in the first place, and why that matters.

That's the *real* challenge of customer consensus today. It isn't just a *quantity* problem. It's a *diversity* problem. Because when these groups come together to make a decision, almost inevitably, it seems, things fall apart.

Take a look at figure 1.1.

FIG. 1.1. Purchase Intent, by Buying Team Size

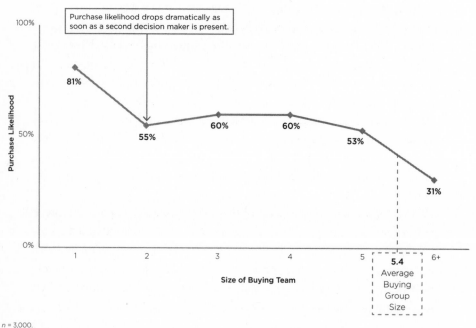

n = 3,000.
Source: CEB analysis.

In a survey of 3,000 customer stakeholders involved in a B2B purchase, we asked respondents the degree to which they agreed with the statement "We will definitely buy from this supplier in the next six months" on a scale from 1 to 10 (we tested other time horizons and got virtually the exact same result. Six months allowed us to capture the largest sample).

We then mapped those responses according to total number of people on the buying team.

Now, the path of that line in figure 1.1 tells a dramatic story, featuring two distinct downward inflection points. The first represents a rapid drop in purchase likelihood just by adding *one* more person to the purchase decision. So going from one to two people means overall likelihood to buy goes off a cliff, dropping from 80 percent to the mid-50s (indeed, apparently mom and pop don't always agree). Then things level out for a bit until we get past person number five. Then there's a second cliff where likelihood to buy sinks like a stone to a dismal 30 percent. As a supplier selling to the 5.4, this is a hard graph to look at. From left to right, this is a one-way ticket to indecision with a final stop somewhere squarely in the center of what some sales leaders have come to call the "solutions graveyard."

From a research perspective, this finding proved hugely important as it gave us the first indication in all our data that suppliers don't have nearly so much of a selling problem as perhaps they do a *buying* problem—brought on largely by the new and wildly diverse cast of characters typically involved today in any solutions purchase.

For suppliers, however, that's a tough finding to digest, as it's hard to know how to manage this kind of challenge. After all, customer diversity isn't something suppliers can make go away by telling their customer, "Actually, we don't think your legal or procurement teams need to look this one over." For even if that attempt were to succeed in the short run, the long-term consequences can be costly. As the chief sales officer at a global manufacturing company recently told us, "We actually tried exactly that just last year. And it worked! We successfully cut everyone out of the purchase other than the head of operations and got the deal done in record time!

"The problem," he went on, "was that when we then went to implement what we'd sold, all those people we'd previously cut out realized what was happening and completely overwhelmed the installation with objections and conflicts that we could have handled in advance if we'd just included them to begin with.

"In the end," he said, "as hard as it may have been, we would have been far better off getting all those individuals on board as part of the purchase process because the bad will we generated as part of a rocky implementation not only undermined this deal, but likely cut us out of future deals for the foreseeable future." It's an incredibly tough thing to find out after it's too late to do anything about it.

But it raises the questions: If suppliers can't fully (or even partially) eliminate customer diversity as part of a sale, then how can they at least manage it more effectively? What's the best strategy for selling to increasingly diverse customer buying groups?

TRACK THEM ALL DOWN AND WIN THEM ALL OVER

Around the world, the strategy for selling to diverse stakeholders follows the same, frustrating reality. It requires a whole lot of work, and it requires a whole lot of time. In fact, most sales professionals agree, the battle for customer consensus plays out across two dimensions, not just one.

FIG. 1.2. Common Consensus-Building Strategy

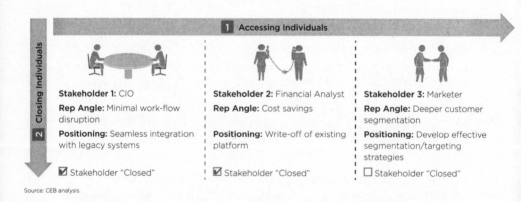

Source: CEB analysis.

The first dimension is a challenge of access—simply winning the right to get in front of all the individuals who matter in the first place. And that's hard. With all those new people involved, the first step is figuring out who they all *are* in the first place. We encourage sellers to begin with the question "Who are our 5.4 for this particular deal?" It's a disarmingly simple question, but often surprisingly difficult to answer. In many cases, these aren't just new individuals, but new roles, functions, and maybe even geographies that that supplier has traditionally never called on before. And chances are pretty good that customer stakeholders' exact role in the purchase may be somewhat murky even to themselves.

Beyond identifying them, however, is the more difficult task of winning the right to speak with them, particularly as a seller may have little to no prior experience or existing connections to fall back on—even in existing accounts with otherwise long-standing relationships. What's worse, from the perspective of that target stakeholder, they may see no especially pressing need to talk to that supplier at all if they fail to see a relationship between their immediate concerns and the supplier's capabilities.

Beyond winning access to each of these individuals, however, sellers still face the even greater challenge of winning each of them over, ensuring they position their offering as precisely as possible, so as to resonate with each stakeholder's priorities and needs. And they have to do that 5.4 times—tracking them all down and then winning them all over.

Now, one might argue there's nothing new here. After all, that's nothing more than just plain good selling, same as it's been for years. But the real challenge is, this is no longer a single sale, but a *serial* sale, each one a little different and carefully positioned to each stakeholder. To be sure, it is great selling. But it's great selling times 5.4! Checking off each stakeholder as they go, ensuring they've bought in before they move on to the next one.

This one challenge has become the heart and soul of most sales managers' check-in calls with their team: "So who have you called on so far? How did it go? Are they on board? How do you know? OK, who's next? How are you going to get in front of them? How are you going to position things for them? How do you think they'll react? What objections do you think they might have [insert role play]? OK, who's left after that?"

So reps work from the known to the less known, the familiar to the less familiar, slowly building consensus step-by-step as they seek to collect a "Yes" from each of those conversations.

A tenured sales manager we interviewed memorably compared it to the plate-spinning act at the circus. You get the first plate spinning on the stick and then move on to the second. You get the second one spinning and move to the third. But somewhere along the line, the first plate has started to wobble, so you have to go back and get it under control as you're simultaneously trying to move on to the fourth. And so it goes across the board, winning one stakeholder at a time. "Check!" "Check!" ". . . aaaaannnnnd check!"

But the deeper into the 5.4 we go, the harder these conversations become. In an all-too-common (but still deeply painful) scenario, the head of sales at a company that sells highly technical instruments for the manufacturing sector told us that his sales reps are almost exclusively trained engineers—which has always made sense in the past as they've traditionally called on engineers inside the customer organization. However, across the last five years, as the scope, impact, and expense of their newer solutions have expanded, they can now rarely get a deal done without also speaking with the customer's head of finance. The problem is, their reps have never sold to CFOs before and find them completely intimidating, so they avoid calling them altogether! But what do you do when your own sales force is literally too scared to call your customer? At first glance it might sound somewhat absurd, but this happens all over the world, every single day. This is what happens when sellers move into the world of the 5.4. Sales reps' familiar comfort zone of selling doesn't expand nearly as fast as customers' required consensus zone for buying.

Likewise, parallel efforts in marketing don't fare much better. A recent move in B2B marketing toward something known as B2P—or "business-to-people"—marketing arises in part from this exact same trend. There, the thinking goes, even in the world of business-to-business buying, it's not companies that buy things, but *people* that do. And with the rapid increase in both number and diversity of people involved in a typical purchase, suppliers have to understand those people today far better and get in front of them far earlier than ever before with content and campaigns that will more specifically speak to each of their unique needs and priorities. In many ways, it's the marketing analog to the "track them all down and win them all over" sales strategy.

So not surprisingly, then, we've observed a strong and renewed interest among more advanced marketing teams in building ever more accurate customer personas, trying to understand individual buyers and their needs. Simultaneously, we've watched marketing organizations dedicate increasing amounts of time and money to building more targeted content, designed to speak to very specific members of the 5.4 about the issues they care about most at each stage of the purchase journey.

Given the scope of the challenge, however, these same teams (often made up of only a handful of people) become easily overwhelmed trying to place highly personalized, original content in all the right places, at all the right times, for all the right people involved in a typical purchase process. Even then, there's often little concrete evidence to show that any of this effort translates into real commercial outcomes, leaving marketers to point to intermediate measures like increased click-through rates or more "likes" on the company Facebook page to justify the added time and expense of their effort.

When we put it together it's no wonder that commercial leaders around the world complain of increased cost of sale, longer cycle times, stalled deals, and smaller deal sizes. The ongoing battle of tracking down each of the 5.4 and then successfully winning each of them over not only takes a huge amount of time and effort, it's fraught with challenge every step of the way. And it leaves commercial leaders around the world thinking the same thing. As one head of sales and marketing put it to us rather poignantly, "There's got to be a better way. All this customer consensus is killing our business!"

But what could that better answer be?

IN SEARCH OF ANSWERS

Given this strong pressure on performance, the CEB sales and marketing practice recently set out to study the dynamics of customer consensus in far greater depth than we ever had in the past.

At the center of this work was an effort to supplement the vast amount of customer research we'd already conducted in the past with new data, aimed at group buying dynamics. And much of that data came from a survey of 1,000 people all involved in some fashion in a typical B2B purchase, representing a wide range of both industries and geographies. More than anything else, the survey was designed to shed new light on the complex relationship across group buying behaviors, commercial outcomes, purchase attributes, and sales rep behavior.

The story that arose from all that work is fascinating as, upon first glance, it is deeply counterintuitive. In fact, when we first ran our analysis, we weren't sure whether we should believe the result. We went back and reran the numbers, remodeled the data, rechecked the sample in an effort to undo a finding that we initially found very difficult to believe. But the findings proved incredibly robust. Though those findings didn't seem to make a lot of sense when we first saw them, as we dug deeper into the data (and continued to dissect the challenge it was meant to address), we came to the conclusion that we'd been thinking about the consensus problem in exactly the wrong way. The implications for sales and marketing were huge.

AN UNEXPECTED FINDING

To show you what we mean, let's start with a concept we'll call a "high-quality sale"—which serves as the backbone for much of our consensus work.

The idea here is: Suppliers aren't looking to close just *any* business. They're looking to close *good* business. So while it is true that suppliers lose to status quo far more often than they'd like, it is equally true that even when they win, they often don't win the way they'd hoped. Perhaps the customer bought a much smaller "good enough" version of their solution. Or maybe the customer so completely beat them up on price that the deal came in way below target margins. So technically, we might call those deals "wins," but they're hollow victories at best. We hear this all the time from commercial leaders. It's not so much the *low quantity* of deals they're doing that causes the real pain, but the *low quality* of the deals that are ultimately sold.

So when we talk about a "high-quality sale" in our data, what we're trying to capture is the kind of deal where customers buy the bigger solution at a higher margin. In our study, we defined a quality sale as a deal where customers:

1. Did not settle for a less ambitious solution, but

2. Purchased a premium offering relative to the base offering

We tested for those attributes through a number of different questions across our various survey instruments.

So now the question becomes, how do suppliers win *that* kind of high-quality deal—especially in a 5.4 world?

Well, let's go back to our strategy for selling to diversity in the first place and see what happens. You'll remember, the conventional sales and marketing approach in the 5.4 world is, we have to track them all down and then win them all over. When we ran the various commercial activities associated with that approach through our model, we found something rather shocking (see figure 1.3).

FIG. 1.3. Comparison of Drivers on Likelihood of Supplier Winning a High-Quality Deal

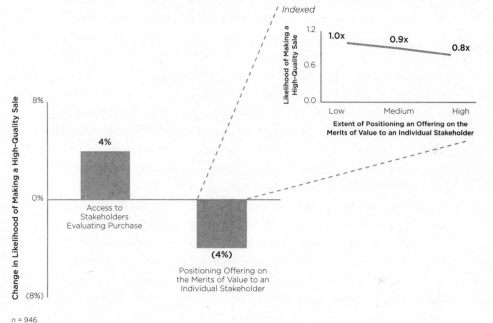

n = 946.

Source: CEB analysis.

ª Change in likelihood of making a high-quality sale is defined as the increase in chance of being selected as a winning supplier and the customer (1) did not settle for a less ambitious solution or (2) purchased a premium offering relative to the base offering.

When we measured each of those two approaches (i.e., winning access, or "tracking them all down," and then better individual positioning, or "winning them all over") against the probability of winning a high-quality sale, we found that winning access to key stakeholders boosts that probability by a positive 4 percent, but positioning our offering to resonate more strongly with each stakeholder actually *reduces* that probability by 4 percent.

Now, what do those numbers mean? Let's take them one at a time. The way to interpret the access number, for example, is this: if we were to move from below-average performance to above-average performance on winning access to each stakeholder across the 5.4, we'd be 4 percent more likely to close a high-quality deal.

In other words, access matters. It has a statistically significant impact on driving up deal quality. Though, you'd likely agree, it doesn't appear to matter nearly as much as anyone might have thought. After all, a 4 percent increase doesn't seem to be all that meaningful. That's kind of strange.

But even stranger is our finding for tactic number two. This is about winning over each stakeholder, one at a time, by connecting our offer as strongly as possible to whatever they care about the most. So we position our offer to meet their needs, emphasizing our ability to address their specific priorities, speak to their individual view of what's important, and connect directly to what they've got to get done (i.e., their MBOs, personal projects, etc.). And the impact here is actually *negative*.

Now what does *that* mean?

Well, what it means is that the better we get at customizing our offer at the individual level, the *less* likely we are to close a high-quality deal. Effectively personalizing our offer to each stakeholder *decreases* deal quality, pushing us deeper into the very commodity trap we were hoping to avoid by personalizing in the first place.

In fact, when we dig into the data one level deeper, we find that if we move from below-average performance to above-average performance on personalization, we're 20 percent more likely to have a *negative* impact on overall deal quality. In other words, the better one positions the offer to the individual, the more likely there is to be a negative impact on overall deal quality. It doesn't seem to make any sense.

We can tell you, our first reaction to these results was a whole lot of surprise, mixed with more than just a little bit of concern. After all, we're the "Challenger guys," the group who found that the best reps are defined by their ability to Teach, *Tailor*, and Take Control. And yet, this data seems to indicate that tailoring can actually hurt you!

So we stared at this for a really long time, trying to figure out what was going on. But it wasn't until we saw the rest of the story—which we'll turn to next—that we figured out what's going on here. And when you see it, you'll find that this result makes a lot of sense. In fact, you'll likely be as surprised as we were that it wasn't more obvious all along.

But before we go there, we first offer one crucial note to provide some important context to our earlier work. Rest assured, today is not the day we disavow ourselves of the Challenger findings and apologetically declare that we got it wrong the first time around. As you'll see as we continue to work through all of our findings, in the world of the 5.4, a Challenger approach—replete with effective tailoring—is arguably more important than ever before.

That said, at the same time, these findings have also led us to realize that we must be far more *precise* about what we mean by tailoring and how we go about it, in order not to inadvertently do damage where we sought to do good. For the data is indeed very clear: tailoring done the *wrong* way can have a significantly chilling effect on overall deal quality. A traditional sales approach of gaining access and then making our pitch 5.4 times is insufficient to drive commercial growth. Yet that's exactly what most sales and marketing organizations are doing right now—all with the very best of intentions of pursuing a commercial strategy that, frankly, at first blush seems inescapably logical.

So what exactly is going on here? Well, remember, all of this research was conducted within a very specific context—not of selling behavior, but of *buying* behavior. Even more specifically, *group* buying behavior. Because what we're ultimately trying to figure out isn't how suppliers can sell effectively to individuals but, rather how they can sell more effectively to *groups* of individuals. And even more important, *diverse* groups of individuals. What we've found is, more than anything else, it's the *diversity* of these groups that makes all the difference. If there's one finding in all of our consensus work that stands above all others, it is that selling to individuals and selling to groups of diverse individuals is not the same thing—but not because the selling is different. Rather, because the *buying* is different.

SOLVING FOR THE RIGHT PROBLEM

You'll remember, the core tenet of marketers' push toward B2P marketing, including more personalized content and messaging, is the broad recognition that, at the end of the day, it's not companies that buy things, but *people* that do. And if we don't understand and connect to those people better than ever before, we'll fail to win them over.

However, based on all of our research, what we've come to conclude is this: while it may be true that, even in business settings, it's not *companies* that buy things but *people* that do, in today's B2B environment, it is equally true that it's not *people* that buy things but *groups* of them that do.

If we don't understand how these groups of people work together—if we sell only at the individual level and not simultaneously at the collective level—there's a good chance we'll miss what has become the most important dynamic in B2B selling today: finding a way to connect the diverse individuals that comprise a buying group around a higher-level vision than where they're most likely to land on their own.

Why is that? There's a very good reason, and it shows up right in the data (see figure 1.4).

FIG. 1.4. Impact of Group Diversity on Group Dysfunction

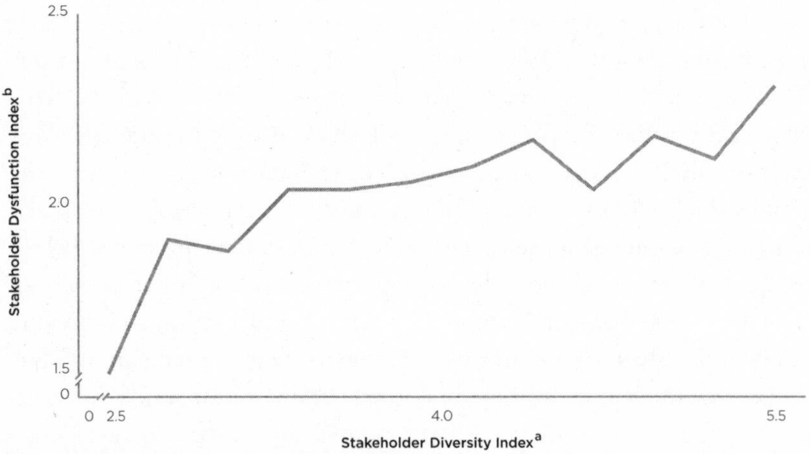

Components of Dysfunction

1	2	3
Stakeholders did not have a fair say in group discussion.	Stakeholders avoided discussions on the most important issues regarding purchase.	Stakeholders had multiple disagreements related to the purchase.

n = 911.
Source: CEB analysis.

[a] The Stakeholder Diversity Index includes the following variables: number of stakeholders from different roles/teams/geographies, total number of functions involved, and differences in stakeholder interests/priorities/goals.

[b] The Stakeholder Dysfunction Index includes the following variables: stakeholders did not have a fair say in group discussion, stakeholders avoided discussions on most important issues regarding purchase, and stakeholders had multiple disagreements around the purchase.

If we map the relationship between stakeholder diversity and something we've come to call "stakeholder dysfunction," we find the relationship between the two to be very telling.

Let's start with a couple of definitions. First, stakeholder *diversity* is based on the range of different functions, roles, teams, geographies, and divergent priorities represented across the various stakeholders directly involved in the purchase decision. Stakeholder *dysfunction*, on the other hand, captures the degree to which members of that buying group struggle to effectively collaborate across a number of important dimensions. More specifically, for the purposes of this work, stakeholder dysfunction goes up when:

1. Various stakeholders don't have a fair say in group discussion.

2. Stakeholders avoid discussions of the most important issues regarding a purchase altogether.

3. Stakeholders outright disagree with one another, multiple times, regarding purchase details.

These are all things that can be measured quantitatively by asking survey respondents a series of questions regarding how they collaborated with other members of the buying group. And really, this is pretty familiar stuff. If you think about a group purchase you've been involved in recently, you'll undoubtedly see some of your own experience in at least one or two of those attributes (think, for example, about the most recent purchase of a new CRM solution in your organization and how that played out).

So let's look at the relationship between these two things: diversity and dysfunction. The data is very clear: as stakeholder diversity increases, so does dysfunction. Pretty dramatically, in fact. Or, put another way, as the diversity of the various stakeholders that suppliers find themselves selling to continues to expand, they can expect to see an equally dramatic rise in the dysfunction of the groups comprised of those increasingly diverse individuals.

This all makes a ton of sense. There are all sorts of reasons why more diverse groups struggle to function effectively. If someone is working with a group of colleagues across their company, all representing different, sometimes even competing, perspectives and priorities, it's almost inevitable that they're going to disagree with at least *someone*. Not personally, but almost certainly professionally, as everyone is working toward whatever priorities make the most sense for their part of the business.

In that environment, there are all sorts of reasons why individuals might fail to connect as that group deliberates. We all have a tendency to think very carefully about the cost-benefit trade-offs of different kinds and levels of group engagement: "I don't want to share my opinion, or advocate too strongly for my position. It's too hard. They won't get it. It's a lot of work for very little benefit. It's just not worth it."

Or perhaps: "I won't speak up because I don't want to look dumb, or selfish, or too dominant, or too weak, or sound too much like I'm not a team player."

On the other hand, other individuals might push too hard, seeking to win over the group by sheer force of will, or rhetoric—or even volume—failing to understand the very different perspectives around them.

Achieving group consensus in an environment like that can be extremely difficult. Over time, everyone loses patience and maybe even gives up. Actually, when we think of it that way, it's a wonder that groups can agree on anything at all!

That said, things don't necessarily have to be this way. When it comes to effectively creating customer consensus, the data provides a ray of hope as well. For just because diversity and dysfunction are highly correlated doesn't mean that they have to always be intertwined. In the end, suppliers may not have an uncontrollable diversity problem so much as they have an addressable dysfunction problem.

Unlike customer diversity, which is largely out of suppliers' control, customer dysfunction is something they can do something about—but probably not very well given conventional sales and marketing strategy. Because imagine how the "track them all down and win them all over" approach plays out in this world of high customer dysfunction. It does nothing to solve for the problem, because this is a problem it was never designed to solve. Current sales and marketing tactics are designed to do something completely different. They are far more focused on better connecting individual customer stakeholders to the *supplier* than they are on better connecting those same individual customer stakeholders to *each other*.

To shed light on just how poorly suppliers' old-world commercial approach is designed to solve for customers' new-world buying dysfunction, let's take a closer look at what these buying groups are struggling to agree on in the first place. Because, as it turns out, the most common source of customer dysfunction has nothing to do with the supplier in the first place.

CLIMBING THE "ME TO WE" MOUNTAIN

If we think about the various stages customer stakeholders must pass through to move a purchase forward, at a high level we can narrow it down to three in particular, each crucially important:

1. Problem Definition

2. Solution Identification

3. Supplier Selection

At any one of those points, things can go off the rails pretty badly as relevant customer stakeholders potentially fail to reach agreement.

So as a hypothetical example, let's say a company has recognized they're unable to make effective strategic decisions due to their lack of quality data-driven insight. So what to do? Well, first, that team has to reach agreement on what exactly the underlying problem is in the first place. Is it data quality? Data quantity? Data gathering? Analysis capabilities? Or maybe they have all the data they need, but it's trapped in various legacy systems that don't effectively communicate with one another. Whatever the case, that buying group has to first define the problem it's trying to solve.

That said, once they've reached agreement on the problem, there's still the question of what to do about it. So let's say, for example, they've settled on a data analysis problem. Now, how to solve for better data analysis? Well, there are all sorts of approaches one might take there, ranging from something relatively straightforward like buying better analytical software to giving staff the *tools* they need to study and play with the data in new ways, all the way to investing in training and development to give them the *skills* they need to perform more sophisticated analysis. Of course, across that very broad spectrum of possible solutions there are myriad other options ranging from less expensive and disruptive to extremely so. Without agreement on a course of action, however, that deal isn't going anywhere.

So for the sake of argument, let's say that that team has identified a solution that they can all agree on—maybe it's the purchase of a new suite of analytical tools. The next step would be to shop that solution with various vendors in order to determine which one can best meet their needs and then eventually select the one that everyone can agree on.

Now, admittedly, any given solutions purchase is far more complicated and far less linear than this, but it's an instructive abstraction nonetheless as it allows us to measure the relative difficulty of each of these decision nodes across a typical purchase process.

What we wanted to figure out in this analysis—in the unforgettable words of a senior manager at a business services company—was at what point across that continuum does the "wailing and gnashing of teeth" reach a crescendo inside the customer company, exposing that deal to the greatest amount of potentially insurmountable customer dysfunction. Or, put in a far less colorful way, when that purchase is most likely to fail.

Now, to figure that out we asked respondents, as part of a much larger survey of 3,000 customer stakeholders involved in a B2B purchase, to rate each of these three critical moments in terms of their relative difficulty. Both with respect to reaching an individual—or "me"—decision and in terms of achieving collective agreement—or a "we" decision (see figure 1.5).

FIG. 1.5. Perceived Difficulty of Decision Making at Each Purchase Stage

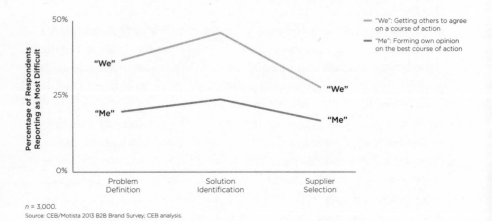

n = 3,000.
Source: CEB/Motista 2013 B2B Brand Survey; CEB analysis.

The first thing we find in our analysis is a much better understanding of just how much harder group decisions are than individual ones. Across the board, at each of those three decision points, the group decision—the "we" moment—proved dramatically harder than the individual decision—the "me" moment. In fact, we can quantify the difference. On average, group decisions are nearly twice as hard as individual ones. If you think about any major purchase you've been a part of in your own organization, we'd imagine this finding will ring true. This is the price we pay for diverse buying groups.

That said, the far more interesting output of this analysis is a clear indication that not all "we" moments are created equal. One in particular stands out as especially difficult, and that's Solution Identification.

So while customer stakeholders might all agree they have a problem, the data (and common experience) tells us there's likely going to be some pretty significant debate on the best way to *solve* that problem. This is a hugely valuable thing for us to know. Because it tells us that if suppliers are going to focus time and effort on creating customer consensus, the place where they really need to rally agreement is around the specific solution to the customer's problem, *irrespective* of supplier.

Now, by the same token, the analysis also tells us the thing *least* likely to create disagreement among stakeholders is Supplier Selection. Why is that? Largely because by the time the group has coalesced around a well-defined, high-priority problem and an agreed-upon, clear course of action, in many cases, from that point forward, the biggest question left to address is simply which of any number of possible suppliers can deliver a well-aligned solution at a relatively reasonable price (welcome back to the 1 of 3 Problem!).

But if that's the case, then this data also tells us something about what most sellers and marketers are likely doing right now to win customer consensus, if they're doing anything at all. Because traditionally speaking, if there's one thing all suppliers are trying to get their customer stakeholders to agree on, it's that their company is great! That they're the best! That they're the leading provider of whatever solution that customer is *already* looking for.

In most cases, that message sounds something like this: *"Our company is a leading, customer-focused global provider of innovative solutions supported by cutting-edge innovations designed to empower organizations with different-in-kind sources of broad-based value creation at their most critical moments of need. And oh, by the way, we're green."*

Sound familiar? If there was one thing we'd all want customers to agree on, surely that would be it! That we're the market leader! The leading brand! The best possible partner! That we can not only meet their needs, but *exceed* them!

So that's the thing all suppliers focus on.

But what this data tells us is, if that's the focus of suppliers' consensus-building efforts, then they're solving for only one of three possible consensus failure points across a purchase path, and of those three, they're almost exclusively focused on the *least* difficult for customers to agree upon, not the most. At the same time, those same suppliers are leaving customers *on their own* to achieve agreement around the two points where things tend to fall apart.

So if a purchase decision is going to stall, more likely than not it's going to stall far earlier than most suppliers would anticipate, particularly if they're focused only on watching for signs of customer disagreement around the value of their offering.

As much as leaders tell us they want their reps to "get in earlier," this data tells us pretty emphatically that if they do indeed manage to get in earlier, they need to take that opportunity to help customers overcome the challenge they're facing earlier. And that challenge has little to do with choosing a supplier and everything to do with deciding which problems are worth solving in the first place and what solutions are worth pursuing to solve them—all *irrespective* of supplier. (This is why the Challenger approach proves so effective, as that's exactly what it's designed to do.)

To give you a sense of just how painful this kind of misalignment can be, the CMO at a medical equipment company told us the following story when he saw this data. Historically, his company has sold to surgeons, who would debate the merits of their product versus those of the competition. It was a straight-up battle over who had the superior capability. But *today*, when they call on those same hospitals, they find they're no longer sitting at the table with just the surgeon, but with a diverse group of buyers comprised of the chief surgeon, the CFO, the head of procurement, and various hospital administrators. So now, instead of debating which supplier's medical equipment to buy, this incredibly diverse buying group is deliberating whether they should buy any more medical equipment at all, or take that money and build a new parking garage as an additional revenue stream for the hospital.

This is what happens when diverse groups get together. Dysfunction almost naturally follows, as not only perspectives but priorities become highly divergent. But more likely than not, it's not even dysfunction or disagreement around which supplier to select, but rather around which problem to address in the first place and how to address it.

It's a painful story, but indicative of how misaligned most suppliers are today in helping customers overcome arguably the number one obstacle in buying their solution. Counterintuitively, suppliers' biggest challenge in winning customer consensus has *nothing to do* with that supplier's solution at all.

Even more troubling, much of the customer's primary consensus challenge occurs far before most sellers are even present to address it in the first place.

MIND THE GAP FROM 37 TO 57

In a well-documented study (see "The End of Solution Sales," *Harvard Business Review*, July–August 2012), the CEB team asked customer stakeholders to consider a typical B2B purchase process from beginning to end and then identify the point at which their organization typically reaches out to a supplier to seek their advice. That answer came back as 57 percent. On average, customers are 57 percent of the way through a typical purchase process prior to proactively reaching out to a supplier's sales rep for their direct input on whatever it is that they're doing (see figure 1.6).

FIG. 1.6. Customer Purchase Progress at Point of Outreach to Supplier(s)

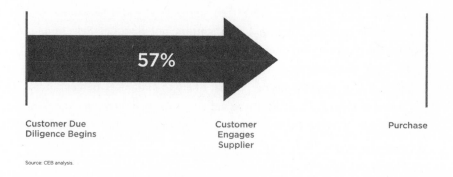

57%

Customer Due
Diligence Begins

Customer
Engages
Supplier

Purchase

Source: CEB analysis.

For suppliers evolving to complex solutions, our data also tells us that the more complex the deal, the later the customer contact. Why? Likely because customers looking to make large investments in a complex solution want to be extra sure they've done sufficient due diligence to avoid being unduly swayed by a particularly charismatic sales rep accompanied by an especially knowledgeable sales technician bent on peddling a general supplier solution rather than addressing a specific customer need.

Now, that 57 percent number has huge implications for suppliers. If we consider what's likely happening inside that 57 percent, chances are pretty good that customers are now doing *on their own* most of the things that suppliers were hoping to do with them together: They're identifying a need. They're prioritizing that need relative to others. They're determining which capabilities they'll require to address that need. They're identifying which suppliers are best able to deliver that capability. In most cases, they're conducting preliminary research on how much each of those suppliers cost. So by the time a supplier is called in at that 57 percent mark, more often than not there's little left to discuss but price. As one senior leader memorably put it, "That 57 percent is a freight train to RFP Station. And we're on it."

Still more troubling, however, is what happens when we place that 57 percent number into the context of customer consensus. Because in follow-up research, we also asked customers to identify the point in a purchase process at which internal conflict most likely reaches a peak—or the "wailing and gnashing of teeth" hits a crescendo—and that deal is in the greatest danger of falling apart altogether. And *that* number came back as 37 percent.

Group conflict peaks at 37 percent. That's the summit of the "me to we" mountain where that deal is most likely to die. And you'll remember, that peak centers around Solution Identification, not Supplier Selection—a problem most suppliers infrequently address.

But let's consider what happens when we put these two numbers together. If a purchase decision is most likely to stall at 37 percent, but a supplier sales rep isn't likely to be called in until 57 percent, then the resulting gap between the two raises a very practical and pretty troubling question: how many times have suppliers lost a deal that they never even knew was in play to begin with as the customer couldn't make it past the 37 percent mark on their own? Or more simply: how many times have sellers lost before they could ever attempt to win? The answer, of course, is unknowable, though deeply disquieting nonetheless. For in that gap—from

37 percent to 57 percent—is a trail littered with deals that have been left to die among the dried-up markers, leftover take-out food, and haphazard piles of double-sided PowerPoints strewn across the floor of customer conference rooms around the world—all bearing witness to the 5.4's inability to reach collective agreement.

That gap has hugely important implications for suppliers. Traditionally, most commercial organizations have considered customer consensus to be primarily a *sales* challenge—requiring reps to win broad customer agreement "on the ground," one person at a time. But if suppliers are largely relying upon sales to stitch together collective consensus once they're called in, then the data tells us they're missing a crucial part of the problem. Customer consensus isn't a sales challenge, it is a *commercial* challenge. To be sure, there are a number of things sales reps can and must do to "crack open the 57 percent" and win earlier access to customer deliberations. But in many cases, if suppliers are doing nothing to simultaneously address the consensus problem earlier through *marketing*, then there's a good chance that that deal can die before sales ever wins sufficient access to get a chance to even try. This challenge must be attacked from both directions simultaneously. For marketing's part, far beyond battling for individual resonance through more personalized campaigns and content, B2B marketers are going to have to find ways to *anticipate* customer disconnects far earlier in the purchase process and avert them proactively. For left unaddressed, these disconnects can be devastating to the supplier's bottom line.

FIGHTING THE LOWEST COMMON DENOMINATOR

When we put it all together, we find the far bigger challenge for suppliers isn't improving their own abilities to *sell*, it's addressing the customer's *inability* to agree.

To understand what's going on here, let's introduce a concept called a "mental model." Now, we'll examine mental models in a significant amount of depth later, but for now, to keep things simple, think of a mental model simply as the way an individual understands their world and how it works. We represent these mental models with three overlapping circles in the form of a Venn diagram (see figure 1.7).

FIG. 1.7. Illustration of Stakeholders' Divergent Mental Models

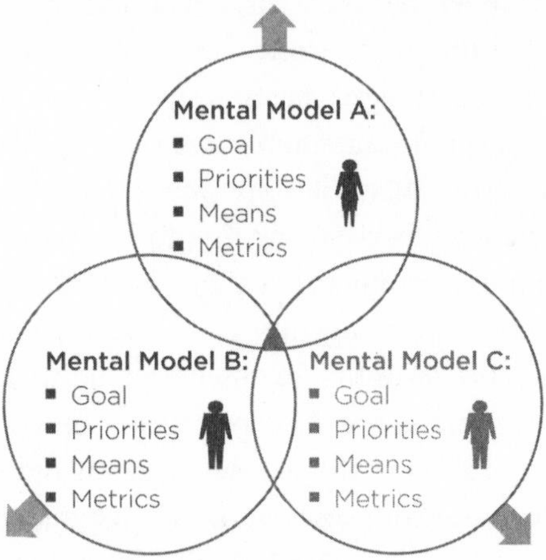

Source: CEB analysis.

So these might be three different individuals in different roles, functions, or geographies. For each mental model, each stakeholder will have their own goals, priorities, means, and metrics, all unique to their particular perspective.

This is the source of dysfunction. It's not these stakeholders' different backgrounds per se, but the fact that those different backgrounds bring with them different, even divergent mental models. (Of course, if a supplier must target 5.4 stakeholders, that potential divergence becomes that much worse.)

It's a very simple concept, but that's on purpose. Because a simple concept like this allows us to visualize very clearly just what suppliers are up against in creating broad-based customer consensus around a high-quality deal. That's because the question we can now ask when looking at a diagram like this is:

Just how much *overlap* is there across the different mental models of the various stakeholders that we have to connect?

Really, that's the question that matters most. Because that overlap is the single point of agreement across all those stakeholders' mental models. It's where they connect. Where they agree.

And if that overlap is very small, then that group can agree on only very little.

So left to their own devices, various stakeholders come together to consider a purchase, and if they find few shared priorities, or little common ground for mutual understanding, they settle on the *lowest common denominator* where they're most likely to agree. Things like: avoid risk, move cautiously, reduce disruption, and save money.

Every supplier knows all too well what it feels like to be on the receiving end of that kind of customer consensus. This is dysfunction. And this is what it gets us.

It's not that diverse customer buying groups can't agree on anything, it's just that, left to their own devices, they can't agree on *very much* and will rarely agree on anything that is highly disruptive or ambitious.

If we think about what all of this means for suppliers, what this tells us is: as they move into a world of increasing stakeholder diversity, suppliers are simultaneously moving into a world of increasing stakeholder dysfunction, brought on by *decreasing* overlap in their mental models.

As the little overlapping triangle at the center of that Venn diagram continues to shrink, it's no wonder that suppliers are all competing with status quo, small deals, and low margins. That's the one thing left in common among an otherwise divergent and dysfunctional group of diverse decision makers.

This is the commodity trap suppliers struggle to escape every single day that sits at the core of the 1 of 3 Problem. An otherwise dysfunctional group of customer stakeholders unable to agree on a common vision but forced to agree on *something* is likely to agree on doing nothing—or at least doing as little as possible—in order to find common ground.

We can see this phenomenon in the data as well. A dysfunctional group is a full 50 percent less likely to pay a premium for a high-cost offering than a functional group (see figure 1.8).

If we think back to where we started, with suppliers' common approach for creating customer consensus, and play it out in this world, we're now in a much better position to understand the findings we saw earlier.

As we considered the "track them down and win them over" approach, you'll remember, we found that while winning greater stakeholder access may help, more careful positioning of one's offering to each stakeholder's needs actually hurts us—at least in terms of driving high-quality deals. And that finding was really counterintuitive.

FIG. 1.8. Impact of Dysfunction on Likelihood of Purchasing a High-Cost (Premium) Offering (indexed)

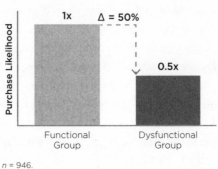

n = 946.
Source: CEB analysis.

But now, using a Venn diagram like the one we describe here, we can see exactly why that's the case.

If we think about aligning a supplier value proposition more closely to each stakeholder's mental model, insofar as those models are divergent to begin with, then they're making things *worse*, not better. They're *exacerbating* the very separation that keeps this group from agreeing on anything but the most basic common ground in the first place. From that perspective, it's *no wonder* the second bar on that bar chart earlier was negative. At the end of the day, suppliers' traditional sales and marketing efforts have likely emphasized difference, rather than overcome it. Underscoring individual separation rather than reinforcing mutual connection.

What's fascinating about all this is that these findings shed light on one of the most frustrating phenomena in complex sales today: watching a deal wither on the vine despite the fact that a supplier has managed to successfully secure the support of each and every stakeholder who seems to matter most.

We see it all the time. All. The. Time. Marketing's personalized content brings in a lead, the first person out of the 5.4. The sales team picks it up and engages that first person who expressed interest . . . and then proceeds to track down each and every member of the 5.4 until they have successfully won them all over. One by one. Everything seems to be in place. Then, somehow, at the last minute, after every stakeholder has said "Yes," the deal inexplicably falls apart. Or, at the very least, it's shrunk down to a much smaller size at a far lower price than what was originally proposed. The seller is left wondering, "What in the world just happened?! We had it in the palm of our hand, and then it all just sort of slipped away!"

As one sales leader put it, "More often than I care to admit, we live in a world where each person says 'Yes,' but then the group ultimately says 'No.' It's like I live in a world where $1 + 1 + 1 = 0$. How is that even possible?"

Well, using the mental model construct, we can now understand exactly how that might be possible. There are a number of different versions of the same story, but one reason that deal may still fall apart is the fact that in winning over each stakeholder, the seller specifically highlighted those components or parts of their offering that spoke most directly to each *individual*'s needs.

And why wouldn't they? After all, they were likely trained to do exactly that.

But think about how that approach plays out across a dysfunctional group. If the seller personalizes the offering so much, then when each of the 5.4 comes together to compare notes, they find that the proposed deal is far bigger, far more disruptive, and far more expensive than anything any *one* individual thought they were signing up for, and then that group will naturally scope it back down to an acceptable size.

If the supplier has done nothing to overcome their divergent mental models—helping them better appreciate the important connections across their otherwise disparate decision-making criteria, then that deal is almost certainly destined for the dustbin—or at least some significant downsizing to something mutually agreeable to everyone.

Bottom line, *if suppliers don't create convergence, their customers will.*

If it turns out that the only thing those customers can agree on is to do nothing, then, at the end of the day, that's exactly what they're going to do.

But notice, that supplier lost not because they failed to connect individual stakeholders to them but, rather, because they overlooked the fact that those same stakeholders weren't necessarily very well connected to *each other*. And that's how $1 + 1 + 1 = 0$. The supplier collects a "Yes" from each individual, but still gets a collective "No" from the customer.

Because, it turns out, *there's a vast difference between a collection of yeses and a Collective Yes.*

So can suppliers get to a Collective Yes? Absolutely. That's what this book is all about. But building that bridge from "me" to "we" will take a very specific strategy, targeted to a very special stakeholder.

FROM "ME" TO "WE"

To show you what we mean, let's think of a typical customer purchase process as moving through the three distinct phases (see figure 1.9).

FIG. 1.9. Purchase Process Overview (illustrative)

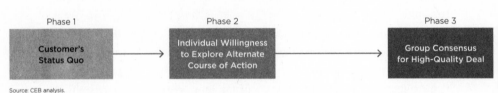

Phase 1 — Customer's Status Quo → Phase 2 — Individual Willingness to Explore Alternate Course of Action → Phase 3 — Group Consensus for High-Quality Deal

Source: CEB analysis.

In Phase 1, we begin with the customer in a state of "status quo." Then through the recognition of some particular need, or perhaps through the exposure to an insight provided by a supplier, at least one or two of the stakeholders in that customer organization come to realize that change is necessary. Indeed, it is in this first movement from Phase 1 to Phase 2 where demand is born, as this is where high-performing sales reps, who we've dubbed Challengers, approach the customer armed with powerful insight to challenge the way they think about their business—research that we've documented extensively in *The Challenger Sale*.

Specifically in this first movement, tailoring one's content and approach is crucial to win these individuals over in the first place. For done well, these stakeholders land in Phase 2, which is "individual willingness to explore alternate course of action." The idea here is that *someone* inside the customer organization has recognized that they have a clear need worth addressing, and they have committed to exploring it further. Of course, the degree to which the supplier has skewed that vision in their favor is critical.

This is where we left things at the conclusion of *The Challenger Sale*—in

Phase 2, with a number of customer stakeholders excited about a new idea and what it could mean for their company.

However, despite the hard-won individual buy-in a supplier may have achieved in Phase 2, that potential purchase is still a long way off from an actual closed deal, as that insight now has to traverse a long second journey from Phase 2 to Phase 3, which may or may not land in group agreement around an actual purchase decision.

It is across this second movement where individual support must somehow evolve into group consensus, moving from "me" to "we" as the supplier works with that stakeholder to build a bridge to the other 4.4.

This can be a tough row to hoe, because it is here that the supplier has to bring in the other stakeholders, get them to meet, convince them to agree, and win them over. Procurement's gotta get involved. Finance has to approve. Legal has to look things over. This is why the distance from Phase 2 to 3 is so much longer than the distance from 1 to 2. One member joked, "This is where good deals go to die." It is indeed the "solutions graveyard."

But it is also here where the seller's tailoring strategy must morph into something else entirely—*tailoring for group consensus rather than tailoring for individual buy-in*. For, if we think about the best way to build that bridge from "me" to "we"—landing in a Collective Yes—at some point in this process, the supplier will have to transition pretty sharply from connecting individual stakeholders to *them* and start connecting those same stakeholders to *each other*.

Yet many of these deliberations and conversations are most likely to happen behind closed doors, and over the horizon, well beyond the direct influence of an individual seller. So influencing these conversations can be incredibly difficult.

Harder still, there's no indication in any of our research that individual stakeholders are created equal in their ability to influence those discussions when the seller can't be there to do it directly. Despite their common support for a particular course of action, in other words, not all customer stakeholders are equally able—or even willing—to fight the good fight of winning over the other 4.4 at the same time.

Quite the contrary; in fact, this is where star sellers make a critical choice. For it turns out, the specific individual they seek out to help them build that Collective Yes truly matters—arguably as much as any other decision they make in driving that deal. For, without the right partner inside the customer organization, they'll likely fail to build a bridge from "me" to "we" able to sustain anything more than the most watered-down of deals.

So who do they choose? That's where we turn next. But lest you think you can skip the next chapter if you're in marketing, read on, as the story you're about to see will have hugely important implications for the entire commercial organization—both sales rep skill and marketing capability.

CHAPTER TWO

THE MOBILIZER

In many ways, the question of who to target as a supplier is as old as sales itself. On the marketing side, the question comes back to the very core of the profession, market segmentation in all its various forms—by geography, industry, strategic fit, customer behavior, psychographic attributes, you name it. On the sales side, perhaps somewhat less scientifically, the question often boils down to a particular sales methodology or recent training program, or—just as likely—the specific guidance from a sales manager based on his or her "thirty years of experience selling in this industry." Irrespective of function or methodology, however, what none of these approaches prioritize in a formal manner is any systematic thought around who to target across the customer organization in order to build a bridge to the other 4.4. That's not necessarily a criticism, simply a recognition of the fact that the world has changed. If not the world of selling, then at the very least the world of buying. A consensus-oriented approach to stakeholder management wasn't as important just a few short years ago when senior decision makers could be counted on more reliably to get the deal done on their own. Given the group buying dynamics we laid out earlier, however, today's sales and marketing executives will have to think far more precisely about who to target as a best candidate across the 5.4 to drive the kind of consensus most likely to get suppliers paid. But who to choose?

It turns out, that's a really interesting question.

BOILING THE OCEAN

The CEB sales and marketing team has spent several years building what is arguably one of the world's largest and most unique data sets around the topic of complex selling. As part of this effort, we ran four separate research initiatives to help us answer the question "How do star sellers win the consensus-based sale?"

Two of those projects focused on sales rep performance and two focused on customer buying behavior. The former started with an expansive study of sales rep behaviors and beliefs, collecting data from more than a thousand star and core performers from over forty companies. In that survey, we ask reps to assess their views and behaviors across everything from opportunity qualification to process execution to stakeholder engagement—all geared toward painting as accurate a picture as possible of what suppliers' best reps do on a day-to-day basis to set themselves apart. This study was all about the actual "motion" of a star performer deal. As always, we built the study to ensure representation across the major industries, geographies, and go-to-market models within the CEB sales membership.

Importantly, we made sure that we weren't biasing our results by surveying just sales reps known to be Challengers. While we know many companies are aggressively pursuing the Challenger model, we wanted to ensure that we were casting as broad a net as possible and that the ensuing results would apply to all companies and sales leaders, not just those who've adopted the Challenger approach. That being said, when you see the results, you'll find—perhaps not surprisingly—heavy overtones of the Challenger profile in what stars are doing.

Once we had the data back from our rep survey, we also ran a number of structured interviews with star performers to corroborate the findings and hear directly from the best about what they're doing so differently— and these conversations proved fascinating.

At the same time, we also conducted two major customer studies. First, because we were studying customer consensus, we ran a survey across roughly 600 individual stakeholders inside B2B customer organizations in order to figure out just how team-based purchase decisions are made— who's involved and how they operate. Second, we conducted a separate survey of over 700 individual customer stakeholders involved in B2B purchases. This latter study was specifically built to determine whether certain stakeholders are naturally better than others when it comes to driving change and building consensus across their organizations. We qualified the respondents by screening out those who did not have previous experience with sophisticated purchases and those who worked for smaller organizations (fewer than 1,000 employees). For those respondents who met these criteria, we asked them to complete a 135-question survey about the actual purchase experience.

These four studies produced a huge amount of data and it took some time to sift through it. But when you step back and take it all in at once, what you find is dramatic: star reps are running a completely different playbook—one designed to *build* consensus and not just *find* it. For our marketing readers, working backward from high-quality deals, and what star performers do to win them, holds crucial lessons for what we do in upstream marketing activities, from value prop construction, to demand generation, to messaging.

THE NEW HIGH-PERFORMANCE PLAYBOOK

There's an old saying in sales that echoes the recent move to B2P marketing: people don't sell to companies, people sell to *people*. Customer engagement is the true heart and soul of sales and marketing. Always has been. At the end of the day, you've got to sit down with the customer, look them in the eye, and try to win their business. It's part art and part science. But either way, it's that magical moment where everything comes together—all the training, all the coaching, all the tools—you've got to run a conversation with an actual person who, at the very least, moves that deal forward.

What we've found in the data suggests that, when it comes to those conversations, stars are not only talking about completely different things in different ways (as we profiled in our Challenger work), but—just as important—they're talking to completely different people. While it is true, in other words, that people sell to people, it is equally true that star reps don't seek out just *any* people. They're just as deliberate about who they sell to as how they sell to them. But before we look at who those people are, let's first turn to people they were most likely told to find.

A CONVENTIONAL APPROACH TO CUSTOMER ENGAGEMENT

If there's one thing suppliers would likely agree on, it's that at some point in the sale, you've got to find and get in front of the senior decision maker to get the deal done. So, much of a rep's time in a sale is typically spent tracking down the people who can grant them access to that person.

But in the painful reality of today's complex solution sale, those "physics" of the traditional sale no longer hold true.

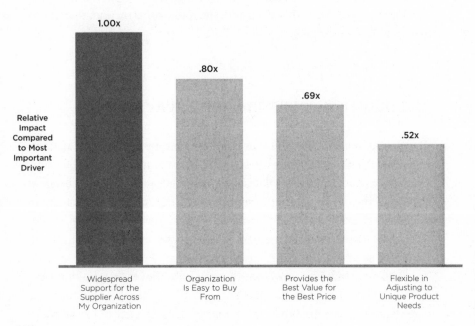

FIG. 2.1. Sales Experience Drivers of Customer Loyalty (for Decision Makers, indexed)

Relative Impact Compared to Most Important Driver

1.00x — Widespread Support for the Supplier Across My Organization

.80x — Organization Is Easy to Buy From

.69x — Provides the Best Value for the Best Price

.52x — Flexible in Adjusting to Unique Product Needs

n = 2,400.
Source: CEB analysis.

In fact, in a survey of senior decision makers across several hundred companies—the central target of this traditional approach—we found that the number one thing they care about most in choosing one supplier over another is whether or not that supplier enjoys widespread support across the customer organization. In other words, the number one thing senior decision makers care about in a complex deal isn't the *supplier* company's solution, it's their *own* company's buy-in. And that makes a lot of sense when you stop to think about it. Who wants to spend potentially millions on the implementation of a new solution, only to find out that everyone's against it? That's a recipe for disaster—and significantly reduced tenure.

So as companies have shifted to selling ever more complex solutions to customers, not surprisingly, decision makers have been ever more wary of going it alone. As a result, we now live in a world where even when a rep does the hard work of clawing his way up to the corner office and makes a powerful, compelling pitch to the senior decision maker, that conversation still ends with something like:

> "This looks great! I'm excited to partner with you! But before we can get this done, I just need you to go talk to this person . . . this person . . . , this person . . . , aaaaaand this person . . . , and then I think we're good to go!"

And that's tough. That's a deal now in significant danger of stalling *despite* the support of the person who typically, one would argue, matters most. Long gone are the days where reps could use advocates to get access to the people who truly matter, then go win them over to get the deal done. In a world of consensus building, everyone matters. There may still be a single "economic buyer" or ultimate "decision maker," but it's a team-based purchase nonetheless.

So now what? After all, salespeople still need to go out and talk to *someone*, but whom?

Who should suppliers tell their salespeople to target first in a 5.4 world? What are most companies doing now?

To find out, we spoke with over a hundred sales leaders, heads of sales operations, and leaders of sales training around the world, asking how they train their reps on stakeholder management. We learned that the attributes suppliers tell their salespeople to look for in an ideal customer stakeholder are remarkably consistent.

Whether we call this ideal stakeholder an "advocate," a "champion," or a "coach," the conventional wisdom out there is that we need to engage with somebody inside the customer organization who can provide guidance on

FIG. 2.2. Conventional View of Critical Stakeholder Profile

Advocate/Coach

1. Readily accessible and willing to talk

2. Provides information typically unavailable to suppliers

3. Prosupplier's solution or products

4. Good at influencing and convincing others

5. Speaks the truth

6. Credible; colleagues seek their input

7. Conveys new ideas to other stakeholders in savvy ways

8. Delivers (often more than asked) on commitments

9. Will personally gain from the sale

10. Often networks reps with other stakeholders

Source: CEB analysis.

how purchase decisions are made and who ideally is willing to help us navigate that process.

We tell our sales reps to look for stakeholders who are readily accessible. We need someone willing to meet and talk with us. We also tell our reps that we want somebody who can provide valuable information typically unavailable to suppliers—for instance, somebody who can provide the inside scoop on the political environment within the customer organization or useful intelligence on how the purchase process will really unfold. And, obviously, we want a stakeholder who's predisposed to support our solution over the competition's offering. It would be an added benefit if this person were good at influencing his or her colleagues—to win them over to our side. To do this, they typically need to be seen as credible by others and, of course, they need to be convincing in articulating the business case for the purchase.

We also guide our reps to look for stakeholders who are truthful and reliable. All of these other compelling traits are for naught if they don't speak the truth to us (or their colleagues) and if they can't be relied on to follow through on their commitments. Ideally, we'd also like this stakeholder to have some "skin in the game"—after all, an advocate is much more likely to help if they stand to profit themselves. And, finally, we'd want somebody willing to network that rep with other stakeholders—to make introductions to other influential folks, in particular the ultimate decision maker.

Piece of cake.

This is a daunting list of attributes. Wouldn't it just be easier to make an end run to the final decision maker herself? While logically that approach seems more straightforward, it's still going to wind up in the same place when that decision maker just sends reps out to build the widespread support she requires in order to make a decision.

What we're looking for isn't just somebody who can help get us into the corner office, we want somebody who can help make our case all over the company—laterally and vertically. This is why a list of attributes like this can get so long. Indeed, that long list of attributes represents the inherited conventional wisdom from years of solution selling, passed down from veteran to rookie and manager to team across at least the last couple of decades. And, honestly, it's hard to argue that any of these things don't apply. After all, who *wouldn't* want a customer stakeholder who did all of these things?

But there's only one problem. When we combed through all of our data from all of our research to find this individual, what we discovered is: they don't exist.

Now, to be fair, each of these *attributes* can likely be found somewhere across the wide range of stakeholders in any given customer organization, but virtually never all in one person.

Why does that matter? Because, as we've told our own sellers, "people sell to people." They don't sell to attributes. So when core reps are working from a list like this (whether it's in their heads or in a training manual), they don't view a list like this as a collection of discrete characteristics. What they likely see is the description of a real person. As a result, they spend a huge amount of time out there hunting for someone who can't be found because they don't actually exist.

But practically speaking, at some point, of course, they have to make a choice. They've got to talk to *somebody*. Since they can't find someone with all these traits, they have to settle for someone who has at least *some* of these traits.

But which ones should they prioritize? Are some better than others when it comes to driving business? How can they tell? How can they be sure?

Without any more guidance, core reps are left to guess on their own. But think about how difficult that choice is going to be. Asking sales reps to go out and find this ideal advocate or coach in nature is like giving them a net, sending them into the forest, and saying, "Bring me back a unicorn!" It's just not going to happen. Now, sales reps at any level are endlessly creative. And most won't come back empty-handed. But at the very best, they're going to come back with either a large goat or maybe a skinny rhino. It'll have four legs and a horn, but it won't be the same thing. Because unicorns don't exist either.

In their sincere effort to get that choice right, we find that core reps inadvertently get it exactly wrong, eventually walking right past the very people star performers consistently rely on to get the deal done.

SEVEN FLAVORS OF CUSTOMER STAKEHOLDERS

In our analysis of over 700 customer stakeholders across hundreds of customer organizations, we asked respondents to assess themselves across 135 different stakeholder attributes, traits, and perspectives. Then, using a statistical technique called factor analysis, we were able to take that data and derive a set of discrete stakeholder profiles. And, finally, we were then able to determine the relative ability of individuals in each profile to drive concrete action around a large-scale corporate purchase or initiative.

What does all that mean? In a nutshell, we wanted to know two things from this analysis. First, we wanted a data-driven understanding of what kinds of customers are out there in the first place—something more reliable than the gut-feel list we saw earlier. And second, we wanted a better understanding of how effective each kind of customer is at building consensus and driving change.

What we found is eye-opening. When all the math was done, we discovered that customers fall into one of seven discrete stakeholder types across a typical B2B sale.

As was the case in our Challenger research (in which we found five distinct rep profiles), we'd emphasize here that these seven types aren't necessarily mutually exclusive. In reality, most people tend to share at least some attributes across these boundaries. That's only natural.

But nonetheless, what the data clearly indicate is that virtually every

FIG. 2.3. Customer Stakeholder Profiles (as determined by factor analysis)

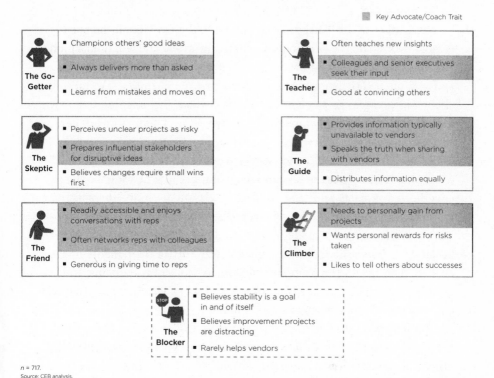

Key Advocate/Coach Trait

The Go-Getter
- Champions others' good ideas
- Always delivers more than asked
- Learns from mistakes and moves on

The Teacher
- Often teaches new insights
- Colleagues and senior executives seek their input
- Good at convincing others

The Skeptic
- Perceives unclear projects as risky
- Prepares influential stakeholders for disruptive ideas
- Believes changes require small wins first

The Guide
- Provides information typically unavailable to vendors
- Speaks the truth when sharing with vendors
- Distributes information equally

The Friend
- Readily accessible and enjoys conversations with reps
- Often networks reps with colleagues
- Generous in giving time to reps

The Climber
- Needs to personally gain from projects
- Wants personal rewards for risks taken
- Likes to tell others about successes

The Blocker
- Believes stability is a goal in and of itself
- Believes improvement projects are distracting
- Rarely helps vendors

n = 717.
Source: CEB analysis.

customer has a "primary posture" when it comes to both working with suppliers and driving change across their organization.

Let's take just a minute to go through each of these different stakeholder types to better understand what makes each of them unique. As we do, chances are that you'll recognize each from your own experience in working with your own customers. Then ask yourself, as you read the descriptions of each, which of these customer stakeholders would you seek out and which would you avoid?

The first profile we found is the "Go-Getter." This person is all about organizational improvement. He's constantly looking for good ideas and champions them when he finds them—no matter where they come from. What's more, he delivers results. This person is the project manager, the pragmatist, the one who immediately starts translating new opportunities into work plans, key deliverables, implementation milestones, and success metrics. When sitting down with the Go-Getter, he will immediately focus on the *how* of what you're proposing as opposed to the *why* of what you're proposing.

Next, we have the "Skeptic." In contrast to the Go-Getter, the Skeptic is more focused on the *why* behind a change proposal and will hold a high bar in terms of burden of proof. The Skeptic pushes back on everything and will often start from the assumption that the change you're talking about isn't going to go as planned—the one whose first reaction to a new idea or opportunity is "Let me explain why that isn't going to work here" or "You know, the last time we tried something like this, it took twice as long, cost twice as much, and delivered half the benefit we expected." Mind you, it's not because he's annoying, but because he's wary of large, complicated projects and tends to take a "glass-half-empty" perspective on the benefits of a given solution, as described by the salesperson. It's typically not because the Skeptic finds the salesperson deceitful, but rather because he doubts his organization can fully realize the benefits of the change. As a result, the Skeptic tends to need a lot of convincing and is especially careful to lay the groundwork and set expectations in order to ensure a successful, measured implementation.

The "Friend" is the third profile we found. Just as nice as they sound, the Friend is readily accessible to reps and willingly networks reps with other stakeholders across the organization. These folks always make time to meet with outside salespeople—whether out of professional courtesy or a genuine interest in expanding their own networks, they are characterized by an openness and willingness to make time for meeting with salespeople. Whereas the vast majority of customers never respond to e-mails or voice mails left by salespeople, the Friend would never deign to be so inconsiderate.

Fourth, we have the "Teacher." The Teacher is all about sharing insights and ideas. Colleagues seek him out for his advice and input. He's good at convincing others to pursue a course of action. Because of their unique storytelling and communication abilities, these people are frequently tapped to help senior leadership craft their own messages. They are the "Blue Ocean Strategy" folks within the customer organization—they love to paint a bold, aggressive vision and see others get as enthused about it as they are. Passion and excitement are the currency of the Teacher.

After the Teacher, we have the "Guide." The Guide willingly provides information typically unavailable outside the customer organization. Their stock in trade is information, plain and simple. They use the information (especially confidential, privileged information) to enhance the perception others have of them (the thinking being that if others see them as "in the know," they'll perceive them as being more senior and important than perhaps the title on their business card suggests). Because of this, they're best thought of as the "oversharers" of the customer organization—the ones who dish the dirt and catch you up on the latest comings and goings of various players inside the company (often sharing information about colleagues and internal politics that makes outsiders a bit uneasy).

Next, we have the "Climber." The Climber is focused almost entirely on personal gain. These are the "skin in the game" stakeholders who actively back projects that raise their profile, increase their influence, or expand their fiefdoms. When they back a project or initiative, they do so out of the belief that—if it goes well—they will be rewarded for their success. The Climber also likes to brag about past successes and accomplishments.

Finally, we have what might be considered the "antistakeholder": the "Blocker." These individuals are wired to avoid change and defend the status quo. They strongly prefer stability and continuity, actively avoiding (and preventing) initiatives that would bring change and disruption. As a result, they rarely help suppliers and almost never go out of their way to speak to outside vendors. Whether they block for personal reasons (e.g., being burned by suppliers in the past or being the person who invented the legacy system or approach) or because they are "pro status quo," it makes little difference. While it's critical to identify and manage Blockers (something we'll talk about later in the book), for the sake of this discussion, we need to throw them out of the mix. Because of how they're wired, they will never be the stakeholder a salesperson will hitch their wagon to.

These are the seven customer profiles we find in nature. We're guessing that if you were to think back across the last few deals your company has sold (or attempted to sell), you could probably put a customer name against each of the profiles you see here.

But while it's a convenient shorthand for thinking about different types of stakeholders, here's the real kicker: the attributes we shared earlier in this chapter—the ten things we tell our reps to look for when finding an advocate or coach—are more or less evenly spread across these seven customer profiles.

Think about what that means in practical terms for core-performing sales reps: if they're looking for a single person who embodies all of those shaded attributes, they're going to be looking for a long time. Not because these attributes can't be found, but because the data tell us that it's extremely rare to find them all (or even more than a few, for that matter) in the same person. Now, one might argue that since these profiles are not necessarily mutually exclusive, technically it is possible to stumble across someone who embodies the whole list, but frankly, that's not very realistic. In fact, we did the math, and we determined that the full combination of ideal stakeholder attributes coexists in the same person less than 1 percent of the time. That's fewer than 7 out of 700 people in our survey. That might not be as rare as finding a unicorn, but it may as well be.

After all, how much time do you want your core reps spending running from account to account searching high and low for the small handful of people that represents all of the ideal stakeholder attributes we tell them are important? Thankfully, in the real world, that's not what actually happens.

So what *does* happen? Here's where the story gets really fascinating. Among the seven profiles to be found, it turns out that core reps and star reps target in nearly opposite directions.

To show you what we mean, let's first do a quick thought exercise.

Go back and look at those seven profiles again. If we were to tell you that star performers focus on building strong relationships with three of these profiles in particular, which three do you think those would be? Next, if we were to tell you that core performers also gravitate to a certain three, which do you think those would be? Here's a hint: there's no overlap *at all* between the profiles core reps target and the ones star reps target. In neither case do they target the Blocker (because, as you'll recall, this person is very antichange and extremely difficult for a sales rep to engage. As a supplier, even if you want to talk to them, they don't want to talk to you).

THE MOBILIZERS

As we dug into the rep data, here's what we found. One of the things we tested in great detail were the attributes sales reps seek out when prioritizing one customer stakeholder over another. Reps were presented with a long list of potential stakeholder characteristics—things like "easily accessible," "budget owner," "senior title," and "willing to share information." We then asked them to rate the importance of each of those characteristics on a scale from 1 to 7 in terms of the relative importance in seeking out the stakeholders best suited to help them advance a sale. We then took those responses and cut them by sales rep performance level to determine which attributes stood out as most important to star performers. The results were surprising. It turns out star performers by and large care about two things far above all others when determining who they're going to rely on to move a deal forward. Relatively *less* important to stars are things like seniority, C-level title, budget ownership, decision-making authority—namely, all the traditional attributes most might assume to be at the top of their list. Instead, star sellers are looking for customer stakeholders who can (1) drive change across their organization and (2) build consensus among their colleagues. These two attributes alone accounted for the vast majority of star rep attention in prioritizing one stakeholder over another. Even more interesting, it's highly unlikely that anyone ever trained them to do this. They just figured it out on their own over time. They've discovered—whether consciously or subconsciously—that in a 5.4 world, the ability to build consensus and drive change stands above all others in predicting the value of a stakeholder in getting a solutions deal done.

Now, that's a hugely valuable finding, because it then allowed us to return to the seven stakeholder profiles we found in the data and ask a very simple but powerful question: who among these seven profiles is particularly good at building consensus and driving change?

To figure that out, we carefully tested each of the seven profiles against their likelihood and ability to drive "organizational action"—specifically, the "likelihood and ability to initiate change and drive agreement around complex purchases and changes."

In practical terms, what this means is that we measured each respondent's ability to drive consensus in a complex deal. To be clear, we didn't just *ask* people how good they thought they were at driving change and consensus. After all, most everyone thinks they do that well. Instead, we let the analysis figure that out by creating a special index score for each respondent based on their reactions to a series of situational judgment scenarios presented in the survey. These scenarios were designed to represent "typical" business situations in which you, as a stakeholder, had to choose a role to play with respect to potential solutions purchases, organizational changes, and large-scale initiatives. There were a wide variety of possible responses—for instance, "I'd support the change if it benefited me person-ally" or "I'd support the change if the project plan made sense" or "I'd work to maintain the status quo and minimize the scope of the proposed change." Respondents would pick which "posture" best characterized how they would engage around the initiative, an exercise that was repeated multiple times to determine a specific person's given proclivity. This method gave us a much more objective measurement of an individual's true likelihood to drive change and allowed us to measure real differences across stakeholders who, had we simply asked them the direct question, more than likely would have all told us they're great at driving change.

When we ran that analysis and then married it back to the sales rep data mentioned above, what we found is: high-performing reps focus on build-ing connections with *Go-Getters, Teachers, and Skeptics*, while average-performing salespeople target *Guides, Friends, and Climbers*.

FIG. 2.4. Seller Preference for Customer Stakeholder Profiles (by seller performance level)

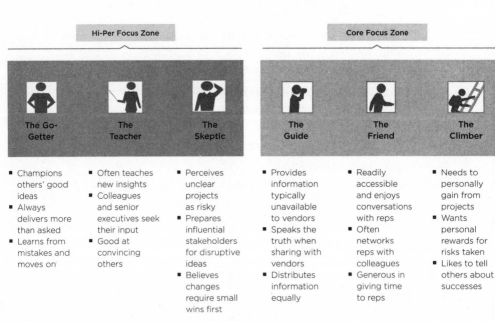

	Hi-Per Focus Zone			Core Focus Zone	
The Go-Getter	The Teacher	The Skeptic	The Guide	The Friend	The Climber
▪ Champions others' good ideas ▪ Always delivers more than asked ▪ Learns from mistakes and moves on	▪ Often teaches new insights ▪ Colleagues and senior executives seek their input ▪ Good at convincing others	▪ Perceives unclear projects as risky ▪ Prepares influential stakeholders for disruptive ideas ▪ Believes changes require small wins first	▪ Provides information typically unavailable to vendors ▪ Speaks the truth when sharing with vendors ▪ Distributes information equally	▪ Readily accessible and enjoys conversations with reps ▪ Often networks reps with colleagues ▪ Generous in giving time to reps	▪ Needs to personally gain from projects ▪ Wants personal rewards for risks taken ▪ Likes to tell others about successes

n = 717.
Source: CEB analysis.

So while it is true that people sell to people, it turns out that core and star performers don't just sell differently to the *same* people, they actually sell differently to *different* people.

It's not so much *that* this happens that makes this data so intriguing; rather, it's the *why*.

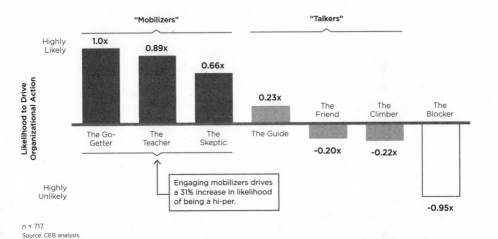

FIG. 2.5. Effectiveness of Customer Stakeholder Profiles for Driving Organizational Action (indexed)

n = 717.
Source: CEB analysis.

It turns out that the Go-Getter, the Teacher, and the Skeptic are fantastic at driving consensus-based change (see figure 2.5). The Go-Getter because she's looking to champion great ideas that can be turned into tangible business results, the Teacher because he can paint a vision that will build momentum for new ideas. The Skeptic—while more cautious—will carefully look something over and then push for change in bite-size increments.

Far and away, these are the key people making things happen inside any organization. In fact, moving forward, we'll refer to these three stakeholders (Go-Getters, Teachers, and Skeptics) as "Mobilizers"—because that's what they are. They are the ones who *mobilize* the organization to act, the ones who forge consensus, the architects and champions for change.

Meanwhile, we have the three profiles that core performers target—the Guide, the Friend, and the Climber—each of whom has relatively little impact on organizational change. They are very interested in talking, but much less so in acting. For short, we'll call them the "Talkers."

This distinction—between Mobilizers and Talkers—raises an important question. If you're selling a large, complex, disruptive solution into a company characterized by these seven stakeholder types, who should you be talking to, Mobilizers or Talkers?

Indeed, if you think back to how high- and core-performing reps map to this framework, you begin to see just how important this finding really is. Core reps sell to Talkers and fail, while stars sell to Mobilizers and win. It's the key to winning the consensus-based sale.

It's not just that people sell to people. It's that *good* people sell to the *right* people. And the difference here can be huge. In fact, when we went back to our sales rep performance analysis, we found that sales reps who engage Mobilizers are 31 percent more likely to be a high performer than those who don't.

When you dig into these profiles in a bit more detail, you begin to see why. Remember our core performer looking for a unicorn? Unable to find all ten advocate attributes in a single person, who's he going to latch on to? Well, if you're a core performer, the easy thing to do is find someone who wants to talk to you, namely, a Guide or a Friend. They're fantastic because they're friendly, open, and accessible. Not just that, but (in the case of the Guide), they're willing to share information. What's not to like?

But if your goal is to get a sale, and not just have a good conversation, the data very clearly suggests that these people can't get you very far. Star performers are out looking for a different kind of conversation altogether. Take another look at the Mobilizers. What do they all have in common? Well, to put it bluntly, none of them are necessarily *looking* to talk to you. These people are focused on getting things done. They're constantly pushing their companies and themselves to think and act differently. In the words of one impressive star performer we interviewed as part of our research, "You've got to have more than someone to talk to. You need someone willing to own the vision and make things happen." What you need, in other words, is a Mobilizer.

Yet, for the average sales rep, a Mobilizer sales conversation isn't necessarily an easy one. In fact, it can be downright unpleasant, if not terrifying. First of all, it's naturally focused on the company's challenge, not the rep's solution. So it requires more than being a good "talking brochure" in the meeting—it requires that you can engage at a meaningful level on real issues of importance to the customer. You're also going to face a ton of questions when you talk to these people. Go-Getters will press you because they want to *do*, Teachers because they want to *know*, and Skeptics because they want to *test*. Skeptics in particular are going to pull an idea apart piece by piece and examine it from every possible angle before grudgingly providing their support. And for core performers, that's a conversation many would rather avoid altogether. Yet for stars, it's the best possible reason to get out of bed every morning. Depending on your perspective, it's either the worst or the very best sales conversation you'll have all year—going head-to-head with a skeptical customer on a new idea, tearing it down and then building it back up specifically in the context of that customer's unique business challenges.

Who wants to have *that* kind of conversation? Well, it turns out, your stars do. In part, because this is the sort of hand-to-hand combat they live for. But more important, because they see Mobilizers for who they are: stakeholders they can rely on to drive meaningful progress and, ultimately, get the deal done. As one high performer said to us in an interview, "If they're not skeptical and don't push me, then I've done something wrong, or they're just not serious." How many of our core performers think that way?

If you step back from this data and think about what's going on here, we're guessing you probably see the same thing we do: when you think about your very best reps—your Challenger reps—it's no surprise that they're naturally drawn to Mobilizers. *Because Mobilizers are just like them. They are the Challengers of the customer organization.* Meanwhile, the Relationship Builder sales rep (as you'll recall, this was the rep focused on identifying and acquiescing to customer demands and, according to our data, the rep least likely to be a star performer) will naturally gravitate to Talkers because Talkers are just like them. They are the Relationship Builders of the customer organization. They're likable and generous with their time. But nothing ever seems to get done.

Core reps don't choose Talkers because they're confused. They choose Talkers because it's *easy*. But it turns out that Talkers are just as bad at getting the deal done on the customer side as Relationship Builders are on the supplier side. One head of sales we work with summed it up this way: "Challengers sell to Challengers and Relationship Builders sell to Relationship Builders. Each looks for its twin within the customer organization and this is the person they will hitch their wagon to." This is how your stars *build* consensus, rather than just find it. They're specifically targeting the people best positioned to create consensus in the first place—to help them climb the "me" to "we" mountain.

THREE KEYS TO UNLOCKING MOBILIZER POTENTIAL

Having studied Mobilizers and their role in the customer buying process for the better part of five years, we've come to conclude that suppliers must get three things right in order to fully unlock Mobilizer potential:

1. Suppliers must *teach* Mobilizers where they learn.

2. Suppliers must *tailor* their engagement efforts to specific Mobilizer type.

3. Suppliers must equip their Mobilizers to *take control* of the consensus-building process.

Why Teach, Tailor, and Take Control?

The framework for this book—"Teach, Tailor, and Take Control"—will feel familiar to readers of The Challenger Sale. *We see three specific reasons for using the same framework to unpack our Mobilizer research.*

First, this book is the "mirror image" of Challenger. *You'll recall from the very first pages that this is a book about buying solutions as opposed to selling them. It's about "customer Challengers" as opposed to Challenger salespeople. So it stands to reason that the same framework would apply—just from a customer perspective, rather than a supplier perspective. In many respects, this book is about the customer "reaction" to our Challenger actions.*

Second, it helps support ongoing change management efforts. No commercial leader who has taken the plunge on Challenger wants or needs a new and potentially different framework distracting the organization from the hard change management work at hand. As we discussed in The Challenger Sale, *adopting this new commercial approach isn't something that happens overnight—the change is difficult and progress is measured in months and years as opposed to weeks and days. For most organizations, they still have not fully digested the first wave of change from Challenger. Dropping a new, competing framework into the mix underserves all parties—salespeople, managers, marketers, CSOs, CMOs, you name it. Our goal isn't to make things more difficult, it's to make it easier for organizations pursuing the Challenger model to adopt these new Mobilizer insights. We'll be taking readers much deeper into the ideas of teaching, tailoring, and taking control than we did in* The Challenger Sale. *We'll provide more data, analysis, perspective, and guidance to those companies already on the journey and, in some cases, provide additional data to those leaders still on the fence about whether a Challenger approach makes sense for their organizations. In that respect, think of this as the 2.0 version of Challenger—not as something different and potentially contradictory to its predecessor.*

Third, well, it just makes sense. We debated this for a long time as a team and kept coming back to one inescapable conclusion: what's happening here is teaching, tailoring, and taking control. As you go through the book, we think you'll agree.

Let's walk through each of these imperatives at a high level, just to orient you to what's ahead.

First, we're going to take a deep dive into teaching. Now, Commercial Insight is a concept we first introduced in *The Challenger Sale*, and our work on consensus and Mobilizers has reaffirmed for us the fact that truly counterintuitive Commercial Insight lies at the heart of the new-world Challenger commercial model. Unfortunately, it's also the single thing we've seen companies struggle with the most when it comes to implementing Challenger—in part because they fail to appreciate that *building insight is an organizational capability, not an individual salesperson skill* (despite the many sales-training vendors out there offering to train your salespeople on how to generate insights) and in part because they mistakenly assume that "thought leadership" is the same thing as counterintuitive insight (when, in fact, the two are quite different).

What's more, our most recent work has convinced us that teaching can't be the job of just salespeople—marketing must be involved not just in *developing* Commercial Insights, but in deploying them as well. Why? Because customers can now learn on their own. And while there's a pretty strong guarantee that your Mobilizer will want to learn, there is no guarantee that they will want to learn from your sales reps. At least not initially. So seeding the world with Commercial Insight is crucial to "catch" a Mobilizer—but only if we know where our Mobilizers are most likely to learn. If they're not going to learn from sales, then marketing is going to have to find a way to get that content into the channels where they *are* going to learn.

Second, once we cover teaching, we'll dig into the concept of tailoring to your Mobilizer. Now, tailoring as we explained it in *Challenger* is, in fact, still very important, but it is specifically important in that first movement to win over the Mobilizer as an individual. Here, we're talking about tailoring content depending on what type of Mobilizer you believe you've found (remember, there are three different types of Mobilizer and each will attach to a Commercial Insight in a slightly different way). But that still doesn't explain what we saw in chapter 1—that better individual positioning can hurt you. In fact, it probably seems like we're saying that salespeople should do the *very thing* that we just told you in chapter 1 is bad!

Well, what we've learned is that tailoring at the individual level is crucially important for winning an individual, but nonetheless dramatically insufficient for winning a high-quality deal. At some point you have to make a big shift from tailoring to win the *individual* to tailoring to win the *group*. Tailoring to win over the group requires a different kind of tailoring technique altogether. Later, in chapter 8, our section on taking control, we will talk about what has to happen to tailoring when we get into that second movement of the sale—when we have to go from winning the individual to winning the group—because in this phase, we are not tailoring to win individual buy-in, we are tailoring to win organizational consensus.

The two kinds of tailoring are, in fact, different. If you do only the first kind of tailoring without the second kind of tailoring, you may win over the Mobilizer but still end up with a low-quality deal—or perhaps lose the deal altogether. Why? Because as good a job as we did connecting that individual to *us*, we failed to connect the Mobilizer and the rest of the 4.4 to *each other*.

Now, how do you do that? Well, one thing we've learned is: your Mobilizer may not fully know either. Just because they're willing to mobilize

FIG. 2.6. Purchase Process Overview (illustrative)

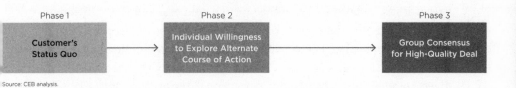

Source: CEB analysis.

doesn't necessarily mean they'll be able to mobilize. Here is where we can help, by essentially taking control of the consensus creation process ourselves and directing the group to agreement. The good news is there's a significant role both marketing and sales can play to tailor their content and their approach to help us take control of the consensus creation process to win in the second arrow. That matters deeply; after all, we don't get paid for individual buy-in, we get paid for 5.4 agreement. That is the ticket out of the "solutions graveyard."

So let's turn now to taking control across that long second arrow. This is where we started our discussion in chapter 1, by focusing on what happens when suppliers try to bridge the second move in the sale—from having one individual on board to building consensus across a *group* of individuals. Because of the diversity of these groups—which creates dysfunction among the 5.4 stakeholders trying to reach agreement—so many of our deals end up, despite doing everything right in the beginning, in the "solutions graveyard."

Why does this happen? As you'll recall, it's because each stakeholder has his or her own *mental model* and the overlap in mental models is likely to be minimal at best. Each person approaches the consensus moment with a different conception of what's important, what needs to be included in the proposal, and what "victory" looks like. Left to their own devices, they will push apart rather than pull together—something that tailoring only to the individual level will actually cause or, at the very least, exacerbate—ultimately landing the group in a place where they can't decide on much of anything. What began for the supplier as a complex, long-term, high-margin solutions deal ends up as nothing more than the purchase of a simple, low-margin commoditized product—because the group, left to bicker about what was really important in the proposal, couldn't reach consensus on *anything more*.

How do we overcome this? Here, we'll go deep into the concept of Collective Learning—one of the biggest eye-openers for us in the past five years that we've been studying the phenomenon of consensus. Collective Learning is a technique for *taking control* of the consensus process. It's about the supplier helping to facilitate that consensus-building process by offering a framework—a new, collective mental model—that anchors a diverse (and dysfunctional) buying group on a common vision, an aspiration they can all coalesce around rather than defaulting to lowest-common-denominator buying. As we mentioned above, this is less about connecting *us* to our Mobilizer—or even to individual stakeholders—and much more about connecting the other 4.4 to *each other*. It's about shifting our sales and marketing approach—historically focused on gathering a "collection of yeses," one from each individual stakeholder in the hopes that they'll come together and hold hands on a decision—to gathering a *Collective Yes* from the group.

But as great an asset as they are in forging consensus, Mobilizers need some help when it comes to *buying* our solutions. So we'll introduce a second concept here, all in the vein of taking control, called "Commercial Coaching." This is really about coaching your Mobilizer on how to buy (versus the conventional wisdom of asking the customer to coach you on how to sell).

Are you ready? Let's start our journey by unpacking the concept of teaching.

CHAPTER THREE

THE ART OF UNTEACHING

If there is one simple truth of every B2B supplier today, it is that they're all selling the same thing: change. Whether it's convincing customers to buy from them instead of the competition, to outsource to them what they've traditionally done on their own, or perhaps to upgrade to their newer/broader solution instead of maintaining their older/smaller one, one way or another virtually every solution sale revolves around a supplier's attempt to convince customers to change.

But think about what that means. What's the one thing most organizations would like to avoid at all costs unless they have absolutely no other choice? Change. Why? It's expensive. It's risky. It's disruptive. It's unknown. Indeed, the one thing all suppliers are selling is exactly the same thing most customers are actively avoiding. From that perspective, it's no wonder that solution selling is so hard. Or, for that matter, that most suppliers' single biggest competitor today isn't so much the competition but the customer's own status quo.

But if we consider the challenge of selling change within the context of creating customer consensus, we begin to see how monumentally difficult selling solutions truly has become. For as hard as it is to convince a single, senior buyer that whatever they're currently doing isn't "good enough," how in the world does a supplier successfully convince a diverse group of 5.4 stakeholders of the exact same thing? Especially when the end result will require some kind of organizational change that some—if not all—would prefer to avoid if at all possible? Remember, if the 5.4 is naturally predisposed to agree on anything, more likely than not it's to *avoid risk, move cautiously, reduce disruption,* and *save money.* How is a supplier supposed to overcome that kind of broad-based resistance to change?

MOBILIZING THE MOBILIZER

When we think of it like this, it's no wonder that star-performing sales reps seek out Mobilizers. After all, they're the individuals inside the customer organization most open to change in the first place. They're looking for new ideas, willing to consider alternate courses of action, and, crucially, able to win over others' buy-in to that alternate point of view. That's not to say, of course, that Mobilizers are necessarily *looking* for a supplier—or even less likely, a *particular* supplier—but they are at least (grudgingly at times) willing to entertain a conversation with a supplier should they believe the supplier might have something worthwhile to share. Simply put, star performers—recognizing that they first and foremost sell change—very carefully target those individuals most open, or least resistant, to that change in the first place, and then lean on those individuals to drive that change elsewhere across the organization. One sales executive called it the "new physics" of sales: "Mobilizers," she told us, "allow me to *minimize inertia* and *maximize momentum*."

That said, if we think back to the three-step model of a customer purchase we introduced in chapter 1 (see figure 3.1), those physics will play out in different ways at different points across the purchase process.

FIG. 3.1. Purchase Process Overview (illustrative)

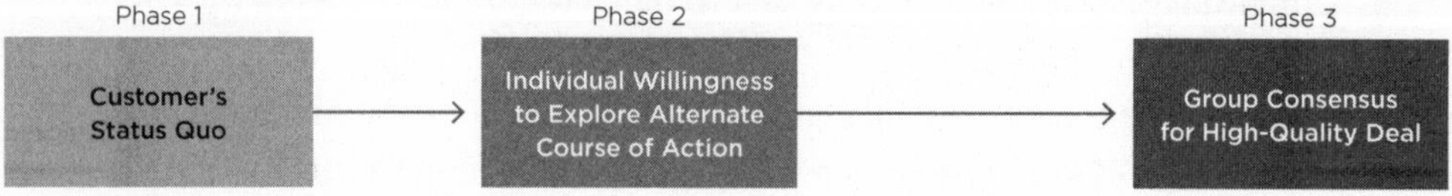

Phase 1	Phase 2	Phase 3
Customer's Status Quo	Individual Willingness to Explore Alternate Course of Action	Group Consensus for High-Quality Deal

Source: CEB analysis.

From Phase 1 to Phase 2, a supplier must first convince *someone* inside the customer organization that change is even necessary. Remember, the goal isn't so much to convince someone to buy a solution but, rather, to persuade them to change their behavior. Just because someone might be predisposed to favor change *in general* doesn't necessarily mean that they'll be willing to support the *specific* change advocated by a given supplier. So the way that supplier's message is constructed—the way it's designed to make the case for change—really matters. As one head of sales told us,

"Look, I might be a Mobilizer, but that doesn't mean I'm going to *mobilize* around every new idea put on the table. Context *really* matters." And he's right. Setting a Mobilizer in motion across that first shift from Phase 1 to Phase 2 requires a convincing vision and credible evidence that that change is even worth it in the first place.

Still, that's just the beginning. For just because the Mobilizer is open to change doesn't necessarily mean any of the other 4.4 are at all. That Mobilizer now faces a real uphill battle building a bridge from "me" to "we" across the chasm from Phase 2 to Phase 3. And the support suppliers provide in that effort can make all the difference in whether the Mobilizer is both willing and able to successfully champion change across the rest of that buying group.

Now, just to make things even harder, *none* of this happens in a vacuum. You'll remember, CEB customer research has additionally found that customers are contacting supplier sales reps later than ever before across a typical purchase process. That's the 57 percent we reviewed earlier: customers proactively seek out sales rep input at 57 percent of the way through a purchase. That single statistic renders this entire three-phase process significantly much more difficult. For, just because sales reps aren't necessarily there to see it happen doesn't mean it doesn't have to happen nonetheless. Just the opposite. It means customers are now left to figure it out on their own.

Now, there are a number of things sellers can do to regain access to the earlier part of a purchase (we'll look at one idea in particular, "social selling," later). From a supplier's point of view, at the very least, the 57 percent number tells us that much of the identification and motivation of a Mobilizer may not happen through person-to-person sales interactions at all, but rather through broader-based *marketing* channels designed to connect with customers far earlier. The lesson being, without tight integration between sales and marketing, it's unlikely a supplier can predictably influence any of this change process at all.

But let's consider for a moment *why* customers are delaying contact with sales reps for as long as they are. The answer is simple but rather instructive: because they can. In fact, based on all of our research, we've come to postulate a sort of "golden rule" of customer-supplier engagement:

Left to their own devices, customers will always engage a supplier as late as they possibly can.

In other words, much of the reason *why* a customer engages a supplier 57 percent of the way through the purchase rather than earlier is that they don't believe that the supplier has anything valuable to contribute to the conversation. At least nothing they couldn't get off that supplier's Web site on their own, without having to speak with a sales rep. "So if I reach out to a supplier," the thinking goes, "all they're going to do is drone on about their product or service and ask me lots of open-ended questions that I don't need their help answering. It's biased information, and it's never really about helping my business, so much as selling theirs . . ." Who wants to sit through that? In a world of information accessibility, customers can get all of that on the Internet. Talking directly to a supplier feels like a waste of time. Let's face it, many of us reading this book sell for a living, and we likely feel exactly the same way about people who sell to us! Why talk to a salesperson unless you really think you have to?

That's exactly where *teaching* comes in, convincingly proving to customers—and especially Mobilizers—that they *do* have to talk to you.

But now we can better appreciate the very specific, and rather complicated, context within which we must deploy that teaching. In this world, suppliers' teaching must:

1. Capture the attention of a Mobilizer, in a way that

2. Motivates them to champion a change in behavior, leading them to

3. Rally the support of the other 4.4, around a vision that

4. Leads that customer back to their unique solution.

That's a very high bar, indeed. In fact, we have a name for this very special kind of content. We call it *Commercial Insight*. The reason we find Commercial Insight so powerful is that it's the only kind of teaching we've found in all of our research that can impact customer buying behavior across all three stages of that buying process *irrespective* of where it's deployed. Whether it's winning the willingness of individual stakeholders to mobilize in the first place, or equipping those Mobilizers to win over the other 4.4 who are potentially even less inclined to change. That's because Commercial Insight is designed to *change* what customers are currently thinking regardless of what that thinking might be—whether it's to do something different or, just as likely, to do nothing at all. In a world where every supplier is selling change, producing content with that kind of impact *really* matters.

But for Commercial Insight to have that kind of broad influence across the customer purchase, it must follow a precise set of design principles. For only a small fraction of the content most suppliers produce today is designed to drive that kind of behavior change. Chief among those design principles is the idea that effective Commercial Insight isn't designed to *teach* so much as to *unteach*.

NOT TEACHING, BUT *UN*TEACHING

Naturally, in order to capture customer attention, supplier content must have something valuable to say. But what exactly must it say in order to drive customer behavior change? What kind of content can do *that*?

To figure that out, our team at CEB conducted a large-scale survey of several hundred customer stakeholders, all involved in a B2B purchase, across every major industry, geography, and go-to-market model.

More precisely, we wanted to identify, with data, the kinds of "content attributes" that have a meaningful impact on customers' current thinking—whether that be the status quo or a particular course of action. In other words, the question we set out to answer was, "What kinds of supplier content can bend the path across the customer's 'me' to 'we' mountain?"

Now, to figure that out, one can't simply ask customers, "What will blow your mind?" Because they likely won't know and, if they do, they probably wouldn't admit to it. So instead, we first asked customers to consider a recent purchase of a more complex solution and then report the degree to which their direction across that purchase process changed, on a scale from 1 to 7.

Separately, we then asked respondents to score the value they place on various aspects of the content they typically consume as part of any purchase process—anything from "readability" to "relevance" to "data quality" to "credibility."

When combined, those two sets of questions allowed us to statistically derive the potential impact of each of those inputs on actually changing customers' purchase direction. And the result was fascinating (see figure 3.2).

FIG. 3.2. Drivers of Changing a Customer's Direction

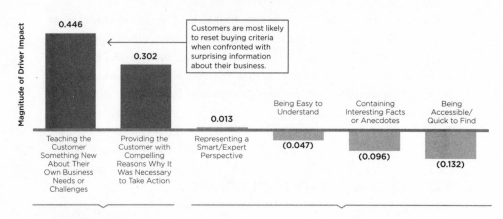

n = 545.
Source: CEB analysis.

Before we turn to what *does* matter, it's instructive to look at what doesn't. For, of all the content attributes we tested, only two turned out to be statistically significant. Everything else had no statistically meaningful impact on changing a customer's purchase direction at all.

So, for example, the fact that content is "easily accessible" and "quick to find" has no bearing on customers' likelihood to change their thinking. Nor does the degree to which content "contains interesting facts or anecdotes" or whether it's "easy to understand."

Now, in many ways, that makes a lot of sense. It seems unlikely that a customer would change course simply because a particular piece of content was easy to find and particularly well written.

But one attribute that *also* doesn't matter was far more surprising. Among the statistically *non*significant drivers of changing customer buying direction was content "representing a smart or expert perspective."

For many suppliers, that finding is far more interesting, as that attribute reflects the stated strategy of most B2B marketers around the world. In a world awash in content of low quality and little relevance, many marketers would argue that the best way to stand out is through high-quality content, representing a smart, distinctive perspective that clearly positions that supplier as a "thought leader" in their industry. The belief being that thought leadership is crucial to a supplier's ability to differentiate not only their content, but also their capabilities. Surely—the thinking goes—a company that produces high-quality thought leadership must also offer high-quality solutions. It engenders trust. It conveys credibility. It tells customers "We know things about the world" and "You should talk to us before you make a decision."

In fact, across the last five years—bolstered by the rise of "content marketing" and new marketing automation technology—marketers have invested an enormous amount of time, money, and resources into thought leadership for exactly these reasons. Indeed, many CMOs have told us, it's their stated strategy for "standing out" in a crowded marketplace where they might otherwise become easily commoditized.

But if that's the case, this data is rather troubling, as that strategy has no statistically measurable impact on changing actual customer buying behavior. Particularly in a world where suppliers compete with customer status quo as often as anything else, that's a worrying finding to say the least.

So what *does* have a statistically significant impact on changing a customer's purchase direction? In our analysis we found only two drivers capable of reliably driving that kind of change:

1. Teaching the customer something new and compelling about *their* business, and

2. Providing customers with a compelling reason to take action

In other words, customers are most likely to rethink their current course or reset preestablished buying criteria only when confronted with surprising information not about the world in general, but about *their own* business. More specifically, information laying out not just the benefits of taking action, but the *costs* of *inaction*.

It's this kind of content we've come to label *insight* (we'll get to the "commercial" part in just a bit). Regardless of whether it's delivered through a sales rep conversation or some other content channel, insight is designed to demonstrate to customers that despite their *own* learning and their *own* expertise, they've missed something materially important to the performance of *their* business—a new way to make money, save money, mitigate risk, or penetrate new markets. All based on information that they themselves would not have discovered on their own.

Insight, in other words, isn't designed just to *teach* customers something new that they've never thought before, but to *unteach* them something that they already have.

Now, we've been talking about insight for a while now, as the concept has played a central role in our Challenger work from the very beginning. While we've been careful to define the term as precisely as possible along the way, in working with companies all over the world, we've learned that as careful as we've been to define what insight *is*, we need to be equally careful to define what insight is *not*.

INSIGHT IS NOT THOUGHT LEADERSHIP

When it comes to insight, we find the term suffers from a strong "false-positive problem," as much of what passes under the name of insight today falls into the much broader, and arguably much less valuable, category of "thought leadership." So let's see if we can put some clear boundaries around what we mean by insight (see figure 3.3).

If we think of all the different kinds of content a supplier might produce in the name of insight, we find there are a number of different "layers" to that content, each separated by a boundary delineating that layer from the next.

Let's start with "general information." General information is, well, just that. Information that covers generally just about everything. It's that overwhelming flood of information out there that customers spend more time filtering out than taking in. So, clearly, the first hurdle suppliers need to overcome in building insight is to be heard in the first place, to capture the customer's attention.

So a supplier's first hurdle in content creation is ensuring that whatever they produce in the name of insight is credible and relevant. If customers don't believe what a supplier is saying, or don't believe it applies to them, that supplier's "insight" isn't going to get a lot of attention.

Of course, the bar for "credibility" may present a moving target in some cases as what we call the "burden of proof" of a supplier's insight will largely determine how credible the information upon which that insight is

FIG. 3.3. Comparison of Commercial Information Types

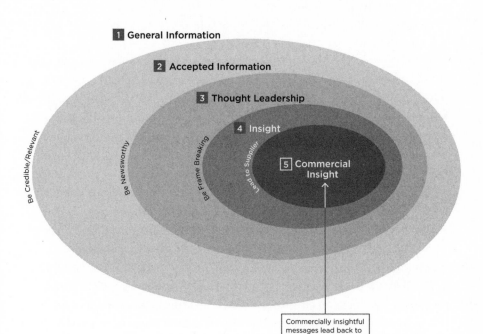

Source: CEB analysis.

based must be. The more counterintuitive or surprising the finding, the higher the burden of proof, and therefore the more robust the evidence must be.

But let's say the information a supplier publishes passes that first test: it's both credible and relevant to the customer. That's fantastic. But it's still not insight. In fact, at this point we've landed at only what we might call "accepted information."

What is that? Accepted information is credible, it's relevant, but frankly it's just not all that interesting. It sounds more or less like everyone else's information—often taking the form of "factoids" or data points. There are a huge number of companies out there every day producing mountains of data—all in the name of insight—that frankly represents nothing more than accepted information. Some examples:

➤ 90 percent of CIOs are concerned about what cloud computing means for their organization.

> ➤ 75 percent of CEOs cite sustainability as a priority, but admit they don't know how to achieve it.

> ➤ 80 percent of global workers report feeling "disconnected from their work."

These are all interesting, relevant, credible statistics, but still, they are statistics. They're not insight. Insight and data are not the same thing. More to the point, this data doesn't tell anyone anything new. Sure, we may not have known that it was *90 percent* of CIOs who are worried about what cloud computing means for their organization, but we could have easily guessed it was a lot of them.

That's the defining characteristic of accepted information: it doesn't tell someone something they didn't know; rather, it largely confirms or validates something they already did.

So customers won't necessarily *ignore* the information. They view it, read it, maybe download it, perhaps "like" it, and possibly even agree with it. But they probably won't *do* anything about it either. At least nothing they weren't going to do already. And yet, it's stunning the amount of content and collateral that's built on this type of information, all in the name of insight.

So what's next? Let's move a step deeper across a boundary we'll call "newsworthy."

Clearly, if we want someone to *act* differently, we have to first get them to *think* differently. To do that, we're going to have to show them something truly newsworthy. And that brings us into the third layer of information: "thought leadership."

Interestingly, above all other categories of content we've laid out so far, thought leadership is the one that can really get a supplier in trouble. Not only because this is the kind of content most suppliers are creating, but because it's the one most suppliers *aspire* to create. Virtually every marketer will tell you, their company strives to be a "thought leader" in their industry.

So what is thought leadership? It's interesting, newsworthy, incremental information that customers themselves likely could not have discovered on their own. So, unlike accepted information, thought leadership is *additive*. It provides new perspectives or new data that *teaches* and doesn't just confirm. So—to be fair—for the first time across our inventory of content, there really is some teaching happening at this third level. And that's great, for what it's worth.

But the real limitation of traditional thought leadership is that it doesn't necessarily drive action. Readers *learn* but they don't necessarily *do*. People may be liking or retweeting the content, but it isn't moving them to action. That's because most thought leadership is largely focused on presenting a *new* idea, rather than undermining an *existing* one. So while thought leadership attracts a lot of attention, it typically has little lasting impact.

We all think, "Wow! That's really interesting!" and then we go back to whatever we were doing before. So it fails to have much commercial impact as it provides only a very weak means, at best, for driving customer behavior change.

So what else is there? Well, the next filter is "Be frame breaking." This is the final bar we need to clear for our content to truly be called "insight." But why that filter, "frame breaking"? What we find is that insight is something else entirely. It's designed to *upend the status quo*. As such, insight isn't about *one* thing, it's about *two* things. It doesn't just convey an idea of what the customer *could* be doing (like thought leadership), but also conveys a story around what the customer is *currently* doing, explicitly laying out why that current behavior is costing the customer time or money in ways they never realized.

That's the key. The contrast. *It's the cost of current behavior juxtaposed to the potential of alternate action.*

Implicit in any good insight is the simple message: "Hey . . . you're doing it wrong!" And done well, it causes your customer to say, "I have to change what I'm doing!" Thus the term "frame breaking."

That's a totally different outcome than one achieves from all of the traditional thought leadership that so many aspire to produce. Insight is a powerful tool to shape or reshape customer demand because it's designed to cause cognitive and emotional dissonance between current behavior and an alternate action.

Customers' reaction to well-designed thought leadership is: "Wow, they're smart."

Customers' reaction to well-designed insight is: "Wow, I'm wrong."

Of course, as we've said all along, the way one delivers that message *really* matters. To be effective (and not offensive!), insight must be delivered professionally, diplomatically, empathetically, and culturally correctly. It's about creating *constructive* tension, not just tension. Otherwise, it's not so much insight as just a plain insult.

Still, when the CEB team is working with member companies on the insights they produce, the first thing we'll typically ask when a company shares an insight for feedback is, "Show me the page, show me the data point, the bar graph, the bullet point, the *moment* where you look your customer in the eye and tell them that they're wrong." If you can't find that moment in your content—no matter how diplomatically formulated— chances are pretty good, you haven't created insight at all.

As the commercial team at CDK Global (formerly ADP Dealer Services) likes to say, "We have to teach our customers that *the pain of same* is greater than *the pain of change*."

Now, that said, we're still not done. We still have to ensure one gets paid for all of this work. So how does that work?

GETTING PAID FOR INSIGHT

It's one thing to drive customers to do something different, but another thing entirely to ensure they do it with you.

So imagine a scenario where a supplier teaches their customer something new, the customer then takes that insight, puts it out to bid, and the supplier's direct competitor wins the business. That doesn't feel so good. And we'd agree. In fact, we call that "free consulting." Few suppliers ever sustainably grew their business falling into that particular trap.

So in order to ensure a supplier *gets paid* for all that insight, we still must pass through one last filter (see figure 3.3). That supplier must ensure that whatever they teach the customer about *the customer*'s business actually leads back to some capability that that supplier is able to provide better than anyone else.

Thus the term Commercial Insight (or what we've called elsewhere "Commercial Teaching"). It's insight that meets the "frame-breaking" bar, but simultaneously leads the customer back to that particular supplier as the only one able to help them take action on that insight.

So when the customer says, "Wow, I gotta do something about this! Who can help me make this happen?" that supplier *must* be able to legitimately look them in the eye and say, "Let me show you how we are the only supplier who can help make that happen."

Much of our work of late has been focused on helping members identify that set of unique benefits in *their* organization to serve as the foundation for this type of Commercial Insight. For it turns out this is not an easy question to answer.

In fact, it's not *one* question but *three* that a supplier must answer to do this well. The first is simply:

1. What are we good at?

Hopefully, that's a question the answer to which can fill a couple of pages, as it refers not only to the features and benefits of the solutions a supplier sells, but to all the capabilities that surround that solution as well—supply chain capabilities, financing opportunities, data-driven market perspectives—whatever the case may be. Think broadly.

The second question, however, is *much* harder.

2. What are we *uniquely* good at?

This is where the pain kicks in, as most companies can successfully answer Question 1 but struggle mightily with Question 2.

One head of sales at a food ingredients company once memorably asked us, "In one part of our business, we sell salt. It's not fancy salt, it's not gourmet salt. It's not sea salt. It's just plain salt. Mountains of it. And our salt isn't any different from anyone else's salt. What's the unique strength in that?"

Our answer was quite simple: "We have no idea." Be that as it may, however, chances are pretty good that that supplier does indeed have some sort of unique strength somewhere in its salt business. But chances are *equally* good that that strength does not lie in the salt itself. In fact, that's almost definitionally the case. Instead, the unique strength of that business likely lies elsewhere in all the various capabilities that that company brings to bear to deliver that salt to market. Maybe it's something about where they mine the salt, creating shorter supply lines, thus enabling just-in-time delivery and reducing customers' carrying costs. Perhaps it's their ability to mine salt around the world, allowing for an uninterrupted supply despite changing geopolitical and climatic conditions. Perhaps it's their uniquely strong financial arm, which enables customers to buy certain financial instruments, allowing them to hedge against risk from fluctuating salt prices.

Granted, these are all strengths we've made up based on pure guesswork, but they're meant to be indicative of the wide net companies must cast when seeking to define their unique strengths. Should they focus too narrowly on their products and services alone, chances are pretty good they may overlook a number of potentially powerful differentiators.

The third, and final, question? It's about time:

3. Which of our unique capabilities is *sustainable*?

After all, an easily copied unique strength isn't much of a unique strength at all.

So to sum it all up, what makes something a true differentiator? At its most basic level a true differentiator is *unique, valuable, defensible*, and *sustainable*.

It's a pretty straightforward list. But consider for a moment what that list rules *out*. Differentiators are not:

1. Features and benefits common in a supplier's market,

2. Outcomes the supplier's product generates, or

3. Vague descriptions or overused descriptions that include *any* of the following words: "innovative," "green," "user friendly," or "solution."

In many companies, we find that once one controls for those three things, there's virtually nothing left. In fact, in a recent CMO survey we found only one-*fifth* of marketers could claim with confidence that their differentiator articulated a true difference in *kind* from the competition (i.e., "we're different") rather than a difference in *degree* (i.e., "We're better. No, seriously . . . we're better") (see figure 3.4).

Not surprisingly, then, only 13 percent felt they could pass what we consider to be the ultimate differentiator test: if we took all the names and logos off of your commercial content and gave it to a competitor to present to a customer, would that customer still necessarily have to buy from you?

When you can say yes to *that* question, you've got something powerfully different to hang your Commercial Insight on.

FIG. 3.4. Heads of Marketing Who "Agree" or "Strongly Agree" with the Statement

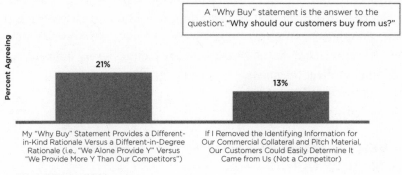

A "Why Buy" statement is the answer to the question: "Why should our customers buy from us?"

My "Why Buy" Statement Provides a Different-in-Kind Rationale Versus a Different-in-Degree Rationale (i.e., "We Alone Provide Y" Versus "We Provide More Y Than Our Competitors") — 21%

If I Removed the Identifying Information for Our Commercial Collateral and Pitch Material, Our Customers Could Easily Determine It Came from Us (Not a Competitor) — 13%

n = 48 Heads of Marketing at 29 B2B Companies.
Source: CEB 2012 CEB Commercial Insight Assessment.

WINNING AS AN ORGANIZATION, NOT AS AN INDIVIDUAL

Notice how these aren't questions any commercial organization would want to leave up to their sales reps to figure out on their own. Indeed, we've watched a number of companies around the world do exactly that—often following the guidance of sales-training vendors—leading almost inevitably to highly limited and potentially dangerous results. Simply putting sales reps through some kind of bootstrapped "insight generation" training with the assumption that building Commercial Insight is essentially a skill to be taught—similar to negotiation or presentation techniques—almost inescapably leads to weak insight.

Building effective, sustainable Commercial Insight requires a much broader organizational capability, if for no other reason than this stuff can be really hard. It takes multiple sources of information. It demands a deep understanding of a company's strategic direction. It requires access to customers well beyond just individual sales conversations. But most important, it requires broad, consistent application across a supplier's vast array of sales, service, and marketing communications. All that is going to take time, patience, multiple iterations, and consistent, focused senior executive buy-in to really work.

What we're talking about here, in other words, is a fundamental review of how a company goes to market. While that question undoubtedly requires front-line input, it is nonetheless an inquiry best guided from the most senior ranks of an organization, up to and including the CEO. Commercial Insight isn't an individual sales technique nearly as much as organizational commercial strategy.

The front end of that effort undoubtedly requires a very different way of thinking about customers.

A VERY DIFFERENT KIND OF "CUSTOMER UNDERSTANDING"

The last ten years have seen an explosion of interest in "customer understanding" led in particular by marketing organizations seeking to ensure their company not only meets customer expectations but *exceeds* them.

Not surprisingly, then, marketers have invested huge amounts of time, effort, and money developing a wide-ranging toolbox to determine whether their organization is "delivering a world-class customer experience," designed to offer memorable "moments of *delight*" across "every possible customer touch point." While this work can span a wide range of activity—anything from interviews, to focus groups, to in-field ethnographic research—much of it relies heavily on the most tried and true of marketing tools: the customer survey. Though, to be sure, those surveys have evolved significantly over time. From customer satisfaction, to customer loyalty, to "voice of the customer," to "Net Promoter® Score," to "customer experience." Indeed, commercial organizations around the world pore over the results of these surveys on a regular basis, often making large-scale strategic decisions and allocating large amounts of company resources based solely on the information they contain.

Yet, as useful as those surveys are in retrospectively gauging company performance, it turns out they're virtually useless for proactively building world-class Commercial Insight. Why? Because every one of those surveys is designed to test for the exact same thing: customers' perceptions of the *supplier*. "Do you like *us*?" "Are you satisfied with *us*?" "Will you remain loyal to *us*?" "Are you willing to recommend *us*?" Granted, those are all important things to know. But notice that they're all supplier focused.

Each one provides an ever more accurate snapshot of how the customer views the *supplier*.

But, you'll remember, the key to Commercial Insight isn't a story about the supplier at all. It's a story about the *customer* and how they've missed something materially important to the performance of *their* business. As a result, in order to build world-class Commercial Insight, suppliers don't necessarily need an ever more refined view of how customers perceive *them*. What they need is a significantly more refined view of how customers perceive *themselves*.

Surprisingly, very little effort in the name of "customer understanding" today is designed to figure that out. In fact, a disturbingly large number of very senior marketers have told us they lack any real sense of how their customers view themselves. Some have even told us that they rarely if ever talk to their customers *at all*!

But it turns out, that kind of customer understanding is absolutely crucial for Commercial Insight to work. Because the only way to (diplomatically) tell a customer that they're "wrong" is to first understand what they believe in the first place. That set of beliefs is something we like to call a "mental model."

BUILDING AND BREAKING MENTAL MODELS

As we saw earlier, selling solutions is all about getting customers to change.

Whether it's getting customers to move from buying nothing to buying something, from buying from a competitor to buying from them, or from buying something from them to buying *even more* from them, commercial teams' primary mission is to move customers off of their current behavior and toward a new, desired behavior.

However, in a world where both individual customer stakeholders and entire customer organizations can learn on their own prior to ever engaging a supplier, the biggest challenge is getting customers to reconsider their current thinking in the first place—irrespective of whether that thinking entails criteria for a particular kind of purchase, or, just as likely, a strong belief that the current status quo is already "good enough."

You'll remember this challenge presents at two levels—or across two different "movements." First, we have to get a (proto) Mobilizer to reconsider their individual thinking, then we have to get the entire 5.4 to reconsider their *collective* thinking.

But how do we do that? How do we get them to believe that change is not only possible but desirable? That undergoing the pain and disruption of shifting from their current behavior (where they are now) to our desired behavior (where they are more likely to purchase our solution) is worth it in the first place (see figure 3.5)?

FIG. 3.5. Customer Mental Models Overview

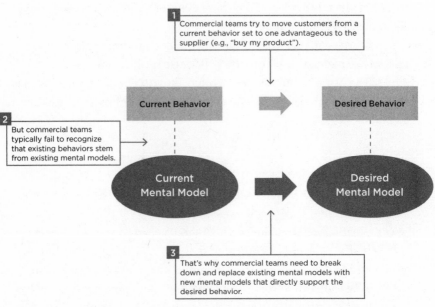

Source: CEB analysis.

Well, the most *common* way is to paint the most attractive picture possible of how wonderful the world of the new behavior could be, if only the customer would just embrace it.

So suppliers invest heavily in extolling the benefits of a world supported by their solution. They develop all sorts of data touting the benefits of the new behavior. They develop ROI calculators showing customers how much money they can save by making the shift. They paint a broad, compelling picture of the unquestionable quality, cutting-edge technology, proven reliability, and "unlocked hidden value" realized only by embracing that new direction. And they provide customer testimonials reflecting how wonderful life in that new world can be.

And yet, suppliers are surprised and disappointed when, despite their best efforts, customers fail to respond favorably, ultimately choosing to remain steadfastly on course with whatever they were doing already. They're left scratching their heads wondering, "Where did we go wrong?" "Do we need a different ROI calculator?" "Do we need better customer testimonials?" "Perhaps we should redesign our Web site." "We need an urgency driver!" Or "What we *really* need is a sharper value proposition." The amount of soul-searching, finger-pointing, and second-guessing that goes on at this point is enough to undermine even the very best of collaborative organizational cultures.

But why is this such a struggle? Why is it so hard to redirect customer buying behavior? Well, what most suppliers fail to fully appreciate is that current behavior is significantly more entrenched than they might realize. Not simply because of some kind of broad "organizational inertia" or failure to appreciate the superiority of their solution. But rather due to an underlying set of beliefs and assumptions about how the world works.

Psychologists call this a "mental model." A customer's mental model dictates virtually everything that they do. That mental model doesn't just matter. It matters a lot. Because that's what's driving that customer's behavior in the first place.

If you want to change behavior, you first have to change the mental model. It's the "frame" in the "frame breaking" we need to do to really call it insight.

Put another way, the only way to change how a customer *acts* is to first change the way that that customer *thinks*.

You'll remember from chapter 1 the degree to which the mental models of each of the 5.4 are highly divergent, that it's not just one way of thinking we have to change but potentially many more.

Be that as it may, what we've consistently found in all of our research is that the best sales reps—Challenger reps—and the best companies—Challenger organizations—see customers' current mental models as the primary leverage point for driving customer behavior change. So rather than engaging customers in a debate on the merits of the supplier's proposed solution, the best suppliers engage their customers in a discussion of the customer's current beliefs. And in that discussion, they diplomatically, empathetically, culturally correctly, yet *systematically* break down their customer's current mental model, show them how it's flawed or incomplete, and then articulate in very clear terms why a move the customer assumes would be too costly or too painful is actually less costly or painful than their current status quo.

It's a careful, credible demonstration that the customer's current mental model is not only flawed, but costing them money or exposing them to risk in ways they never fully realized. That, indeed, the pain of same is greater than the pain of change.

This is the true power of Commercial Insight when it's done well. Not only does it paint a picture of how great life *could* be if they change, but far more important, it teaches customers that it's not nearly as good as they think it is, were they to stay the same. At the same time, this is what virtually every supplier is currently missing in their current content creation efforts—a disciplined, systematic approach to *understanding* and then *replacing* a customer's mental models.

Bottom line, the only way to get customers to think differently about you is to first get them to think differently about *themselves*.

This is why efforts to understand how customers perceive *themselves* in the first place are so important. Without that very different kind of customer understanding, a supplier can't build the mental model in the first place. And without that mental model, a supplier can't effectively overturn a customer's current thinking. One can't *change* the way a customer thinks of themselves if they don't even *know* how that customer thinks of themselves in the first place.

So what exactly is a mental model and how would one build one? We'll cover that with some very concrete, practical examples in chapter 5. But for now, let's sum up everything we've learned about Commercial Insight in a single, simple, but powerful diagram.

BREAK DOWN THE A, THEN BUILD UP THE B

To simplify what, admittedly, at first glance must feel like a relatively complex idea, let's boil this down to two simple things: the customer's *current* beliefs and behavior on the one hand, and their *desired* beliefs and behaviors on the other.

Here, "desired" refers to what a supplier essentially *hopes* a customer will believe and do, as that behavior will most likely lead directly to the adoption of that supplier's solution.

We represent this model with a large "A" connected by an arrow to a large "B."

FIG. 3.6. Overview of Shifting the Customer Mental Model

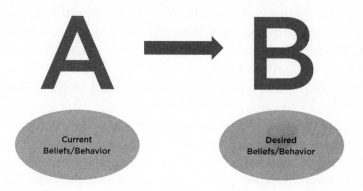

We like this model because it allows us to ask a very simple, but rather telling question: if you were to consider all of the collateral, all of the "pitch decks," all of the content your organization currently creates in an attempt to get customers to buy your solution, what's it mostly about? Is it primarily about the A? Or is it largely about the B?

For most organizations, the predominant answer is, by far, the B. For reasons we just discussed, suppliers bend over backward extolling the virtues of the B—painting as attractive a picture as possible of life over there on the right, in a world supported by their solution. So they walk through its utility, calculate its return, demonstrate its value, and enumerate its benefits. All in an attempt to convince customers through sheer force of persuasion that whatever they're doing over on the left couldn't *possibly* be as good as what the supplier suggests they *could* be doing over on the right. By and large, it is a battle for the B.

But the strange thing is, more often than not, suppliers will win that battle but still lose the war. Customers will look them in the eye, emphatically agree that B is indeed better, but still not budge off their current behavior. When that happens, suppliers' natural inclination is to conclude that their articulation of the B must need further refinement. For, clearly, if it were more compelling, then that customer would make that move. But all that added effort rarely returns additional benefit. As one senior leader memorably told us, "If our value proposition got any 'crisper,' we'd have to write it on a cracker—but it's *still* not enough!"

After studying this problem for the better part of five years, we've come to conclude the real challenge in changing customer buying behavior isn't a better articulation of the benefits of B. It's a better articulation of the pain of A. Without that, the B may seem great, but the A still remains "good enough." Winning a solution sale, in other words, isn't so much a battle for the B nearly so much as a battle for the A.

Or, as we like to say: you have to break down the A before you build up the B.

Again, that's the moment where you must tell the customer (diplomatically, empathetically, and culturally correctly) that they're *wrong*.

Notice how different this kind of message really is. One CMO looked at this diagram and said, "There's nothing new here. This is just 'Marketing 101.' It's a basic value proposition." But that's not the case at all. In fact, for many sales and marketing professionals, the A-to-B statement is completely counterintuitive relative to everything they've been trained to do in the past.

How exactly? Consider this. When done well, who is the A about? It's about the *customer*. But then, who is the B about? It's *also* about the customer.

But if that's the case, then where in the world is the *supplier* in all of this?

Now, some like to say, the supplier is in the arrow. But that's not really correct either. For what that arrow really represents is the behavior change the *customer* would have to undergo to get from A to B.

So where *is* the supplier in the A-to-B statement? The answer is: they aren't there at all.

The A-to-B statement isn't a story about the supplier; it's a story about the *customer*. Done properly, it's "supplier agnostic." That's pretty counterintuitive. Who ever heard of a supplier value proposition that doesn't include the actual supplier? But that's not really what the A-to-B represents. It's not so much a value proposition designed to articulate a supplier's capabilities as it is a value proposition designed to articulate the return from customer behavior change. And that makes a lot of sense, since, at the end of the day, that's exactly what a supplier is selling anyway.

So if you wanted to assign a letter to the supplier, then arguably they would be the C. They're the natural end point of the A-to-B story. For, if a supplier effectively breaks down the A and then successfully builds up the B, that customer is going to look at that supplier and say: "I've got to change! But who can help me with this?"

That supplier *must* be able to say, "Let me show you how we are the only supplier that can help you with this."

That's the power of Commercial Insight.

So how does a commercial organization build something like *that*? We'll look at some very concrete examples in chapter 5, but here's a simple four-question exercise to get you started.

FOUR QUESTIONS TO BUILD COMMERCIAL INSIGHT

Admittedly, building Commercial Insight is not easy. It takes broad-based commitment and collaboration across the entire commercial organization—everyone from marketers, to product managers, to sales managers, to sales reps, to senior leaders (and, arguably, more). In fact, based on a widespread demand, CEB has been running a series of sold-out workshops around the world for our members designed to help companies think through a step-by-step framework for building Commercial Insight. Our consulting arm has worked hand in hand with countless organizations to build not only Commercial Insights, but more sustainable Commercial Insight capabilities across those organizations.

All of the work can be boiled down to four questions that can kick-start any company's Commercial Insight design efforts. Each question is designed to pick up a part of the story. We think you'll find these questions to be especially helpful as you start your own journey toward building Commercial Insight.

Question #1: *What are our sustainable, unique strengths?*

Remember, think broadly.

Question #2: *Of those unique strengths, which ones are currently* underappreciated *by our customers?*

This one is especially counterintuitive, as it forces you to think in the exact opposite direction of where you might naturally go on your own. After all, once you identify your unique, sustainable strengths, it seems like you'd be done. Put that in the value proposition and "away you go!" But remember, we just saw how that plays out. That's a story of the B. What we're looking for is a story of the A.

Question #3: *What is it that the customer fails to fully understand about* their *business that leads them to underappreciate our unique, sustainable capability now?*

Note the emphasis. This isn't a question of what the customer fails to understand about the *supplier*'s business. It's a question of what the customer fails to understand about their *own* business. This is where a very different kind of "customer understanding" is absolutely crucial. This is the A—with a view toward what the customer is "missing." A different way to ask the same question might be: "What is their A, and how is it broken?"

A clear understanding of the customer's current mental model allows us to then ask:

Question #4: *What would we have to teach that customer about their business that would lead them to value that capability more than they do now?*

Or, put another way, "How can we credibly break down their A and build up their B?

We've run those four questions in workshop format with sales and marketing teams around the world, and the results are always fascinating. As a result of the exercise, commercial leaders are almost always surprised by both what they already know—if they just think about things a little bit differently—and what they *don't* really know—because they'd never thought to ask. It's an exciting yet simultaneously humbling exercise. But it's virtually always a productive one.

For, if nothing else, it leads to a series of natural follow-on questions that can provide productive work streams for members of the commercial team. Things like:

- ➤ What kind of evidence would we need to credibly convince customers of what we're saying?

- ➤ How high is the "burden of proof" of our argument?

- ➤ How much of that evidence do we have now?

- ➤ How/where could we build or buy the evidence that we're missing?

For, if we bring things full circle, remember that this is a story of activating Mobilizers, engaging them in a conversation that they'll find compelling enough to want to act on, and then equipping them with the evidence they'll need to win over the other 4.4, despite potentially high levels of internal dysfunction.

That is why Commercial Insight matters so much. It's less a solution for how suppliers struggle to sell, and far more a solution for why customers struggle to buy—or more accurately, why they struggle so mightily to *change*.

So let's turn to chapter 4 and break down the process of Commercial Insight creation in more detail with some concrete examples.

CHAPTER FOUR

BUILDING COMMERCIAL INSIGHT

In working with suppliers around the world to apply Commercial Insight concepts, the most common questions we hear from marketers are: Where are we supposed to find this insight in the first place? Where does it come from? For many, it all feels like a big mystery.

In working with these organizations, if there were one lesson we'd want to impart more than any other from all of our work, it is: *You don't find Commercial Insight. You make it.*

One doesn't "search" for Commercial Insight—among reps, customers, subject matter experts, or anyone else. One builds it. To be sure, it's a science with no small element of art mixed in. It can be somewhat messy. It requires multiple inputs. It is unquestionably organic. And it will most certainly require iteration to get it right.

Yet creating Commercial Insight is nonetheless a highly structured, eminently replicable, highly learnable process that follows a set of core principles that can be combined in all sorts of powerful and creative ways. That's good news, for it puts suppliers in control of their own destiny. They don't have to wait around for "insight" to somehow magically fall from the heavens. They can proactively go out and make it, test it, revise it, test it again, broadly deploy it, and ultimately scale it as an organizational capability. All using tools, tactics, and frameworks designed to answer one simple but very powerful question:

What do our customers fail to fully understand about *their* business, but should?

That's the central question Commercial Insight is trying to address. At its heart, creating Commercial Insight doesn't require a deeper understanding of how customers see *your* company, it requires a much deeper understanding of how those customers see their *own* company. As we saw earlier, the best way to get someone to think differently about *you* is to first get them to think differently about *themselves*.

So as we work through two real-world examples of Commercial Insight—one from DENTSPLY and one from Xerox—the manner in which each company answers two key questions about their customers will serve as our central focus: What are our customers thinking? What are they missing?

Because as different as these two examples may appear superficially, at their core, they're both built off of the exact same approach: a deep examination of how customers view themselves. To get there, both examples feature a powerful application of the "mental model" concept.

CASE STUDY: DENTSPLY

DENTSPLY International Inc. is a leading manufacturer and distributor of dental and other consumable health care products. Their broad global product platform helps dental professionals serve patients' oral health care for a lifetime, from preventive services to tooth replacement. DENTSPLY oral health products range from general dental consumables and laboratory products to products supporting the dental specialty markets of orthodontics, endodontics, and implants. DENTSPLY sales reps call on dentists, educating them about DENTSPLY's wide range of products, including the company's latest innovations.

Now, one can imagine, for a dentist, a capital cost like new instruments is a pretty big expense, so it's not something they're looking to change or upgrade very often. While they certainly want to have the best instruments, they also want to get as much use and value out of those instruments for as long as possible as well. So if an instrument isn't broken, then there's no need to replace it.

Indeed, from the perspective of the dentist, an instrument is likely the least of their worries. It's something they'd rather not have to think about at all as they go about the day-to-day job of running a successful dental practice. So if you're a DENTSPLY sales rep, selling new instruments into that kind of environment can be tough. Like so many other suppliers, DENTSPLY's biggest competitor is the status quo itself.

Now, the one thing dentists *do* worry about, of course, is the success of their dental practice. After all, they're all small-business owners, and the health of their business—along with the health of their patients—is largely what's on their mind all the time. Recognizing this, DENTSPLY has found a way to change how dentists think about their business that leads back to the unique benefits of DENTSPLY's product. But the key to that story is something you might not expect, as the story isn't really about DENTSPLY. In fact, initially, the story isn't even about instruments.

To show you what we mean, let's go back in time a few years to DENTSPLY's launch of a brand-new dental instrument and play things out step-by-step.

A Tough Sell for a Great Product

Several years ago, after a great deal of research and development, the DENTSPLY product development team introduced a truly remarkable new product—a dental instrument designed to be balanced, lightweight, and more ergonomic than anything else available on the market to date. Better still, the research and development team had discovered a way to shrink the motor driving that instrument to a sufficiently small size, allowing it to be mounted directly into the handle of the instrument itself. Typically, that motor—due to its size—was located outside of the instrument, attached by a long, cumbersome cord. With DENTSPLY's innovative new technology, however, they were able to offer an instrument that was completely cordless.

As you might imagine, there was a great deal of excitement across the team as they geared up to take their new product to market. After all, they now had a lightweight and ergonomically designed handpiece—and it was cordless. This thing couldn't lose! It was the instrument to beat all instruments! After putting the right kinds of patent protection in place to protect from potential fast followers, the DENTSPLY team set about building a go-to-market strategy designed to capitalize on the many unique features and benefits of their brand-new instrument.

As DENTSPLY sales reps started talking to potential customers about the new instrument, however, something unexpected started to happen.

Everyone loved it! But very few people actually bought it. Try as they might to convince dentists of all the ways the instrument was better, DENTSPLY sales reps struggled mightily to persuade them to make the investment to install the new instrument in their dental practices. At least not nearly in the numbers they'd hoped for given the step-change improvements represented by the instrument's new technology. And that was really strange—not to mention deeply frustrating. But even stranger—and more frustrating—was the fact that nearly every one of those potential customers agreed right up front that the new product was unquestionably better in almost every way possible compared to what they were using already. So clearly, the problem wasn't DENTSPLY's inability to articulate its features and benefits, or convey its utterly new and unique value.

Instead, the problem was something else entirely. As much as dentists thought the new instrument was great, they also believed that whatever they were using right now was *good enough*—or, at least, "good enough for now." Indeed, a typical DENTSPLY sales conversation might end with the customer saying something like,

"You're right! It IS amazing! Wow, it's even lighter than I thought! I love it!"

What do you think the first question was that dentists asked upon seeing the new miracle device? You got it: *how much does it cost?* When the sales rep answered that question, the dentists hedged.

"Tell you what. I don't need any new instruments right now, but why don't you check back in a year or so, and I'd love to talk to you about it then!"

And that's painful. After all, DENTSPLY's growth strategy wasn't tied to the promise of customers potentially buying more instruments *tomorrow*. Their growth strategy was built on DENTSPLY sales reps' ability to sell more of them *today*. Yet they'd just landed in the very conundrum we laid out in chapter 1: what do you do when your customer looks you in the eye, stipulates right up front that you're better, and still won't pay you for it?

It's an all-too-common but nonetheless incredibly tough place to be as there doesn't appear to be any easy or clear solution. After all, a clearer, "crisper" articulation of the new instrument's features and benefits wouldn't help, because customers already agreed to those benefits in the first place! In this case—like in so many others—efforts to create an even better articulation of the instrument's potential value would simply provide an ever better solution to the wrong problem.

So what was the "right" problem? Over time, what DENTSPLY came to realize was that their biggest obstacle in selling more instruments wasn't how those dentists thought of DENTSPLY—or their instrument. The problem was, how those dentists thought about *themselves* and the dental practices they were running. *That* was the right problem.

Reframing the Conversation

Through our consulting team, we were lucky enough to have a front-row seat in helping DENTSPLY devise a solution to this challenge. Their solution is absolutely fascinating.

They discovered the only way to get dentists to think differently about DENTSPLY—and their new instrument—was to first get them to think differently about the economics of the business they were running. While it is true that dentists were very focused on running a successful and profitable dental practice, they were completely unaware of the connection between that goal and the potential value of a lightweight, ergonomically designed, and cordless instrument. The connection here isn't necessarily obvious.

How did DENTSPLY help dentists make that connection? By starting with a problem that dentists are *all* aware of, namely, the frustratingly high rates of absenteeism and early retirement among their dental hygienists. In a typical dental office, hygienists are the ones tasked with much of the routine, day-to-day cleaning of patients' teeth and can spend hours at a time, day after day, with their hands held at awkward angles while doing their job. Perhaps not surprisingly, the job often results in very sore wrists and, over time, even chronic carpal tunnel syndrome, forcing many hygienists to take time away from work to recover from the pain of doing the job. In the worst-case scenarios, the problem can be so severe it can lead to surgery and early retirement.

Beyond the all-too-real impact on individual hygienists' quality of life, however, the issue also impacts dentists' ability to operate their practice efficiently, as hygienists' health problems can flare up unpredictably, forcing them off the job with very little notice, for unforeseeable amounts of time. Yet, as common as the problem is, dentists tend not to give the problem a great deal of thought as it's typically seen as a cost of doing business in the dental industry. "It's just the way things are" is the most common sentiment among dentists around the world who recognize the issue.

Having studied dentists' thinking—and the potential impact of their new product on this problem—this is where DENTSPLY found an opportunity. To that end, DENTSPLY sales reps now pick up the conversation with their customers in what some might find a surprising manner, by first helping dentists' understand that the problem is far worse and far more costly than they ever realized.

So a DENTSPLY sales rep might begin with:

> "I wanted to talk to you today about some findings we've had in our research about the true costs of hygienist absenteeism. We're finding virtually all of the dentists we work with are having the same issue, and I'm guessing you're seeing it too?"

Now, because DENTSPLY has done their homework in advance, they know the answer to that question is almost guaranteed to be "Yes," as virtually every dentist has the same problem.

At which point the DENTSPLY rep might say, "You know, we've been looking into this issue in a lot of detail lately, and the thing that surprised us about it is just how expensive the problem is. Have you ever sat down to calculate how much that absenteeism is costing your business?"

To which the dentist is more likely than not to reply:

> "I'm not sure. What do you mean?"

> "Well, let me show you. This is actually kind of scary . . ."

The DENTSPLY sales rep then walks the dentists through a step-by-step calculation of just how much money the absenteeism problem is costing that particular dental practice. With the dentist's input, they use that practice's actual wages, overtime costs, number of hygienists on staff, and absenteeism rates to calculate *in the moment* the fully loaded costs of the absenteeism problem. It's a powerful exercise, as it's one dentists themselves have likely never done on their own.

As the DENTSPLY sales rep digs deeper into the problem, however, they help the dentists make all sorts of connections to the issue that they wouldn't have necessarily made on their own. There's health care costs, the cost of lost business, the impact on employee morale and engagement, the impact on receptionists having to reschedule appointments with disgruntled customers, the frequency with which those disgruntled customers defect to another practice—possibly taking their entire family with them (especially, the research indicates, if they're a mother, who takes four to five patients away from the practice), the cost of bad "word of mouth." It's a daunting list. When it's laid out step-by-step, with an actual, believable cost associated with each item, the dentist can't help but feel a little overwhelmed by the time the discussion is over. And that's the point. The goal of the rep here is to demonstrate to the dentist (empathetically, professionally, culturally correctly) that this problem is far worse and far more expensive than they'd ever realized on their own—all in a highly credible manner backed by data-driven industry research, practical experience gained from working with hundreds of other similar practices, and the dentist's own numbers.

When it's over, the average dentist feels a little sick.

"Holy mackerel! I knew this was a pain, but I had no idea this was costing me so much money! This is killing my business!"

"Yeah, it's surprising, isn't it?" says the rep. "We had no idea the problem was this bad either, until we started digging into the numbers. It's kind of scary."

"You're right! I have to do something about this. But what can be done? After all, it's just kind of the way this job works."

"Well, what if there *was* something you could do about it?" the rep might ask.

"What do you mean?"

"We've been studying this problem in a lot of depth, and one of the surprising things we've found is that there might be a solution to this problem."

"I'd love to hear it, if you have one."

At this point, the rep shares with the dentist brand-new, credible research conducted by third-party sources, which demonstrates that a large portion of hygienists' work-related injuries isn't the result of the job itself, but the instruments used by hygienists while they're performing their job. That's a connection that dentists themselves had never made on their own. Partly because the universal nature of the problem had led them to never investigate the issue in the first place. Partly because all of the instruments heretofore available on the market were similar enough to preclude any possible implications. Again, it was all simply the way things worked. So for dentists, to find out that much of this problem is the result of the instruments they choose to put in the hands of their hygienists is a bit of a head-snapping moment.

"It's the *instruments*??"

"Yeah, it turns out it's the instruments that are causing this problem."

"Wow, but what exactly *about* the instruments?"

"It's a number of things. It's their overall weight. And their shape. They're not designed to get after this particular problem. They're great for cleaning teeth, but now we realize, at considerable expense in the process— not just to your people," the rep says, pointing down to the calculation still lying on the table between them, "but to your business as well."

"Huh. So you're telling me, if I think differently about my instruments, I can make some of this problem go away?"

"That's what we're finding. But the instruments have to be specially designed to alleviate the problem."

"What do you mean?"

"First of all, they're going to need to be a lot lighter. Much of the problem is fighting the weight of the thing all day long. It doesn't seem like a lot, but over the course of hours and days, it adds up."

"Makes sense."

"Second is the shape. No matter how light the instrument, if you're forced to hold the instrument at a bad angle, straining your wrist, the damage is potentially just as bad."

"OK . . ."

"But there's something else too. Something that surprised us when we looked into this. The real culprit is the cord."

"The cord?"

"Yeah, that thing weighs more than you might think. When you spend your entire day bearing the weight of that cord to keep your elbow at just the right angle, the impact on muscle fatigue is dramatic."

"Wait a minute. So you're saying, if I want to find a way to solve this problem"—glancing again at the cost calculations still lying on the table—"then I've got to have an instrument that's lighter, more ergonomic, and . . . what? Cordless? Where am I going to find an instrument like that?"

"Well, let me introduce you to DENTSPLY's new line of instruments. We're excited about them, because they were specifically designed to solve this very problem . . ."

[. . . aaaand scene]

And this is how DENTSPLY sells its new instrument today. Now, to be sure, we've glossed a number of areas in the conversation. And added a bit of extra flair for dramatic effect. But by and large, that is the flow of a typical sales conversation today as DENTSPLY sells its new instrument.

You'll notice, it's very different in a number of important ways. First and foremost, the conversation isn't about DENTSPLY at all. It's about dentists and their practice. More specifically, it's about a very real problem that they never knew that they had. Or, to be more accurate, it's about a problem they knew they had, but never appreciated in terms of its cost and impact.

So where does the story of DENTSPLY's new instrument come into the conversation? Not at the beginning, but at the very end. The story doesn't lead *with* DENTSPLY, it leads *to* it. That's a key element of any good Commercial Insight. As we laid out in great detail in *The Challenger Sale*, every good Commercial Insight conversation follows a very specific path, or "choreography." This choreography leads the customer to appreciate the supplier's strengths more than they ever would have on their own. That's because the choreographed story is designed to change the way the customer thinks about *themselves* first, before they're ever asked to consider the supplier. As we like to say: *don't lead* with *what makes you unique, lead* to *what makes you unique.*

The results for DENTSPLY have been dramatic. They're selling more instruments at higher margins in less time than ever before. But to understand the true power of Commercial Insight, here's a kind of trick question: at the beginning of the story, before DENTSPLY changed their approach, what were they selling? The answer is: they were selling their newly designed instrument. Pretty straightforward. But here's the tricky part. After changing their sales approach, what are DENTSPLY reps selling? A solution? An idea? A new opportunity to save? All that may be true. But practically speaking, what they're selling at the *end* of the story is the same thing they were selling at the beginning. It's the *exact same instrument*. Nothing's changed. They didn't go back to the drawing board to redesign anything. But they're now selling more of that same instrument than ever before, at higher margins, and in less time. Not because they changed *what* they sell, but because they changed *how* they sell it.

That's the true power of getting Commercial Insight right. It doesn't necessarily require a complete revamp of your product portfolio. In fact, it likely doesn't require you to think very differently about your company at all. What it does require, however, is helping customers think differently about *their* company. And that can come only from a deep understanding of how those customers think of their business in the first place.

So with that example in mind, let's turn to that question more systematically now and break down the DENTSPLY story in terms of the customer's mental model. It's an instructive exercise, as it's a highly replicable technique any supplier can use for their own customers.

Building a Mental Model

First things first, if we're going to overturn a customer's mental model, then we need to construct that model in the first place.

Now, we don't want to put anyone off with the rather academic-sounding name "mental model," as we think you'll find that this concept is actually pretty straightforward.

So what *is* a mental model? Technically, it's a representation of how someone thinks of their world, ranging from very simple to very complex. But more often than not, we like to draw mental models as root-cause diagrams—a simple diagram of cause and effect.

To do that, the first thing we need to establish is the customer's goal. What is the customer trying to accomplish? In many cases, the goal will be denominated in some sort of commercial metric (revenue or margin), but it doesn't have to be (for marketers, for example, a typical interim goal might be higher net promoter scores; for sales, it might be increased funnel velocity). Of course, for any given customer, there are a number of different goals they're seeking to achieve, so picking the right one matters. In the next chapter, we'll show you in more detail how Xerox thought through this very question. But in the case of DENTSPLY, you'll remember that we started with dentists' goal of running a profitable dental practice.

Now, once we've established that end goal, we can then work backward from there to identify primary and secondary "drivers" of that goal and begin to map out their relationships to one another. You'll find this to be a relatively organic process as you gather more information, test what you've found, debate its implications, and iterate on your thinking over time.

By way of example, let's think through a simple mental model for a typical dentist in our DENTSPLY story (see figure 4.1).

FIG. 4.1. Existing Mental Model for a Dental Product Customer

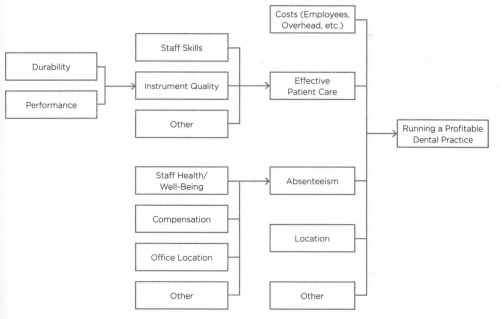

Source: CEB analysis.

So if we start with a dentist's primary goal as running a profitable dental practice, that puts us in a pretty good position to make practical headway. To be sure, dentists have other goals as well—chief among them improving the health and well-being of their patients—but we'll start with profitability here as that outcome best allows us to reverse-engineer the story above. Indeed, you'll find that different outcomes allow you to engineer different stories. So which outcome is "right"? As long as it's an outcome that your customer would agree with and has some degree of inherent urgency tied to the customer business, the "right" one is likely the one that can best be made to lead back to your unique capability.

In the case of DENTSPLY, once we've established profitability as the outcome, we can then lay out the primary drivers of running a profitable practice. So there's operating expenses, effective patient care, followed by employee absenteeism, location, and others. These models can be built out with almost endless amounts of detail. However, you'll find there are significant diminishing returns after nailing down the top three or four nodes.

Once we've done that, we're then set to dive deeper into primary nodes. So if we follow "effective patient care," for example, what do dentists believe to be the drivers of that? Well, primarily that's likely a result of both staff skill and the instruments they use (and probably a few other things too).

If we then go deeper still down the instrument node, we find that "instrument quality" is thought of by dentists in terms of its durability and performance.

So once we've built out the mental model a few layers down, we can then reverse direction and work back up the tree to pressure-test the logic and be sure we aren't missing anything important. We can ask things like: as a dentist, why do I buy instruments?

Well, according to our mental model, I buy instruments that perform *well* enough and last *long* enough to ensure that I'm providing effective patient care, then—at least as far as the instruments are concerned—I can ensure I'm running a profitable dental practice.

So as long as I have effective, durable instruments, I don't need *new* instruments.

There's the customer's logic laid out right there, step-by-step, in a single, simple easy-to-read diagram.

Think about how useful it is to know *that* logic if you're in the business of selling dental instruments to dentists! It's like having a map to their mind. It's not voice of customer—it's *mind* of customer. It's how they think—the logic they use when running their business. To be sure, it's a simple diagram, but it's a very powerful one.

In terms of the "absenteeism" node, maybe dentists recognize this driver as an important element of running a profitable dental practice, and maybe not. But either way, they likely wouldn't rank it nearly as important as operating expenses and effective patient care. So why include it at all? Because we'll eventually use that node to teach dentists something they likely underappreciate about practice profitability. So on the absenteeism node, we might include things like staff health, maybe compensation, and office location.

Now, if your first reaction when thinking through an exercise like this is "How in the world would I construct something like this for one of *my* customers?" we'd encourage you to give it a try. It doesn't have to be perfect. It's better if your first attempt *isn't* perfect. That's because the next thing you'll want to do is *test* it. Put the mental model in front of some of your best sales reps and ask them what they'd add. What would they take away? Where do they think it's wrong, based on their experience? Show it to your implementation teams, your product managers. Get their feedback. This is a team exercise, and the broader the input you have, the better. Test it. Push it. Blow it up and start over. Each change will likely make it better. Again, it doesn't have to be perfect, but it does have to be accurate and believable enough for your customers to be able to see themselves in it.

Why? Because once you think it's pretty strong, that's exactly what you do next: put it in front of your customers. Find a few whose feedback you trust and ask them, "We think this is a pretty accurate view of how you think about your world. Are we close? What would you add? What would you take away?"

Having made it that far, you can dig in and start exploring the relative importance of different branches. Ask your customers: "If I were to give you 100 points to distribute across these top nodes according to relative importance, how would you distribute them?" "Why that way? What's hard about that exercise? What trade-offs do you find yourself having to make?"

It's such a powerful exercise. Even better, practically speaking, conversations like that can be run in person, over the phone, as part of a broader survey, via the Web, built in to a customer diagnostic. You name it. But notice, above all else, the essence of this exercise is built around gaining a far better understanding of how customers think of *themselves*, not how they think of you. Mind of customer, not voice of customer.

In terms of the A-to-B model we introduced in chapter 3, this is a map of the customer's A.

It's a map of how they currently think their world works. It is *the* most important building block of Commercial Insight. As you'll remember, the fundamental movement of any good Commercial Insight is "breaking down the A" before "building up the B." And this is the A we need to break down.

So what do you do with a mental model once you have it? You break it.

Breaking a Mental Model

Without retelling the entire story, let's use the mental model we just constructed to review how DENTSPLY teaches the customer a completely different way to think about their business. This is the art of "unteaching" (see figure 4.2).

FIG. 4.2. Desired Mental Model for a Dental Product Customer

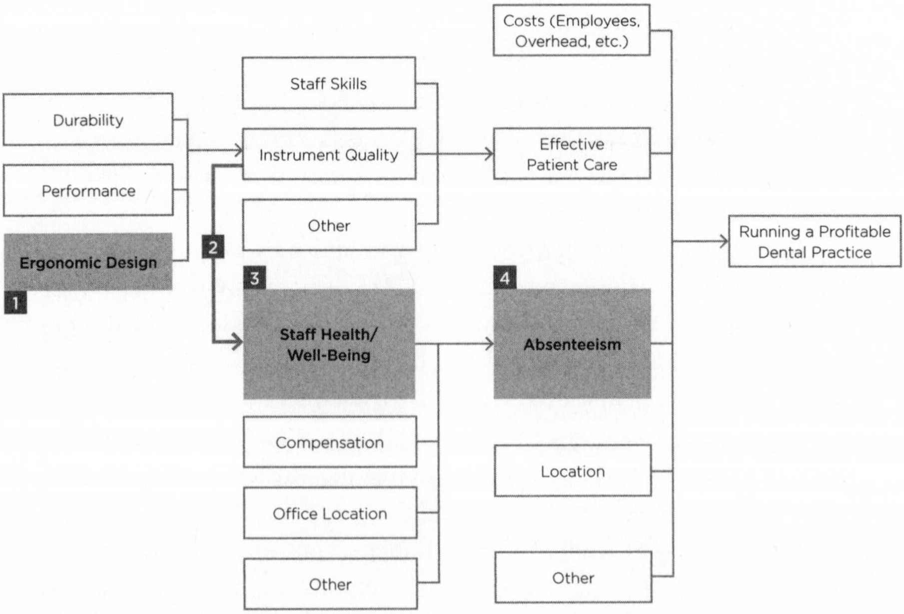

Source: CEB analysis.

You'll remember, the first part of the DENTSPLY story is about building out the total—often hidden—costs of hygienist absenteeism. In terms of our mental model, what they're doing here is dramatically increasing the size of that particular box, or node. That is, they're teaching dentists that the problem of hygienist absenteeism costs them a lot more than they ever realized. By demonstrating how absenteeism impacts the dentists' overall profitability, DENTSPLY significantly elevates the importance of this box in the mind of the dentist.

The next step is associating that absenteeism with hygienist health. Something we glossed over in the customer conversation above, but nonetheless vitally important to the chain of logic, the DENTSPLY rep provides data demonstrating that the number one driver of absenteeism, by far, is wrist pain and not, say, poor work-life balance. However, in the case of the DENTSPLY story, this particular step is largely a relatively easy one for most dentists to follow, as they're likely already aware of this particular relationship. The "burden of proof" on this particular point isn't particularly high. So this is a step that DENTSPLY can move through relatively quickly with very little objection.

Importantly, however, that's a question you'll have to examine carefully for each step in your own story. "What's the burden of proof?" The higher it is, the more evidence you'll need to move your customer through that part of the narrative.

For DENTSPLY, it's the *next* step that's the game changer. The truly surprising part of DENTSPLY's story for most dentists is the unexpected evidence that hygienists' sore wrists and carpal tunnel is not an unavoidable consequence of having their hands awkwardly poking in people's mouths all day long, but instead a largely *preventable* consequence of the instruments hygienists have in their hands at that time. For most dentists, this is a head-snapping moment, as it's a connection they've never made on their own. As you might imagine, unlike in the previous step of our story, here the burden of proof is relatively high.

You might be wondering how DENTSPLY came up with this connection. The DENTSPLY team did a very clever thing—they hired a savvy dentist to help them with developing the strategy from a practice perspective. It's amazing how quickly you can refine and pin down a customer mental model when you have big chunks of uninterrupted time with seasoned customers! Between the dentist's deep understanding of how his peer dentists *think* (and what they take for granted) and having an out-side party like CEB there to drive inquiries that test accepted wisdom, DENTSPLY was able find the hidden connection between absenteeism and dental instruments.

Not surprisingly, then, DENTSPLY has worked to bring the proper evidence to bear to demonstrate this point both credibly and emphatically. For any supplier constructing Commercial Insight, when the burden of proof is especially high like this, the quality of the evidence matters. Is it data backed? Is it from credible sources? Is it conveyed in a convincing manner, with sufficient context to be understandable, believable, and share-able? Because what DENTSPLY is doing here is building an entirely new causal connection in the customer's mental model. It's a relationship between "instrument quality" and "staff well-being" that dentists them-selves had never appreciated, or perhaps even recognized. Ensuring that dentists "come along" on this part of the journey is crucial.

Once they've made it that far, DENTSPLY is finally ready to talk about the nature of the instrument itself. What kind of instrument would you have to have in order to reduce the risks to staff well-being? The answer isn't about durability *or* performance at all—the two things, you'll remember, dentists are focused on most when it comes to instrument quality. Instead, it's something else altogether that dentists probably hadn't given much thought to in the past. It's about instrument ergonomics. So DENTSPLY is adding a whole new box, or node, to the mental model as a key driver of instrument quality—again, checking along the way that they've met the burden of proof for that particular point.

But when we step back and put it all together, notice where we've just landed. DENTSPLY can now draw a compelling—but completely brand-new—causal chain across the customer's mental model. A path that—prior to that conversation—wasn't there at all:

1. Ergonomics have a huge impact on instrument quality,

2. In a way that improves employee health,

3. Thus reducing absenteeism, and

4. Driving potentially dramatic increases in overall long-term profitability.

Step-by-step, DENTSPLY has deconstructed the customer's mental model and rebuilt it around a compelling, actionable idea that doesn't just change the way those dentists think of *DENTSPLY*'s business, but far more importantly changes the way they think of their *own* business.

This is how you break down the A before you build up the B.

If you were to distill this process into its basic building blocks, you'd find the entire process boils down to three ways to change a mental model:

1. You can add a node—meaning you're introducing a root-cause driver that the customer previously hadn't known was there.

2. You can increase the importance of a node—you're showing a customer that a root-cause node is far more important than they previously believed.

3. You can add a causal link—you're making a connection between different nodes in the mental model that the customer previously believed had no connection to one another.

Or, if you're drawing your mental models with boxes and arrows (as we do), in even simpler terms, you can:

1. Add a box.

2. Make a box bigger.

3. Add an arrow.

This is the power of a mental model. Sure, it's just a diagram. But it's a diagram that holds a huge amount of power, as it crystalizes in very simple terms how customers think of themselves.

One important piece of advice as you think about your customer's mental models—don't get overly detailed or make the exercise overly complex. It will stunt the entire point of simplifying how they generally view their business, and the opportunities you have to upend their thinking. If you're five or six levels away from the outcome, the likelihood of the customer caring is slim to none. The closer to the outcome that you can find disagreement, the more impactful your insight will be. However, be forewarned that such insights will inherently carry a higher burden of proof, requiring very strong evidence. The further away your disagreement rests from the outcome, the lower the burden of proof, as well as lower likelihood of the customer truly caring. The sweet spot for insight is typically around one to three levels below the economic outcome.

Now, you may be wondering how to decide where to apply mental modeling. After all, customers likely have a whole range of potential outcomes they care about. How would you land on the equivalent of "running a profitable dental practice" in the first place, as opposed to any other outcome that dentists might care about? To answer that question, we'll turn to the Printing Solutions division at Xerox.

CHAPTER FIVE

COMMERCIAL INSIGHT IN ACTION

CASE STUDY: XEROX PRINTING SOLUTIONS

While the DENTSPLY example focuses on mental model mapping specifically, this case example from Xerox pulls back to look at the broader set of steps that commercial teams can take *around* the mental model mapping, so to speak. It illustrates the "Monday morning" set of practical steps that marketers can take, collaborating with colleagues in sales and product, to generate and deploy Commercial Insight.

For context, Xerox Technology Business, a division of Xerox, is a leading provider of enterprise printing capabilities to a variety of vertical markets, from health care to high tech to education. When Leah Quesada, a VP of marketing in Xerox's Enterprise Business Group, sat down with her team to plan a campaign to promote its offerings to the kindergarten-to-twelfth-grade (K–12) education marketplace, she felt conflicted.

She was thrilled with the latest advancements in a technology that Xerox had developed—the next generation of cartridge-free solid-ink-based printers, called "ColorQube." This kind of technology enables dramatically less expensive color printing, putting color on *nearly* equal footing to low-cost black-and-white printers in use at most school districts.

It's a marketer's dream, right? Similar to DENTSPLY's new instrument, this Xerox solution offered a *differentiated* product that delivered *order-of-magnitude* improvement in printing costs. And, in a huge market. The K–12 education market prints in high volume, but almost exclusively using black-and-white devices, which come with thinner margins for Xerox and other print vendors.

But there was a nagging question running through Leah's head: in an era of declining school budgets, how on earth was she going to position a premium *color*-printing solution to a school district's head of technology who was far more concerned with eking out a few more years from the technology they already had, rather than exploring the latest and greatest benefits of newer technologies coming over the horizon? Leah had observed that not just Xerox but *all* technology suppliers were having trouble selling premium color solutions into the K–12 space. And Xerox's new offer was clearly a premium play against what the competitors were selling.

The classic response in an engineering-led organization, with a rich history in R&D, would be to get *even crisper* in articulating the technology features and benefits—the "speeds and feeds," as it were—that underpin the product's value proposition. But as Leah appreciated, that was never going to work in an era when customers will grant that your solution is better and still not pay for it.

What Leah and her team came up with was a Commercial Insight that not only changed the kinds of conversations Xerox was having with its customers but, just as important, changed the stakeholders with whom they were having those conversations. Ultimately, Xerox saw a 17 percent lift in sales in a vertical market that had been flat to declining.

In the balance of this chapter, we'll outline how Leah and her team created the Commercial Insight itself, and then in chapter 6, we'll dive into how the team put that insight into action through both marketing content and front-line sales teams.

Expanding the Target

Leah and her team relied on a simple model—two concentric circles—to guide their efforts for creating Commercial Insight (see figure 5.1), which we developed here at CEB. Leah's team members taped this model to their cube walls as a touchstone across the six months they spent researching and planning the ColorQube K–12 campaign, as a constant reminder to think well beyond the traditional horizon where ColorQube's capabilities most obviously met educators' relatively straightforward operational needs.

The idea underneath the model is to "mine for surprise." To find a way to *reframe how customers assign value* to your points of differentiation. This reframing sounds simple, but the devil is, as always, in the details.

The way the model works is: the inner circle is meant to capture the key components of the supplier's value proposition and should include key

FIG. 5.1. Xerox's Insight Model

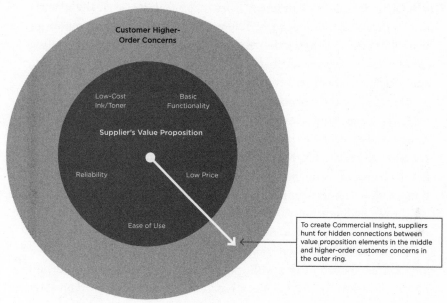

Customer Higher-Order Concerns

Low-Cost Ink/Toner

Basic Functionality

Supplier's Value Proposition

Reliability

Low Price

Ease of Use

To create Commercial Insight, suppliers hunt for hidden connections between value proposition elements in the middle and higher-order customer concerns in the outer ring.

Source: Xerox Corporation; CEB analysis.

points of differentiation. As Leah says, "These are things that our customers would expect us—and our competition—to talk about." Things like functionality, running cost, reliability, and ease of use. These represent the core building block of virtually every company's traditional value proposition.

The outer ring, on the other hand, is what customers care about at a higher-order level, *independent* of any supplier's capability. As Leah says, this is "what's *really* on customers' minds." The idea here is to create connection points—literally draw arrows—between elements in the outer ring and elements in the inner circle, but always with a view toward making surprising or underappreciated connections that the customer is unlikely to have recognized or fully appreciated on their own. Those arrows are, in essence, Commercial Insight candidates. They can be pressure tested and adopted or rejected, based on how well they resonate and help suppliers to alter customers' view of themselves. (Note: while that outer ring is blank now, we'll come back to fill it in across the next few pages.)

Now, in many ways, it's a completely straightforward exercise. However, when you think about what most companies might do to articulate their value—especially when promoting an important product in their line, Leah told us her team was no different. They focused almost exclusively on the inner circle—the product's key differentiators and the value proposition that ties them together. Why? Because that was the most obvious and easy-to-defend connection between their products' attributes and their customers' stated needs.

Think about the customer messaging this classic approach inevitably leads to—you've heard this before, right? "Our leading-edge, cartridge-free technology produces 90 percent less waste than laser, and creates vibrant, smooth images quickly. No matter your setup, we can integrate that solution with any one of our software options in order to offer a broader education solution that fits your needs." That was the message. It appeared across a wide range of content channels in an early attempt to generate market demand for the new technology.

But at the end of the day, that school district's technology administrator, reading about this in a white paper she downloaded over a working lunch at her desk, or finding it in a brochure she casually picked up at the Xerox booth at an educators' trade show in Orlando, or sitting in a sixty-minute in-person sales meeting across the table from a Xerox sales professional is likely going to react with the exact same thought irrespective of the channel through which they heard that statement: "I believe you. There's no question in my mind that you do produce that much less waste, and I'm sure the colors are vibrant. Vibrant!! But our tech budget just got cut, and our research tells us we need to replace our old printing system for $X or less, with an improvement in performance. Period."

Now you're stuck. You've just boarded the express train to Commoditization Station. It's so frustrating.

But how does one bend that conversation in a different direction? Better yet, how does one *avoid* that conversation altogether?

Here are the steps that Leah and her team used to create a Commercial Insight that reframed the way customers thought about the value proposition and led to a very different kind of customer conversation:

Step 1: List your differentiators.

Step 2: Create a list of outcomes your customers care most about.

Step 3: Prioritize and choose an outcome as a starting point.

Step 4: Map customer beliefs about outcome drivers.

Step 5: Hypothesize connections between your differentiators and customer outcomes.

Step 6: Test and validate connections.

The first three steps in this process are the work that you'd do *before* you get to the mental model mapping we discussed in the DENTSPLY example. Step 4 is the mental model mapping itself. Step 5 is where you figure out how to break the mental model. That's the Commercial Insight. And Step 6 is all about pressure testing and validating the insight.

Let's dive into how Xerox executed these steps.

Step 1: List Your Differentiators

Leah's team started with the inner circle of that concentric circle model, listing Xerox's differentiators. They included differentiators at the solution level (e.g., low-cost color ink technology), as well as differentiators enabled by broader Xerox-level capabilities (e.g., easy replenishment because of Xerox's logistics and geographic footprint).

The team went broad here, casting as wide a net as possible. It included differentiators that, in some cases, separated Xerox from most, but not all, competitors. Vibrant color? Sure, some of Xerox's competitors can provide vibrant color, but no one but Xerox can provide it at such low cost, thanks to their low-cost ink technology.

Going broad here was important, because it enabled the Xerox team to better see what often ended up being a *bundle* of several differentiators that delivered unique value only when combined—something that no competitor can match.

Another reason to go broad on differentiator identification is because it gives more anchor points for potential connections out to the outer ring, or what customers care most about. At this stage, Leah's team was looking to be *expansive* in generating ideas for these hidden connections between the inner circle and outer ring—between Xerox's differentiators and the higher-order outcomes that customers care most about.

Step 2: Create a List of Outcomes Your Customers Care Most About

An outcome is best thought of as an action verb and something that could be measured in some fashion. For example, "Improve teacher engagement," "Modernize school facilities," and "Increase school rank" are all outcomes.

The Xerox team's next step was to create a list of the outcomes that customers care about most. That sounds straightforward, but so few marketing teams get this right. It's absolutely imperative that they do.

The first failure point for most marketing teams is thinking too narrowly about the term "customer." Marketers are trained to obsess over a target decision maker—a persona—most often the one that has always been the key decision maker in a purchase in the past. For Xerox, that would be the IT manager or business manager at the school district level. On the face of it, it feels so right, doesn't it? Why *wouldn't* you want to understand the inner logic, the pain points, the desired outcomes of your key decision maker? The single person who holds the go/no-go authority?

But if you're trying to create Commercial Insight, if you're trying to reframe the way the customer organization views its own business, you have to get outside of the classic decision maker to understand the outcomes the broader organization values most. Moreover, in the era of the consensus purchase, suppliers have to understand the outcomes that the broader set of stakeholders hold most dear. That's going to enable suppliers to more closely knit them to each other, to forge the consensus that is needed to sell more complex solutions. For Xerox, that meant getting to the superintendent, the principal, the business manager, and lead teachers—figuring out, what higher-order outcomes do these stakeholders care about most?

Beyond thinking of the target customer too narrowly, the second frequent failure point in working with customer outcomes is thinking of the outcomes themselves too narrowly. Suppliers tend to anchor on the metrics that their sales force has urged them to anchor on, because these are the ones that show up in 90 percent of the RFPs! For Xerox, this would include things like printing cost per page, machine uptime, and printing speed. These are the ones their sales reps are most used to hearing about in customer win-loss analyses.

But if, like the Xerox team, suppliers stop to think about *higher-order* outcomes—those that a *broader* set of customer stakeholders cares about—they arrive at larger outcomes like "Improve student performance" or "Improve teacher effectiveness." These are the outcomes that the broader stakeholder group cares about most, *irrespective of printing solutions.*

How did Leah's team figure out what these broader, higher-order outcomes were for *their* customers? Well, the first thing they found is that they didn't know in all cases what this broader set of stakeholders really cared about, and certainly not in order of importance. So they went out and asked. They conducted several dozen customer interviews. They talked to their leading sales reps. They plowed through industry research. They did more customer interviews.

It's startling to us at times how many leading marketers tell us that they rarely talk to their customers—for all sorts of different reasons (budget, focus, internal politics, you name it). But Xerox provides one more corroborating piece of evidence that this kind of direct interaction between marketing and customers is absolutely vital in order to successfully build Commercial Insight. In fact, there are many different opportunities to do this—think of the customer interactions that happen every day around your organization—at trade shows or between customers and sales reps or between customers and subject matter experts. Many organizations have customer advisory councils that meet once or twice a year. These are ideal opportunities to ask customers these kinds of questions, in a structured way. *Here's a list of objectives we hear from our customers. Are these right? Which ones do you care most about? What's missing? What would you change? How would you prioritize them?*

With some work, the Xerox team landed on a whole set of broad, higher-order outcomes that revolved around concerns like modernizing school facilities, boosting student engagement, balancing budgets, and so on (see figure 5.2).

Step 3: Prioritize and Choose an Outcome as a Starting Point

Next, the Xerox team rank-ordered those outcomes based on importance *from the customer's point of view.* When they spoke to customers, they asked them to rank the outcomes based on importance. They'd always

FIG. 5.2. Xerox's Insight Model with Xerox Customers' Concerns

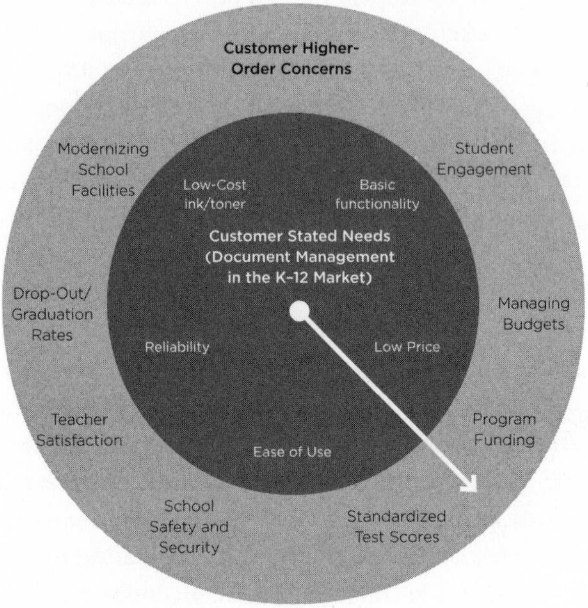

Customer Higher-
Order Concerns

Modernizing
School
Facilities

Student
Engagement

Low-Cost
ink/toner

Basic
functionality

Customer Stated Needs
(Document Management
in the K-12 Market)

Drop-Out/
Graduation
Rates

Managing
Budgets

Reliability

Low Price

Teacher
Satisfaction

Program
Funding

Ease of Use

School
Safety and
Security

Standardized
Test Scores

Source: Xerox Corporation; CEB analysis.

follow up with "Why?" to get the context on that rank ordering. No need to overengineer this or be overly precise here. At this point, you're just trying to get to an approximate importance of one outcome versus another, and where there might be shared outcomes across buying group stakeholders, so that you can sort them and consider the most important ones first as you look for potential connections with your differentiators.

Also, at this point, Leah's team went through a process of assessing the outcomes for their *likelihood of having hidden connections to Xerox's differentiators* (in other words, connections from the outer ring to the inner circle). For example, "Maintain safety of school facilities" is a fairly important outcome to school leaders, but it's not one that the Xerox team could imagine plausibly connecting to its differentiators in the inner circle. It's just hard to imagine a connection there. So the team crossed that one off the list.

On the other hand, for the "Improve student performance" outcome, the team did see a potential connection. School printers produce classroom materials, which teachers rely on to teach students. So the team decided to focus on this outcome as a starting point.

Note the parallel to the DENTSPLY example here. In choosing an outcome to focus on, Leah's team has chosen the equivalent of the far right box in the dentist's mental model, "Running a profitable dental practice." Next comes the equivalent of the mental model mapping—identifying customer beliefs about outcome drivers.

Step 4: Map Customer Beliefs About Outcome Drivers

As Leah's team was engaging in those customer conversations to understand outcomes, they were also asking customers what they believed *drove* those outcomes. Again, the team aimed to understand these mental models across a variety of stakeholders, creating a list of the top drivers of student performance based on their interviews. That landed them on drivers like "student engagement," "motivated, inspired teachers," and "individually paced lessons." This was the customer belief set, so to speak—the equivalent of DENTSPLY's dentist mental model on running a profitable practice.

This can be the toughest part, because we have to get inside our customers' minds. At CEB, when we run members through workshops that simulate this methodology, this is where they struggle most. Many marketing and sales leaders realize their teams just aren't close enough to customers to be able to do this. This should be a giant wake-up call. Recall from the discussion on A Very Different Kind of "Customer Understanding." Suppliers don't necessarily need an ever more refined view of how customers perceive *them*. What they need is a significantly more refined view of how customers perceive *themselves*.

Step 5: Hypothesize Connections Between Your Differentiators and Customer Outcomes

This is where the Xerox team set about trying to break the mental model. Having mapped the drivers customers believe drive the "Improve student performance" outcome, Xerox moved to a "what if" exercise, asking, "What if there was a connection between student performance and our differentiators?"

The team held brainstorming sessions and engaged leading sales reps with their filled-in mental model, hunting for potential hidden disconnects or possible opportunities for reframe. To do that, they used a simple set of brainstorming questions that would prove invaluable to any team working through a similar effort:

> ➤ What impact can we have here that we haven't yet realized?

> ➤ What do we know about this area that customers are overlooking?

> ➤ What is changing in this outcome that customers aren't aware of? What changes are customers missing?

> ➤ What recommendations would our customers' customers (pupils, teachers, parents) make here?

That said, in engaging internal stakeholders in these questions, Leah cautions against listening too closely to the loudest voices. She says some of their leading reps had hypotheses about connections between color and the ability to print yearbooks, for example. Not necessarily the best starting point, because yearbook printing is far from "higher order"—yearbook printing is typically funded through the PTA or fund-raisers, so it doesn't register as an outcome that key internal stakeholders care about. This is very much like detective work, and sometimes it's the small clues that are the most important ones.

As they dug deeper into these conversations and brainstorming sessions, it dawned on the team that there might indeed be a connection between vibrant color and improved learning in the same way that interactive learning aids improve students' knowledge retention. What if today's children, having grown up using high-resolution tablets before even walking, have an expectation of vibrant color in all of their classroom materials? What if they perform better—higher knowledge retention, better classroom engagement—when using color instead of monochrome materials?

It would make sense that senior K–12 decision makers, who themselves grew up and likely raised children in the pretablet era, would miss this kind of effect in their mental models of student performance. This was something that had changed in the environment relatively recently. That idea got the Xerox team excited. They now had a strong hypothesis for what felt to be a potentially highly valuable reframe.

Step 6: Test and Validate Connections

Yet it was cautious excitement. For Leah's team knew that, as with any significant change in customer mental models, the burden of proof would be high. Lifelong senior educators and school district leaders don't shift mental models easily, especially not about something like student performance, which many of them have been focused on for decades.

FIG. 5.3. Xerox's Commercial Insight Prototype

Commercial Insight Prototype

A — Business Problem and What Customer Is Currently Doing

Highlight What Customer Is Missing

B — New Customer Approach (Leading to Xerox Solution)

Customers care most about: Improving student learning and test scores by investing in interactive learning tools and scalable customization of lesson plans and materials

But, customers don't realize: Digital technology is resetting students' expectations, causing a decline in attention and interest when information is delivered in black-and-white

Therefore, customers should: Increase access to color printing in classrooms

Quality Evaluation Questions

Does this reflect customers' top-of-mind concerns?

Does this disrupt the customers' thinking and teach them something new?

Does this lead back to a specific set of Xerox differentiators?

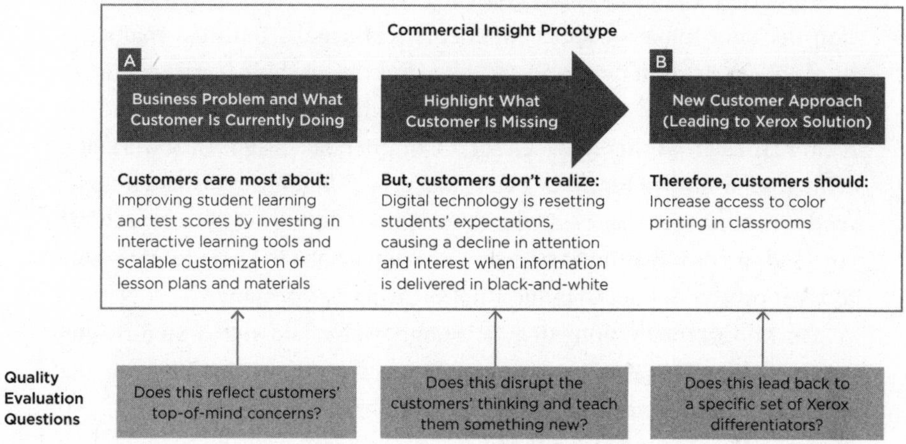

Source: Xerox Corporation; CEB analysis.

So the team began pressure testing its hypothesis. They wanted to ensure it reflected customers' top-of-mind concerns, challenged customer thinking about those concerns, and led back to Xerox's differentiators.

Here's a checklist of questions the team used:

➤ Do we have customer permission to speak about this idea?

➤ Can we prove the validity of this idea and the new approach?

➤ Can we energize customer stakeholders to act on this idea?

➤ Will this idea require the involvement of new stakeholders?

➤ Does this idea surface any major risk or cost objections?

➤ Does this idea carry any new change management concerns?

To answer these questions with more than a gut response, the Xerox team fielded surveys. Knowing the difficulty of changing long-held customer mental models, the team started by surveying customers' customers—students, in this case. Presenting surprising insights or underappreciated connections to customers about *their* customers is an incredibly powerful change motivator. With a little research, that's exactly what the Xerox team was able to do. Xerox found, for example, that 77 percent of students agree that color documents boost their focus, interest, and memory.

The other audience Xerox surveyed was the broader group of education decision makers—superintendents, principals, business managers, heads of curriculum development—beyond those whom Xerox traditionally engaged in the technology office of school districts. Leah and her team realized that this raw idea for a Commercial Insight they were hovering over would be highly relevant to a very different set of stakeholders. And crucially, that these stakeholders could hold the key to a very different kind of conversation for Xerox to have with its K–12 customers—one focused on student performance, not printing performance.

It's important to note that, although we've laid out a step-by-step approach here, this entire process for Xerox was a highly iterative one that took place over the course of several months, with plenty of testing and rewinding happening along the way.

Leah's team structured these surveys to simultaneously help with individual steps throughout the entire sequence. For example, the education decision-maker surveys tested Xerox differentiators. They validated the rank ordering of the customer outcomes by importance. They tested decision-maker beliefs about drivers of those outcomes. They tested several different prototypes of Commercial Insights for plausibility, credibility, and newsworthiness. They also tested a set of practical *objections*, uncovered in conversations with sales reps, that decision makers would have about a connection between student performance and color—namely, the perceived high cost of printing in color. That, of course, played right into Xerox's differentiators, in being the only supplier that could provide a color-printing option competitive to black-and-white, thanks to the ColorQube technology.

The Xerox team hit pay dirt with its student performance insight. It commissioned additional research to further investigate the connection between color and student performance, building out an evidence base that was equal to the size of the mental model shift it was seeking to drive.

We'll see how the Xerox team deployed that evidence in a content and demand generation strategy in the next chapter.

It feels like a lot of work to create one insight, doesn't it? Yes and no. Yes, it took the Xerox team several months to do the homework on customers, construct and field the surveys, conduct the detective work, and validate the insight. But it wasn't a huge team—it was four people:

➤ A product marketer

➤ A marketing communications specialist

➤ A sales trainer

➤ A project manager trained in Lean Six Sigma

We'll come back to the people later, because it turns out the mix of talent is *make or break* when it comes to creating great Commercial Insight.

But think about what's at stake here—from flat growth to 17 percent growth. You can imagine how school district Mobilizers gravitate to Commercial Insight like the one the Xerox team created. This kind of insight speaks to the higher-order outcomes that Mobilizers are motivated to drive in their organizations, and *they* are the ones who are equipped to drive the underlying change. If you can win that Mobilizer—whether it's a school principal or a head of curriculum development or even a district business manager—through Commercial Insight that redefines how they themselves (and then their organizations, in turn) assign value to what you do best as a supplier, that's the key to sidestepping commoditization and price-based competition.

Moreover, if you can get into the minds of the broader group of stakeholders and understand how they think about their business, you can craft insights that form the center point of consensus. That's incredibly powerful in an era of consensus purchase, when buying solutions is even harder than selling them.

One of Xerox's sales agents, John Golitz, shared a quote about just how powerful this Commercial Insight was in his ability to engage customers:

"The deals that I get involved in, I'm winning almost all of them. Once I reframe the conversation around student learning and how Xerox can

help, there's no more talk of competition. It's as if the door closes. I'm on the inside and everyone else is on the outside."

Because the Commercial Insight changed the nature of the conversation (see figure 5.4), Leah and team report consistently getting "ahead of the RFP" as a result of deploying the student performance insight. Beyond that, the K–12 example served as a proof point within Xerox, lighting the way for other product groups to pursue a Commercial Insight–led go-to-market strategy.

With stakes like these, the question isn't "How can we afford to build Commercial Insight?" but "How can we afford *not* to?"

Once you've created a Commercial Insight, that's the starting point.

FIG. 5.4. Xerox's Shift from Product-Centric to Insight-Led Sales Interactions (illustrative)

Feature-Centric Interaction

"Our leading-edge cartridge-free technology produces 90% less waste than laser, and creates vibrant, smooth images quickly...and we can integrate that with one of six software options and other education solutions to fit your needs..."

Xerox Solutions:

Hardware Options

Software Options   Service Options

Sales Rep

- Leads with value of features and options
- Focuses conversation on known customer needs

Before
Leading *with*
Unique Benefits

Insight-Led Interaction

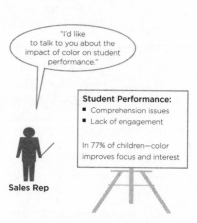

"I'd like to talk to you about the impact of color on student performance."

Sales Rep

Student Performance:
- Comprehension issues
- Lack of engagement

In 77% of children—color improves focus and interest

- Leads with issues affecting customers' top priorities and economic concerns
- Tells customers something they don't know about themselves

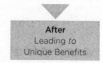

After
Leading *to*
Unique Benefits

Source: Xerox Corporation; CEB analysis.

You can equip sales reps with that insight, and they can take it out to the field to fight the good fight. The problem is, many customers aren't engaging meaningfully with sales reps until they're 57 percent of the way through a purchase, and by that point buying criteria are typically already well set. Even with world-class Commercial Insight, it can be a challenge to shift buying criteria at that point.

So with that in mind, the question is how do suppliers deploy Commercial Insight so they can engage and teach Mobilizers *before* the customer buying group is ready to meaningfully engage our sales reps? We're going to look at how suppliers can redesign their entire content-marketing strategy around Commercial Insight. All with the purpose of seeding the "57 percent arrow" with content that attracts and teaches Mobilizers, and that gets them excited to drive change on your behalf.

CHAPTER SIX

TEACHING MOBILIZERS WHERE THEY LEARN

Where do your customers, and Mobilizers especially, learn? We've put that question to hundreds of commercial organizations, sales and marketing alike. It's a deceptively simple question, but you might be surprised at how few commercial organizations have a firm grasp on the answer. And for good reason. "Where customers learn" has been a moving target with the explosion of both digital and social media channels that customers tend to trust far more than classic marketing channels.

Moreover, when you nail down the answer to this question (and make no mistake, you do have to know this), engaging Mobilizers where they learn *is going to feel hard*. Because they are learning in lots of different places. They're following varied learning paths. They're learning from peers and subject matter experts in social networks, where the rules of engagement are different than what marketing or sales are used to. According to CEB research, the average B2B customer consults *nearly a dozen* sources of information, spread across all varieties of touchpoints on the path to purchase. Only half of that information comes from suppliers, *in total*. So if you're an individual supplier, and say you're one of four that a customer knows to seek information from, you've got about 12 percent "share of information" that customer is consuming. No wonder it feels hard just breaking through all the noise.

On top of that, you have to teach customers *at arm's length* in all these places? In other words, with little to no human engagement. How are you going to do *that*?

"Sounds like a job for great content," you say. Well, yes and no. "Yes" on content. That's going to be critical to teach customers, to change their direction while they are learning in a noisy information marketplace. But "No" in that almost all the conventional wisdom on content marketing

FIG. 6.1. Information Sources B2B Customers Consult on the Path to Purchase

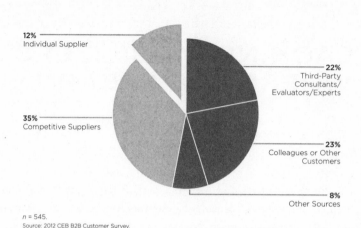

12%
Individual Supplier

22%
Third-Party
Consultants/
Evaluators/Experts

35%
Competitive Suppliers

23%
Colleagues or Other
Customers

8%
Other Sources

n = 545.
Source: 2012 CEB B2B Customer Survey.

leads us *away* from the kind of intervention suppliers need to be doing with Mobilizers to change their direction in that 57 percent.

THE DARK SIDE OF CONTENT MARKETING

At the risk of oversimplifying, there are three high-level points of guidance we repeatedly hear in the massive amount of content and marketing created to explain content marketing:

1. Look smart—"You need to be a *thought leader.* By representing an expert perspective, when the customer is in the market for a solution in your space, they'll think of you first."

2. Be useful—"Create content that speaks to customer pain points. Look to customer search patterns and create content that provides answers to what customers are looking for. Have content that is practically useful in the customer's day-to-day routine."

3. Be present—"Create customer personas. Publish content on a regular cadence to engage those different personas on what is relevant to each of them in the information sources they use."

Each in its own way is a tiger trap for suppliers looking to teach Mobilizers where they are learning. Let's take them in turn.

LOOK SMART. The problem here is that the vast majority of content written in the name of thought leadership focuses on building up the B and completely overlooks tearing down the A. Bottom line, customers aren't going to change unless we give them a good reason to. That's the tiger trap of thought leadership.

Think about it. If the Xerox marketing team had pursued a classic thought leadership strategy, they would have created content about the trends related to their differentiators. It would have been blog posts with titles like "5 Things You Didn't Know about Document Security," or a customer testimonial on the benefits of adopting distributed printing, or an (entertaining?) video of a lab-coated chemist talking about trends in use of solid-ink printing. Those are all about the B—"what life would be like if only you appreciated what's going on at the cutting edge of printing these days." That may be enough to get the customer to view you as an expert supplier, but is it enough to fundamentally change their current behavior? CEB research suggests no, not even close.

BE USEFUL. By definition, this line of conventional thinking has suppliers speaking to customer pain points that customers *realize* they have. What are they searching for? Let's write content that speaks to that. Even if it doesn't relate directly back to the supplier's solution. It's an attention play.

That's well-intentioned advice—in a very noisy marketplace, many marketers will take that attention. But it's grossly insufficient. If suppliers are going to upend mental models with their Commercial Insight, they ought to be talking about problems that Mobilizers *don't realize* they have. Mobilizers won't know to be searching on it in the first place, so analyzing search patterns and writing content that speaks strictly to those search terms isn't going to help us shift how Mobilizers think about their business. In other words, suppliers who follow the *be useful* advice might be ringing up blog clicks and "engagement" metrics, but none of that is feeding through to any kind of meaningful sales activity.

Marketing qualified lead? Sure.

High-quality deal closed? Not likely.

BE PRESENT. This is all about coverage. The problem here is the sheer volume of content that suppliers have to create and deploy. The back-of-envelope math on this gets really ugly, really fast.

For example, take a conservative calculation: 4 personas × 5 touch-points × 4 pieces of content per month × 4 business units = 320 pieces of content per month, or close to 4,000 pieces of content annually. And that probably understates by at least half what most midsize or large enterprises would be facing.

Very quickly, the content tail wags the dog, as a big flashing light on the editorial calendar starts flashing red because no new blog post is in the queue for next week's submission deadline. You're left thinking in a panic, "We need more content!" Fill the hole in the content calendar. Make the deadline. Get it done.

We speak with marketers all the time who find themselves in this "feed the content beast" rut. They inexorably fall prey to putting content *quantity* over content *quality*. That's the tiger trap of "be present." If this sounds familiar, you aren't alone. From all of our structured interviews with marketing organizations, we estimate over 85 percent are in some form of the coverage rut.

The real devil with all of these content approaches is the opportunity cost. Every ounce of energy and resources that goes into creating and deploying "look smart, be useful, be present" content *crowds out* the energy and resources needed to create surprising content that has a chance to truly change the customer's direction. To give that Mobilizer the surprising insight about her business, and the agitation that "pain of same is greater than pain of change." If suppliers don't hit that mark, their content is unlikely to actually redirect the train from rolling into Commoditization Station.

But how do suppliers create content that does that? What does that look like?

CREATING CHALLENGING CONTENT PATHS

If the primary goal of marketing content is to break down the customer's A and then build up a B, then suppliers should ensure that all of their content is somehow tied to that goal. In other words, *once they have created a Commercial Insight, marketers need to step back and create a related content strategy.* That strategy will lay out the content paths that lead Mobilizers on an ever deeper exploration of a Commercial Insight that simultaneously changes the way they think about their business and leads them ever closer to valuing the supplier's unique strengths. Not that every piece of content must "get them to buy," per se. But imagine if every piece of content were built back from a single, powerful insight, all thematically aligned, leading to an ever deeper treatment of that topic. The goal there is to "get them to explore." As long as the exploration is designed to lead them exclusively back to you, the deeper the exploration, the better.

However, most supplier content, thematically speaking, is just the opposite. It's scattered all over the place. That's no surprise given the "look smart, be useful, be present" conventional wisdom in content marketing. That kind of approach leads marketers to create content on a very *wide array* of topics, for very different personas, and to scatter it as far and wide as possible. This is B2P marketing run amok, as marketers seek to match the speed of their content output to the increasingly complex diversity of the 5.4 stakeholders.

Yet notice how this strategy doesn't build a consistent path or message to *anywhere*, as each piece is largely independent of every other. As a result, customers may come away with the notion that you have a lot of smart things to say, but that's about it. They may think differently about you, but they're far less likely to think any differently of *themselves*.

On the other hand, when you lay a purposeful path with your content, so it's all tied together thematically to a single, provocative insight, you get a different output altogether.

In this world, all the content is linked—almost like a trail of bread crumbs—leading back to a single Commercial Insight purposefully designed to change the way customers (and specifically, Mobilizers) think about *their* business. What's especially powerful here, each one of these links in that narrative chain provides a potential hook to catch a Mobilizer, and a possible rallying point for forging consensus.

So how do marketers build that path? Take a look at figure 6.2. It's a simple model that identifies the steps to overturning a customer's mental model. Let's unpack this and then bring it to life with the Xerox example.

First off, the whole idea here is to have all of the content you produce, publish, and curate—all the blog posts, all the testimonials and case studies, all the white papers, all the infographics, you name it—lead to a Commercial Insight.

There are three mental steps that Mobilizers (or any customer stakeholder, for that matter) go through to have their A state challenged, creating

FIG. 6.2. Spark-Introduce-Confront (SIC) Content Path

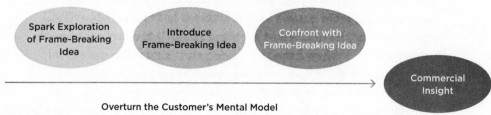

Overturn the Customer's Mental Model
Hook the customer into (re-)exploring their mental model; show where it is wrong and quantify the pain.

Source: CEB analysis.

the drive for them to rally other stakeholders and mobilize change toward a B state.

The first step is to spark exploration of the frame-breaking idea at the heart of your Commercial Insight. You need your content here to hook the Mobilizer into revisiting her mental model in the first place. That might be a killer infographic or an intriguing tweet. Individual sales reps increasingly have a role to play here as "micro-marketers," deploying marketing-curated "sparks" in social networks. The thought bubble you're looking for that Mobilizer to have is "Huh . . . I never thought of it that way before . . . I need to learn more" or "I'm not sure I believe it, but I'm kind of intrigued . . . tell me more."

Having gotten the Mobilizer to want to learn more from the Spark content, the Introduce content (second step) lays out the idea in more detail. It presents the rational evidence and makes a powerful emotional appeal that breaks the customer's frame. That could be an animated video or an interactive white paper or a trade show booth. You want your Mobilizer to come away from this content with the thought bubble "I 'get' the insight conceptually . . . I believe it could be true generally . . . but I wonder how that plays out in my world—in *my business.*"

That's when you path the Mobilizer to Confront content, the third step. This is where you confront the Mobilizer with the frame-breaking idea *in her own terms.* You dial up *her* pain, so that she can't escape the sense that the pain of same is greater than the pain of change. By the way, this isn't about pressuring the Mobilizer *as a person* in any way; rather, it is diplomatically but convincingly leading the Mobilizer to *pressure-test her own ideas, assumptions, and beliefs about her business.* Often, these kinds of content are online diagnostics or interactive pain calculators, which enable the Mobilizer to plug in information about her own reality, so that she can see where the gaps are or how big the pain really is. The thought bubble coming off this content should be "Holy cow! I had no idea we were taking this kind of hit. I need to learn more about fixing this."

We'll refer to this Spark-Introduce-Confront content progression as an SIC content strategy. Through a progression like this, you've blown up the Mobilizer's mental model through compelling content at arm's length. You've broken down the A state.

At this point, you can path Mobilizers to content that builds up the B state. But we can't overstress that customers who consume only B state content are unlikely to feel the need to break from current course and speed.

When you put it all together, if you're looking to teach Mobilizers with content like this, it boils down to three rules.

Rule 1: *All content should be tied in some way to a Commercial Insight.*

Rule 2: *Content that isn't itself frame breaking should directly path back to content that is.*

Rule 3: *All other content should be discarded or never created in the first place.*

This won't be easy to do. It means discarding content that doesn't fit the model. As we've spent time with CEB members, running content audits on their existing content portfolios, we find that there are often pieces of existing content that can be repurposed for Spark, Introduce, or Confront. White papers that can be atomized into bite-size pieces, with some atoms being repurposed and others disappearing altogether. Blog posts that can be repurposed. Sales decks with pages that can be torn out and used.

And then there will always be the practical spec sheets that are necessary for the transactional parts of the selling process. Those can stay (but you can't lead *with* them . . . you have to lead *to* them).

But we don't want to understate the importance of staying tightly aligned to these SIC content paths. Stay on message. Keep beating the drum. Tear down the A before you build up the B.

This is a big shift for marketers. For the majority of content types you produce, following this content strategy will *shift the focus from supplier-centric to supplier-agnostic.* That will feel really unnatural, at first.

For example, most marketers are used to creating customer testimonial videos focused on the B. Over 90 percent of the testimonial videos we review from marketers focus on the B. To create content paths that break mental models and drive urgency instead, they'll have to start creating testimonials about the A. Imagine creating video testimonials of Mobilizers talking about how they discovered a hidden connection in their business and how it was costing them so much more than they realized. And then, how they rallied the 5.4 around a consensus view of the drivers of that pain and what kind of solution it would take to solve it. You want these kinds of A state testimonials to lead back to your Commercial Insight and the differentiators underneath that insight. It's a really different approach, but it's so important to breaking down the A and changing the customer's direction.

Testimonials are but one kind of content. We've seen marketers apply SIC principles all over the content portfolio, from trade show booths to white paper design to online buying toolkits.

LESS IS MORE

Done well, a tightly managed SIC content strategy should lead marketers to create *less* content than they currently do, but drive *greater* impact on the commercial metrics that matter. Why would that be?

Among other things, disruptive ideas naturally garner more earned media attention. They are more likely to get shared, or earn coverage from other outlets with broader reach than what suppliers can achieve alone through their (often modest) owned and paid media efforts. We know this from data, not just experience. Based on empirical research into what gets shared in today's digital environment, two of the most important traits that predict sharing are tightly aligned to disruptive content. That is, content that is *awe inspiring* and *surprising* gets shared much more often than typical news or practical information. This comes from a fascinating study by Jonah Berger and Katherine Milkman, of the University of Pennsylvania, about which articles got shared and which didn't by *New York Times* readers.* According to the authors, awe-inspiring content is defined as having two components: its *scale is large,* and it *requires "mental accommodation"* by forcing the reader to *view the world in a different way* (italics are ours).

These two traits are nearly perfectly aligned to Commercial Insight and our model of content. Commercial Insight is, by definition, surprising because it counters existing mental models.

That kind of attention is critical in today's noisy marketplace, because what gets shared or picked up by non-supplier-affiliated sources tends to get more attention and trust. With B2B marketing budgets what they are—well short of what it would take to satiate a hungry content beast—surprising content will make marketing resources go much further. *Less* can be so much *more.*

To show you how, let's take a look at some examples of how a Spark-Introduce-Confront content strategy plays out in practice.

Example 1: DENTSPLY

The SIC content framework becomes a very powerful tool for determining which content to create and which content should never see the light of day. As an illustrative example, take the DENTSPLY Commercial Insight. Please note, this example is not necessarily reflective of DENTSPLY's actual marketing efforts and is merely meant to illustrate how DENTSPLY's insight could potentially be turned into an effective content path. Recall that DENTSPLY's insight is related to dental hygienist absenteeism causing dentists more pain than they ever realized and how it's actually controllable with the proper dental instruments.

Now, suppose you're a DENTSPLY marketer charged with developing a content strategy that will upend the mental models of Mobilizers inside of dental practices. Figure 6.3 shows what kinds of content would be "in" and what would be "out."

---

* Jonah Berger and Katherine Milkman, "What Makes Online Content Viral?," *Journal of Marketing Research*, 2011, http://ldi.upenn.edu/uploads/media_items/virality.original.pdf.

FIG. 6.3. Hypothetical Content Path for DENTSPLY Commercial Insight

	Accepted Disruptive Content	Rejected Content
Spark Exploration of Frame-Breaking Idea	▪ Infographics, data, factoids, blog posts, etc., about the average yearly cost of hygienist absenteeism or the linkage between carpal tunnel syndrome and hygienist absences	▪ Blog post on "Why You Need Your Own Dental App" ▪ Trade show booth that displays all products in a showcase format ▪ Web link to government data on average dental hygienist wages by region
Introduce Frame-Breaking Idea	▪ Evidence about hidden impact of absenteeism on patient satisfaction and loyalty ▪ Evidence from a third-party medical study on how the ergonomics of dental tools impact hygienist health ▪ Video testimonials from other dentists talking about their absenteeism problem and the steps they took to solve it	▪ Guide for "Using Social Media to Attract Patients" ▪ Sponsorship of hygienist continuing education classes offered by the American Dental Association ▪ Pitch deck focused on product performance and benefits ▪ E-book about new trends in dental practice management
Confront with Frame-Breaking Idea	▪ Pain-sizing calculator using customer data to quantify customer's specific pain resulting from direct and indirect absenteeism costs ▪ Study by a third party showing the savings on hygienist absenteeism when using ergonomically designed tools	

Source: CEB analysis.

Spark content, for example, would include infographics on average yearly cost of hygienist absenteeism, including a breakout of all the hidden or indirect costs that a dentist faces with that absenteeism. You'll want to build numerous Spark content pieces like this, to provide on-ramps for your customers and Mobilizers in all the places they go to learn. Again, you're just trying to get the Mobilizer who sees this to think, "Huh, I didn't realize the cost was that high, I wonder why . . ." By contrast, Spark content would not include a blog post on "Why you need a dental app" for your practice, or a Web link to government data about average hygienist wages by geographic region. These don't spark exploration of DENTSPLY's Commercial Insight.

Introduce content might include evidence about the hidden impact of absenteeism on patient satisfaction, or maybe testimonials from other dentists. But not about how great DENTSPLY's new instrument is, rather about the process of realizing that absenteeism was costing that dentist more than he ever realized. It would not include a pitch deck about the unique benefits of DENTSPLY's instruments. Likewise, it would not include a trade show booth displaying DENTSPLY's instruments by product category. These are all leading with the supplier's products and do very little to break down the customer's A state.

Confront content would be an online pain-sizing calculator, where a Mobilizer could plug in a few attributes about her dental practice—number of patients, number of hygienists, average days absent, percentage of patients with families, percentage of hygienist hours that are overtime, hygienist cost per hour, average time to fill a hygienist position—that sizes up the true, all-in costs of hygienist absenteeism. That makes it real for the Mobilizer. Thought bubble: "I've got to do something about this problem in *my* business!"

Confront content would not include a standard ROI calculator—which is just the return on buying the supplier's stuff . . . not the return on removing the pain the customer is feeling in his A state.

Ultimately, you're trying to create a content path tied directly to your Commercial Insight. In other words, it leads a Mobilizer down a *teaching* path that breaks down the A, toward a B state that that supplier is best positioned to fulfill.

Example 2: Xerox

While the above DENTSPLY example is hypothetical for teaching purposes, here's an example of content that is real. It's Part 2 of the Xerox story from chapter 5.

To set the scene here, recall that Xerox wants to engage Mobilizers about *student performance*. Here's what the Spark-Introduce-Confront model looks like in Xerox's context, laid on top of a simplified purchase journey.

In Xerox's case, the purchase journey has a few high-level steps to it. This should look familiar. Before the Mobilizer or broader buying center ever enters the formal due diligence process, there's a period of Passive Learning. Then, you have a stage of Need Awareness and Exploration, followed by Evaluating Solutions, and on to purchase.

FIG. 6.4. Opportunities to Spark Customer Exploration of Commercial Insight Content

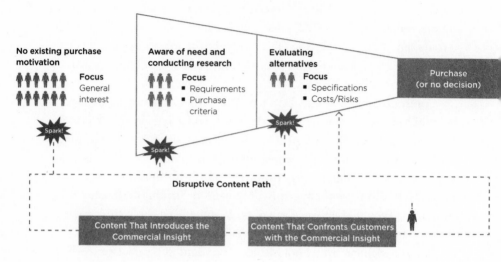

Source: CEB analysis.

The Xerox team realized that across thousands of potential customers, there'll be large audiences in each of these stages. The idea is to create "on-ramps" that spark a Mobilizer, no matter where she is in the journey, to travel down a teaching content path that challenges her mental model.

For Xerox, that sparking content took multiple forms:

➤ Provocative data points promoted through social media, where Mobilizers are doing that Passive Learning

➤ A series of e-mail scripts that sales reps could use to promote the research findings on the link between color and student performance

➤ A K–12 segment microsite with resources and banner displays promoting Xerox's Commercial Insight content

➤ Third-party affiliates posting comments and blogs about the Xerox K–12 color research

As well, note the implications of a Commercial Insight content strategy on your search engine marketing and optimization efforts. Because your

FIG. 6.5. Sampling of Xerox's Spark, Introduce, and Confront Content

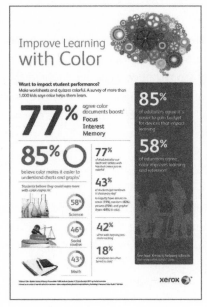

Screenshot from customer video discussing purchase of Xerox ColorQube

Insight-led pitch deck

Source: Xerox; CEB analysis.

content is focused on surprising or unexpected aspects of the customer's business, those customers won't naturally be searching on your content keywords. So the key is to find adjacencies between your insight-related content keywords and the keywords that your Mobilizers are naturally searching on. For Xerox, that might have meant purchasing search terms like "interactive classroom" (a term that school principals might naturally search on) and linking to content on the surprising link between color and student performance. The idea is to locate Mobilizers where they are searching on adjacent terms and "spark" their exploration of your Commercial Insight—take them to your infographic or a mention of your insight somewhere in earned media. Once you've sparked a Mobilizer into exploring your insight, you can pull her in more deeply with Introduce content.

Xerox's Introduce content included a blog series, a white paper titled "Improving Student Performance in Unexpected Ways," and testimonial-style videos like its "Huephoria" video that depicts educators talking about use of color in the classroom. This content portfolio unpacks the

Commercial Insight by using a combination of evidence that appeals to a Mobilizer's rational side and narratives from peers that appeal to a Mobilizer's emotional side.

In this case, the power of Xerox's Commercial Insight meant it was achieving strong engagement with Mobilizers on the Spark and Introduce content alone. Leah and her team found they could rely on sales reps and account executives to do the work of Confront content. It equipped them with extensive sales tools and training to help engage customers and help them understand what they were missing, and the pain they were experiencing, as a result of a flawed mental model about student performance drivers.

By the way, as of the writing of this book, much of this content can still be viewed at www.xerox.com/k12.

Sometimes the strength of a Commercial Insight will win early engagement between Mobilizers and sales reps. Here, it'll be about having sales tools that are custom-built to Confront the Commercial Insight and how well sales reps use them. At the same time, marketing will need to create Confront content so Mobilizers can engage with the personal ramifications of the Commercial Insight before they speak with a sales rep. The disciplines of field marketing, content marketing, product marketing, demand generation, and sales ops/training all need to work closely together to co-create these SIC content paths that transition seamlessly into sales conversations.

We'll finish this example with a really important lesson Xerox shared involving editorial discipline. The Xerox team had to keep a ruthless focus on creating content that tied back to their Commercial Insight. As will be the case with most suppliers, Xerox had a broad set of people and partners creating and curating content. The tendency will be for that dispersed set of content players to drift into the "feed the content beast" mentality, leading to creation of content that doesn't build out those clear learning paths. As Justin Doyle, the sales program training manager on the K–12 team, put it:

> *"There were opportunities where we could add more information in our content deliverable set. But we wanted to make sure we had a laser-clear message and laser-clear offering that got back to how color improves student learning. So it was . . . a ruthless editing process to say, 'This is THE*

message that we want to go to market with.' We made sure we stayed true
to that."

Example 3: SMART Technologies

The growth in digital communications is opening up all kinds of creative surface area for marketing teams to reach their Mobilizer target audiences. It's even allowing marketing teams to create powerful content paths, from Spark to Introduce to Confront, within *single* pieces of marketing content.

One of our favorite examples comes from SMART Technologies. SMART is a leading provider of technology solutions that enable collaboration in schools and workplaces. This supplier is perhaps best known for its SMART boards—interactive whiteboards that enable people to better collaborate.

Jeff Lowe is the CMO of SMART Technologies, based in Calgary, Canada. We've long admired the work that Jeff and his team have done with Challenger. In this example, Jeff had recently arrived at SMART Technologies and hoped to embed a Commercial Insight–led approach to SMART's go-to-market strategy.

To set the context, Jeff and his team began crafting a Commercial Insight they came to call the Tragedy of Disengagement. The idea is that in business these days there's a greater need for collaboration across work sites and functions, yet a growing percentage of employees are working remotely. That's leading to disengagement when those remote employees can't effectively participate in collaborative work, and it's costing employers far more than they realize in productivity, higher talent acquisition costs, and opportunity costs of great ideas that never come to fruition.

It's a great example of a Commercial Insight. But Jeff and the team realized they needed to penetrate the 57 percent arrow, because buyers of office equipment were increasingly doing their own research and setting buying criteria around very basic kinds of whiteboards and virtual conferencing capabilities.

The content piece that Jeff's team created, in partnership with SMART's agency, gyro, is a brilliant example of an effective content path. It's a video-enabled direct mailer, about the size of a CD case (remember those?).

So this colorful item lands on your desk via mail, inviting you to "Discover the Power of Inspired Collaboration," which is itself an intriguing

FIG. 6.6. SMART Technology's Direct Mailer

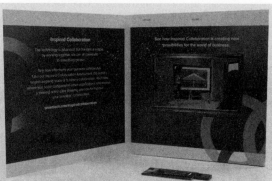

kind of event that can spark exploration. When you open the mailer, a video plays on a screen about the size of a credit card. The video lays out the Tragedy of Disengagement story in an engaging way, bringing both rational and emotional elements to bear to break down the A. The video goes on to paint a vision of inspired collaboration, building up the B. That's the Introduce piece. Then at the end, it asks the viewer, "How inspired is your collaboration?" and invites the viewer to take a collaboration appraisal. The viewer can enter a URL into a browser, or use an enclosed USB stick, to navigate to the appraisal, which is an interactive diagnostic. The viewer can input information about her business and get an assessment, highlighting strengths and gaps, with benchmarking against other organizations that look like hers. That's the Confront piece.

In one fell swoop, SMART has overthrown a Mobilizer's mental model by breaking down the A and provided a reason and urgency to take action. Pain of same greater than pain of change. It's a great example of the huge creative surface area that marketers have—to mix digital with physical—as they go about creating SIC content paths.

This would all be very impressive on its own, but if you think about the data set that SMART is building here, you can appreciate why this single marketing vehicle is so brilliant. Over time, SMART has gathered data from 1,500 participating organizations on the ins and outs of their collaborative dynamics. Now SMART can provide more specific Confronting insights to particular vertical markets or geographies, making it that much more difficult for competitors to attack this Commercial Insight space that SMART has come to own. It's like building a data moat around your Commercial Insight. Now that's smart.

DEMAND GENERATION AND "CONSUMPTION OF DISRUPTION"

At this point, you may be wondering how a content strategy that teaches Mobilizers ties into demand generation—lead generation, lead scoring, lead nurturing, marketing automation, and all that comes with it. We'll take a deeper dive into this in chapter 10. That's because it helps to have a working knowledge of the chapters on tailoring and taking control to really appreciate the full set of implications for demand generation.

But to give you a preview, one of the biggest implications for demand generation is for marketers to shift lead-scoring criteria away from sensing *purchase readiness*, and toward sensing mental model disruption. By focusing lead scoring on indicators of purchase readiness, marketers are in essence handing over to sales customers who haven't necessarily had their mental models overturned. They're more likely to be the ones who have done the research on their own in the 57 percent and are narrowing to the three suppliers they are going to pit against one another on price.

The activities covered in chapters 3, 4, 5, and 6 so far have all covered the teach part of Teach, Tailor, and Take Control. Commercial organizations that excel at teach—successfully creating Commercial Insight and then laying down SIC content paths with demand generation efforts oriented to those paths—will have attracted and activated Mobilizers, engaging them in a conversation they find compelling enough to want to act on. In other

FIG. 6.7. Purchase Process Overview (illustrative)

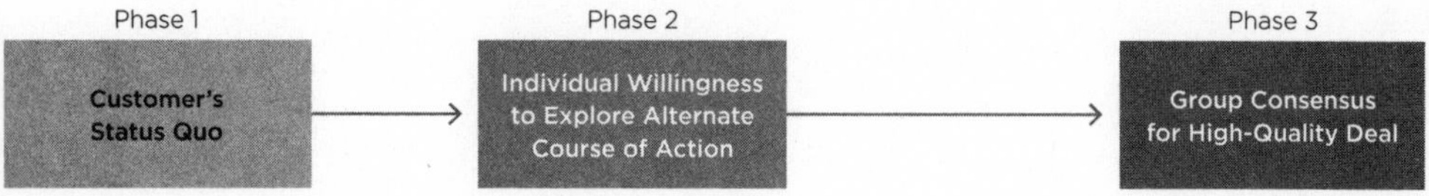

Phase 1	Phase 2	Phase 3
Customer's Status Quo	Individual Willingness to Explore Alternate Course of Action	Group Consensus for High-Quality Deal

Source: CEB analysis.

words, you'll have covered the ground from Phase 1 to Phase 2 in the simple purchase model from chapter 1 below.

Chapter 7 is all about tailoring. This is where we start to transition from winning the individual to winning the group. Again, sales and marketing will both have important roles to play here. All with the ultimate goal of generating high-quality deals.

CHAPTER SEVEN

TWO TYPES OF TAILORING

Now that we've laid out an organizational framework for building and deploying Commercial Insight, let's examine how suppliers might tailor that insight to better connect to individual customer stakeholders.

The ultimate goal in any solutions sale, of course, isn't to get stakeholders to believe your insight, it's to get customer *organizations* to buy your solution. To do that, however, requires customers to do something else—to change their behavior. That decision to change organizational behavior isn't an individual choice but a collective one. So does that mean that tailoring insight for individual stakeholder resonance no longer matters in this world? Not at all. In fact, just the opposite. But it matters in context. To demonstrate how, let's place Commercial Insight back into the context of a customer purchase.

You'll remember, in chapter 1 we introduced a simple framework for a typical customer purchase process spanning two movements (see figure 7.1).

FIG. 7.1. Purchase Process Overview (illustrative)

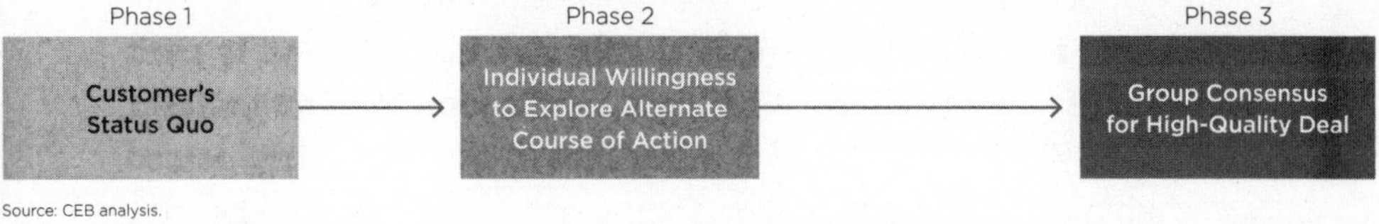

Phase 1		Phase 2		Phase 3
Customer's Status Quo	→	Individual Willingness to Explore Alternate Course of Action	→	Group Consensus for High-Quality Deal

Source: CEB analysis.

In the first movement, from Phase 1 to Phase 2, a supplier is looking to win agreement from one or two customer stakeholders that change is even necessary in the first place. Think of this as establishing a beachhead in the battle against status quo. Yet, as we saw in chapter 2, in this early stage of the purchase process, all customer stakeholders are not created equal. After all, suppliers aren't looking to get the 5.4 to *agree*, they're looking to get the 5.4 to *change*. So carefully connecting to the people most willing and able to drive that change not only matters, it matters deeply. These are the Mobilizers. And this is exactly why connecting with Mobilizers matters so much.

However, five years of customer research tells us that tailoring to Mobilizers is far more important than tailoring to stakeholders more generally. First and foremost, suppliers must tailor their approach to identify and appeal to those with the highest potential to either be or become a Mobilizer. In a moment, we'll turn to the steps a supplier might take to create that kind of tailored message in the first place.

That said, there isn't just one type of Mobilizer, there are three—the Go-Getter, the Teacher, and the Skeptic. Each a little bit different, requiring a different approach and different kinds of support. At this level, sales reps in particular can very precisely modify their approach to (1) test whether they're even meeting with a Mobilizer in the first place at all, and then (2) ensure that they're tailoring their approach to resonate most effectively with whatever type of Mobilizer they're meeting with at that moment. So after we look at creating more tailored appeals to Mobilizers in the first place, we'll then turn to more precisely look at how sales reps can effectively identify and type those Mobilizers in the moment, allowing them to tailor their interactions with far greater precision than relying on more traditional stakeholder attributes such as title, role, or seniority.

That said, notice that even when done well, this kind of tailoring is only half the battle. Once a supplier has effectively identified and connected to a high-potential Mobilizer, they still must find a way to connect that Mobilizer more closely to the rest of the 4.4. In terms of the customer's purchase process, in other words, we still have to cross the long second chasm from Phase 2 (Individual Willingness to Explore Alternate Course of Action) to Phase 3, the actual collective purchase decision. This is where any definition of tailoring, no matter how precise, is nonetheless still incomplete. For in the second movement of a typical purchase process, the goal here can't simply be creating better individual resonance; it must evolve to ensuring profitable collective consensus. Indeed, as we saw in chapter 1, ·

an ever more precise articulation of individual value at this stage may backfire insofar as people across the 5.4 aren't aligned already. So at this stage tailoring efforts must shift dramatically toward aligning mental models around the need for change.

BUILDING MOBILIZER MESSAGES

When it comes specifically to tailoring for individual Mobilizers, perhaps the smartest marketing application we've seen thus far comes from Jeff Lowe, CMO of SMART Technologies, whom we first heard about in chapter 6. To provide some context, SMART is in the collaboration business. Their solution enables people to interact and collaborate more effectively across multiple locations around the world—whether it be conference rooms, classrooms, or coffeehouses. Particularly on the B2B side of their business, SMART provides a combination of hardware and software that allows physically dispersed employees to interact with one another as if they were all in the same conference room, working on the exact same whiteboard. Among other things, it's a powerful solution because it's designed to overcome the high level of detachment felt by most remote workers as they struggle to effectively contribute to group discussions through more traditional conference calling and videoconferencing technology.

However, like any technology provider, SMART has a 5.4 problem. In the B2B setting, for example, they've got to win over the facilities manager, the CIO, the CFO, the head of procurement, and, likely, a wide range of potentially diverse end users. It's only natural, then, that the team would seek out a logical "first point of contact" to help connect them all. That person could then serve as the primary target of the company's marketing campaigns, sales tools, and positioning statements. But who to choose? The head of IT? After all, it's a tech-driven solution. The head of facilities? After all, they're the traditional buyer of this type of equipment. The CFO? After all, SMART's full-blown solution can require a sizeable investment. It's a tough choice. No one candidate seemed like the best choice *at scale* above all others.

After an analysis of past "won" deals for some clues, however, Jeff and the team came to a powerful conclusion. They found they were asking the wrong question. The deals they were most likely to win weren't due to the backing of any one of those individuals versus another. The deals they won were due to the backing of people who actively championed the cause of effective collaboration inside their organization. Effectively, they were "Collaboration Champions," as SMART came to call them. These are SMART's Mobilizers. But note, completely consistent with CEB research, Jeff and the team discovered they weren't necessarily mobilizers for a *supplier*; they were mobilizing around an *insight*—specifically, the belief that more effective collaboration can have a dramatic and underappreciated impact on employee performance and engagement. Just as important, they weren't mobilizing because of their role, or title, or function, but *irrespective* of those things. They were Jeff, or Deb, or Kevin, or Joanne. Simply individuals who found the surprising benefits of more effective collaboration to be important enough to make them willing to go fight the good fight among the other 4.4 to acquire the kind of solution necessary to help their company make good on that compelling insight.

But at that point, all Jeff had so far was an understanding that when these kinds of people appeared in *past* deals, the company was more likely to win. What he really wanted to identify, however, was a way to predict *in advance* (1) who *else* might be a Collaboration Champion, and (2) how to identify them, and (3) what kinds of content might predictably motivate them to mobilize on SMART's behalf. As a marketer, in other words, Jeff was looking for a way to predictably identify and effectively tailor to potential mobilizers *at arm's length* and *at scale*.

To do that, the SMART team did something rather clever. Having identified a number of Collaboration Champions from previous deals, Jeff invited them to join a customer advisory panel, which meets in person on a periodic basis to allow SMART to understand their needs and priorities. Consistent with everything we saw in chapter 3, however, the purpose of getting that group together wasn't to best determine how they viewed SMART but, rather, to figure out how they viewed *themselves*.

Those discussions allowed Jeff and the team not only to formulate a clear mental model of a Collaboration Champion but then, even better, to begin testing language, messages, insights, and ideas to determine their resonance with the kinds of people most likely to mobilize for SMART's solution. That work allowed the team to tailor their Commercial Insights not to CIOs, or facilities managers, or procurement officers, but to *Mobilizers*. It also resulted in a kind of "Mobilizer identification toolkit," which enables SMART sales reps to identify additional potential Mobilizers with just a few simple questions—all based on insights gleaned from working with proven Mobilizers from past deals.

It's a simple but powerful idea that we especially like for a number of reasons, but in no small part because it's not all that different from what many companies who convene customer panels might do already. That's good news, as it means implementing an idea like this may not prove all that disruptive to whatever a supplier may be doing already. The crucial difference, however, is the makeup of the group convened. By identifying Mobilizers from past deals (i.e., SMART's Collaboration Champions), Jeff was able not just to tailor to *stakeholders*, but to very purposefully tailor to *Mobilizers*. That view can then be incorporated into all of the various marketing campaigns, content-marketing efforts, and sales support tools necessary to identify, attract, and even create Mobilizers in the marketplace.

So now that marketing has built a strong *hypothesis* for who might be a Mobilizer in the first place and tested the types of messages most likely to resonate with them, the sales team is in a much better position to go out and *test* those hypotheses in real conversations with real people. All with an eye toward identifying and connecting to the people most willing and able to drive the change necessary to get the deal done. So let's turn to that next—and look at deploying tailored Commercial Insight in the field. As we go through this, you'll notice the same principles can be applied equally well *indirectly* through both marketing campaigns and channel partners as well. In both cases, the principle is exactly the same, centering on the careful observation of customer stakeholders' reactions to a supplier's Commercial Insight.

IDENTIFYING AND TAILORING TO MOBILIZERS

If we were to break down the reasons why core reps naturally gravitate to Talkers (and not Mobilizers), it's largely because core reps aren't thinking so much about *driving customer change* as they are *gaining customer access*. For core-performing reps, access equals action. Not surprisingly then, they take the very fact that a stakeholder is talking to them as an indication of that stakeholder's ability to drive change. But the two aren't the same thing.

Moreover, a conversation with a Mobilizer isn't necessarily guaranteed to be an easy one. Unlike the Talker, they're going to challenge the rep—and the insight. They're going to test the logic, seek to poke holes in the argument. All to ensure that that idea is rock solid before they take it to anyone else on the team.

But it's not just a matter of finding someone willing to have that conversation in the first place. Who reps choose to engage with this kind of conversation really matters. As one star rep told us, "A lot of my colleagues take whoever they can get. The problem is, if you let the wrong person carry your message, you forever get lumped in with their bad ideas and cut off from influence. Having a bad contact is worse than nothing at all." But how do stars identify the exact type of stakeholder they're engaged with? If you just ask stars, they'll tell you it's "gut feel" or "years of experience," or they'll say they've never thought about it, they just *know* who they're talking to. But when you dig deep enough—as we did in a series of structured interviews with high performers at a variety of companies—you find stars' ability to assess stakeholders is based on a deep and nuanced understanding of how customer organizations operate.

READING BETWEEN THE LINES

In the structured interviews we ran with high performers to better understand how they choose stakeholders in the customer organization, it became very clear to us that they naturally have (or perhaps have developed over time) a skeptical mind-set. They tend not to accept people at face value. They're always going to dig a couple of layers deeper. High performers look for a handful of "tells" to know what kind of stakeholder they're engaged with. They're a lot like poker players in that regard.

We worked with high performers to get them to help us identify these tells and then worked backward to build a Mobilizer identification tool that any salesperson or manager could use to sort out whether a customer stakeholder is a Mobilizer or not and, if they are a Mobilizer, what kind they are.

To understand how to make sense of the identification tool—and how to tailor to the different types of Mobilizers—we've got to dig a little deeper into each of the stakeholder profiles—so that we *really* get to know these profiles and, therefore, know what to look for in identifying them. Let's start with the three flavors of Mobilizer: the Go-Getter, the Teacher, and the Skeptic. Each has a unique set of traits that makes them stand out from other stakeholders in the organization.

FIG. 7.2. Summary of the Three Mobilizer Profiles

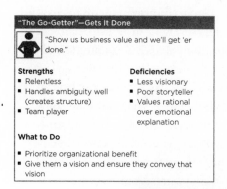

"The Go-Getter"—Gets It Done

"Show us business value and we'll get 'er done."

Strengths
- Relentless
- Handles ambiguity well (creates structure)
- Team player

Deficiencies
- Less visionary
- Poor storyteller
- Values rational over emotional explanation

What to Do
- Prioritize organizational benefit
- Give them a vision and ensure they convey that vision

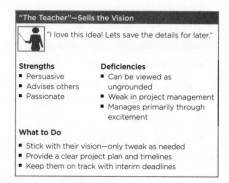

"The Teacher"—Sells the Vision

"I love this idea! Lets save the details for later."

Strengths
- Persuasive
- Advises others
- Passionate

Deficiencies
- Can be viewed as ungrounded
- Weak in project management
- Manages primarily through excitement

What to Do
- Stick with their vision—only tweak as needed
- Provide a clear project plan and timelines
- Keep them on track with interim deadlines

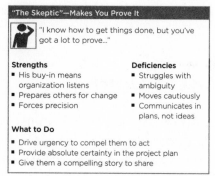

"The Skeptic"—Makes You Prove It

"I know how to get things done, but you've got a lot to prove..."

Strengths
- His buy-in means organization listens
- Prepares others for change
- Forces precision

Deficiencies
- Struggles with ambiguity
- Moves cautiously
- Communicates in plans, not ideas

What to Do
- Drive urgency to compel them to act
- Provide absolute certainty in the project plan
- Give them a compelling story to share

n = 717.
Source: CEB analysis.

As we explained in chapter 2, Go-Getters are relentless and excel at taking ambiguous ideas and translating them into work plans. A Go-Getter isn't the most visionary person and can tend to explain things with data rather than stories (more "trees" than "forest," in the way they view things). They're far more rational than emotional. While they can help convince others *how* something will get done (addressing implementation hurdles, resourcing questions, success measures, etc.), they are decidedly less skilled in terms of selling an idea and convincing colleagues *whether* something should be done.

The Teacher is almost the polar opposite of the Go-Getter. The Teacher is *all about* the emotional part of the idea. The Teacher is passionate and persuasive—a dynamic force within the customer organization who prides himself on his ability to advise others, even on matters far outside his area of responsibility or expertise. He gets excited about the idea of taking a contrary position to the group and, through compelling argument, bending the group to his will. The Teacher, however, for all his passion and excitement, lacks (in some cases, severely) in terms of project management. He can't be bothered with minor details like resources, budget, timelines, or metrics.

Last, we've got the Skeptic. The Skeptic feels like a bit of a hybrid of the Teacher and the Go-Getter. She's all about precision and having complete certainty in the plan before moving forward. The rest of the organization knows this and sees her support as a huge vote of confidence in any idea. Unfortunately, she sometimes allows the perfect to be the enemy of the good and gets bogged down in seemingly minor details, causing decision delays until open questions can be resolved to her satisfaction.

BEWARE OF SWEET TALKERS

What about Talkers? You'll recall that we've got three flavors of Talkers too—Guides, Friends, and Climbers—and each is a bit different.

First, let's look at the Guide. This is the stakeholder who traffics in information. They know the ins and outs of the customer organization— not just the rules and formal processes that everybody knows, but the *informal* rules that only those who are really deep (and, typically, very tenured) understand. They aren't action oriented, per se, so while it's highly likely to hear them dish the dirt on internal politics and power struggles, it's just as *unlikely* to hear them talking about championing or driving a big change initiative in their organizations. They are more copilot than pilot, in other words.

The Friend is exactly who he sounds like. He seems to go beyond the call of duty in terms of offering help—for instance, making introductions

FIG. 7.3. Summary of "Talker" Profiles

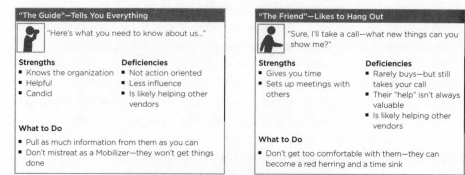

"The Guide"—Tells You Everything

"Here's what you need to know about us..."

Strengths	Deficiencies
▪ Knows the organization	▪ Not action oriented
▪ Helpful	▪ Less influence
▪ Candid	▪ Is likely helping other vendors

What to Do

▪ Pull as much information from them as you can
▪ Don't mistreat as a Mobilizer—they won't get things done

"The Friend"—Likes to Hang Out

"Sure, I'll take a call—what new things can you show me?"

Strengths	Deficiencies
▪ Gives you time	▪ Rarely buys—but still takes your call
▪ Sets up meetings with others	▪ Their "help" isn't always valuable
	▪ Is likely helping other vendors

What to Do

▪ Don't get too comfortable with them—they can become a red herring and a time sink

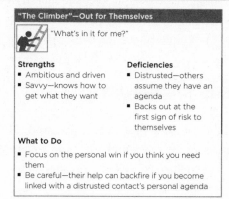

"The Climber"—Out for Themselves

"What's in it for me?"

Strengths	Deficiencies
▪ Ambitious and driven	▪ Distrusted—others assume they have an agenda
▪ Savvy—knows how to get what they want	▪ Backs out at the first sign of risk to themselves

What to Do

▪ Focus on the personal win if you think you need them
▪ Be careful—their help can backfire if you become linked with a distrusted contact's personal agenda

n = 717.
Source: CEB analysis.

to others across the organization or carving out time from his schedule to sit down and meet with salespeople (even when it seems like everybody else in the company is too busy with important business—like, perhaps, closing the financial year, preparing for the rollout of a new enterprise-wide system, or working on postmerger integration). Sometimes, it can be surprising how unbusy he seems. One high performer we interviewed told us about a particularly eager Friend from one of his customer organizations: "There's a guy at this company I've been trying to get in with for a few years now . . . whenever I call, he makes time for me. He's super helpful. He usually calls me to let me know when he's going to be in town so that we touch base on things and talk selling strategy. Great guy to have a beer with, but I figured out pretty early on that he wasn't going to help me get a deal done. He'd rather sit on the sidelines than be in the game mixing it up."

Then we have the Climber. Every organization has its Climbers. These are the "WIFM" guys ("What's in it for me?"). It's all about their careers, building their fiefdoms, enhancing their own position, currying favor . . . you get the picture. They are savvy and certainly know how to get what they want—and if a certain supplier's solution helps accomplish that, they will advocate for it—but as soon as they figure out that there's no personal upside for them, they will leave the salesperson hanging in the breeze.

These sorts of tells can be very helpful to the average seller as he navigates the customer organization, trying to ascertain who to hitch his wagon to. If we're going to ask our sales reps to identify Mobilizers, they need to know exactly what they're looking for.

PROGRESSIVELY DISQUALIFY

After we derived these "profiles" of our Mobilizers and Talkers, we worked with high performers to build a simple decision tree that can be easily employed to sort stakeholder types out from one another and identify types of Mobilizers within the customer organization.

There are two ways to use this tool. The first is as a qualification tool—in other words, we can use it to sort out whether we're engaged with a Mobilizer in the first place. The other use is as a Mobilizer identification tool to assist us in our tailoring efforts.

Obviously, we can't put the cart before the horse, so before we can even talk about tailoring, we need to make sure we're not mistakenly engaging with a Talker. Let's first talk about qualifying your stakeholders. One surprising (if not a little frustrating) thing we learned in building this tool is that it's easier to identify *Talkers* than Mobilizers. So the way to think about the tool is more of a Talker *disqualification* tool than a Mobilizer *qualification* tool. It will get you to the point where you have high confidence that your stakeholder is, in fact, a Mobilizer, but it isn't guaranteed. We'll pull up and talk more about how to test your conclusions after we talk through the first few steps of the tool itself.

Now, as we discussed, the idea here is to use certain "tells" to disqualify Talkers until we're certain we're left with only Mobilizers.

FIG. 7.4. Mobilizer Qualification Screens

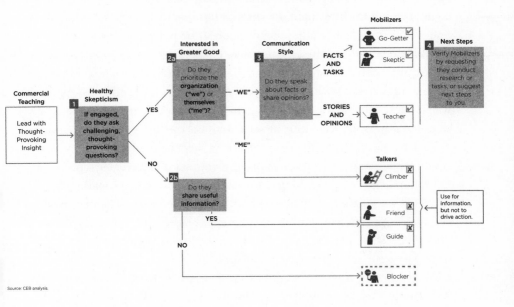

Source: CEB analysis.

Hopefully, by this point in the book, you're on board with the importance of Commercial Insight to any Mobilizer engagement effort. It's central as well to the process of qualifying Mobilizers. The first step in this exercise is to lead with a thought-provoking insight and gauge the customer's reaction to it. Remember, Commercial Insight is the Mobilizer dog whistle—only they can hear it and only they will understand the potential it holds for their organizations.

This is what you're looking for right off the bat—engagement around the insight you've just put on the table. You've approached the customer with an insight or set of insights that teaches them something new and changes the way they think about their business. Done well, this is a *provocative* insight—provocative because it challenges the customer's current worldview, the mental model they have about how things are *supposed* to work. It's not unlike what you might see in one of those detective shows. The detectives have the suspect in the interrogation room . . . warming him up with some softball questions and then . . . *BOOM!*—they drop a critical piece of information on the suspect just to gauge his reaction.

Just like a master detective, that's what we're looking for. We want to gauge our stakeholder's reaction to our Commercial Insight. If you approach the customer with valuable insight, how do they react? Do they tune you out, or do they stay engaged? Someone who doesn't even engage with the content of your teaching is almost certainly unlikely to drive change around that idea across the customer organization. If they don't engage at all, or simply accept the insight at face value, chances are pretty good you're dealing with either a Blocker (we'll talk more about how to handle Blockers later in the book), who's likely against the idea, or a Friend or a Guide, who is never going to dig deep enough to forge consensus around the idea.

Alternatively, do they lean forward and ask thought-provoking questions? Do they dig deeper? Do they seem a bit skeptical at first? If so, that's a good sign. Because, while it scares the daylights out of the average rep, customer skepticism is a good thing. It means that our insight is resonating. Or, at least, it's resonating enough to get a reaction. Even better, skepticism is observable. It's concrete. It means that the stakeholder is engaged—not with the supplier, but with the idea. That's so much more important, because that's what's going to ultimately mobilize action.

So the first step on the identification journey is the customer saying "OK, this is interesting. But before I do anything with this idea, I'm going to make sure it makes sense and that it's in our best interest." Star performers told us that if a stakeholder behaves this way with a vendor, chances are pretty good they behave this same way with their colleagues. That's good, because it means that any idea this person brings to the table inside the company is much more likely to be seen as credible, as colleagues know this person has high standards for good ideas.

But just engaging with your Commercial Insight isn't enough to know that you've got a Mobilizer. Instead, we need to surface a second "tell." What we need to know next is how they talk about their needs and their challenges. Do they talk about the greater group, department, or company as a whole? Or, are they in it for themselves and talk only about their needs? If they focus just on themselves, that is *not* a horse you want to hitch your wagon to.

Why?

If the customer isn't thinking about other people, they're likely in it for themselves, and that's something their colleagues have probably come to recognize over time as well. This person, who is undoubtedly a Climber, is the worst person your idea could be associated with, as the distaste colleagues carry for the Climber can easy rub off on you. If others see a supplier as being joined at the hip with a Climber, it can be the kiss of death for a deal since others (typically out of personal spite) will line up to fight the Climber on the proposal or solution they're advocating for, irrespective of whether it makes business sense. Not a good place to be.

So what next?

Well, before we go any further, take a step back and look at how far we've already come—with just two tells. By simply observing carefully how a stakeholder reacts to quality, thought-provoking insight, we have largely determined whether or not we're speaking with a Mobilizer. As long as we start in the right place, we're only two questions away from finding the right person.

The conversations we had with star performers taught us that even if our stakeholder clears these hurdles, we still can't be certain that we've got a Mobilizer. Only once we test the willingness and ability of our would-be Mobilizer to *actually mobilize* can we be certain. How do we do that? By giving them an assignment and seeing if they come through.

Give them something they value and then ask them to do some homework in return.

This isn't "download your org chart from your intranet and e-mail it to me"; rather, it's something like "Go out and research something that's happening in your company, and come back to me with your point of view." If they don't do the homework, it's a real red flag. Either they can't get it done, or they're not on board. Another idea is to test the customer's influence in the organization. Throughout the course of any given sale, reps have several meetings with customers, often with larger groups of stakeholders. But unlike the core reps, high performers will use these group meetings as tells. They'll ask the customer to set up the meeting, then watch who shows up. If the people who matter most aren't there, your customer stakeholder has a lot less influence than either he'd thought or you'd hoped.

Now, we could stop here because at this stage we have several pretty good signs that this person is both credible and influential enough to be a Mobilizer. But as we think about tailoring to Mobilizers, it turns out we can dig still one level deeper based on what type of Mobilizer we're dealing with.

Don't Let the Title Fool You

In perhaps one of the most counterintuitive findings of all of our Mobilizer research, we found that neither title nor seniority is statistically predictive of Mobilizer tendencies. Normally, it would be logical to assume—given their particularly strong ability to drive organizational change and build consensus—that most Mobilizers would be relatively senior. But that's not the case (see figure 7.5).

FIG. 7.5. Distribution of Customer Stakeholder Profiles
(by title and role in purchase)

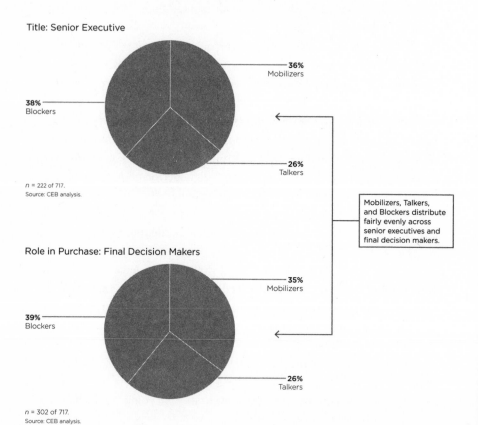

Title: Senior Executive

36% Mobilizers

38% Blockers

26% Talkers

n = 222 of 717.
Source: CEB analysis.

Mobilizers, Talkers, and Blockers distribute fairly evenly across senior executives and final decision makers.

Role in Purchase: Final Decision Makers

35% Mobilizers

39% Blockers

26% Talkers

n = 302 of 717.
Source: CEB analysis.

When we examine the distribution of Mobilizers, Talkers, and Blockers across senior decision makers we find they're actually spread pretty evenly. In other words, neither seniority level nor role in the purchase is predictive of being a Mobilizer. A senior executive with decision-making power is just as likely to be a Blocker as a Mobilizer. Even more troubling, they're just as likely to be a Talker.

This last finding in particular is especially concerning. For when a core-performing sales rep bumps into a senior-level Talker, they've unknowingly fallen into a perilous position. Given their natural predilection—and classic training—to find and meet the "senior decision maker," from the core rep's perspective, they've just found the Holy Grail. A senior decision maker not only willing to take a meeting but to openly share information. One can almost guarantee that that rep will come out of that meeting walking on air: "Next stop: Closed Deal! Friday of next week, at the latest!" Yet that rep is surprised when, two months later, that deal still hasn't gone anywhere. All because they failed to realize the difference between a senior executive and a Mobilizer. The potential cost of conflating the two can be huge—if nothing else, in lost time and false expectations. Bottom line, in the world of complex, consensus-based sales, an old-school strategy of finding friendly, senior-level advocates will no longer cut it. As one head of sales put it to us, "If we want to get anything done, we've got to take our 'senior leader goggles' off and put our 'Mobilizer goggles' on—in every deal we do."

To sum it all up, you can't find Mobilizers on an org chart. They're not the VP of this or the senior director of that. Role and title don't matter. They're individuals who mobilize irrespective of the org chart, not because of it.

IDENTIFYING AND TAILORING TO MOBILIZER TYPES

So now that we've *qualified* our stakeholder as a Mobilizer, the next step is to *identify* what kind of Mobilizer we're talking to. Simply put, even though we've likely found a Mobilizer, we haven't determined yet how exactly to *engage* them, depending on the type we're talking to. That all depends on what *kind* of Mobilizer they are—and, you'll recall that there are three different types of Mobilizer.

So if we continue to move through the process, the third tell is their communication style. Do they speak in terms of actions and facts, or in terms of stories and opinions. Are they more rational or emotional? This will tell us whether we've found a Go-Getter or Skeptic on the one hand, or a Teacher on the other. This is important. Tailoring our approach to the type of Mobilizer we're dealing with will ensure not just that they are fully engaged with what we're saying but, as we'll see in the coming chapters, that we're going to have to support each of these Mobilizers a little bit differently to have the best shot at forging consensus.

Let's spend a bit of time talking about the basics of how to tailor to the three different Mobilizer types.

A great way to think about how to tailor your approach to these Mobilizer types is to map their styles against the steps in a typical customer purchase process as we've done in figures 7.6, 7.7, and 7.8. First, let's look at the Go-Getter. A Go-Getter is going to be interested in the big picture, but they are going to quickly want to understand the implementation

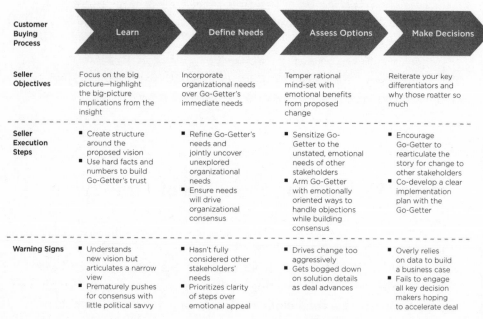

FIG. 7.6. "The Go-Getter" Engagement Road Map

Customer Buying Process	Learn	Define Needs	Assess Options	Make Decisions
Seller Objectives	Focus on the big picture—highlight the big-picture implications from the insight	Incorporate organizational needs over Go-Getter's immediate needs	Temper rational mind-set with emotional benefits from proposed change	Reiterate your key differentiators and why those matter so much
Seller Execution Steps	■ Create structure around the proposed vision ■ Use hard facts and numbers to build Go-Getter's trust	■ Refine Go-Getter's needs and jointly uncover unexplored organizational needs ■ Ensure needs will drive organizational consensus	■ Sensitize Go-Getter to the unstated, emotional needs of other stakeholders ■ Arm Go-Getter with emotionally oriented ways to handle objections while building consensus	■ Encourage Go-Getter to rearticulate the story for change to other stakeholders ■ Co-develop a clear implementation plan with the Go-Getter
Warning Signs	■ Understands new vision but articulates a narrow view ■ Prematurely pushes for consensus with little political savvy	■ Hasn't fully considered other stakeholders' needs ■ Prioritizes clarity of steps over emotional appeal	■ Drives change too aggressively ■ Gets bogged down on solution details as deal advances	■ Overly relies on data to build a business case ■ Fails to engage all key decision makers hoping to accelerate deal

Source: CEB analysis.

details. The salesperson must be mindful of this—if the vision sounds too "pie in the sky" for the Go-Getter, she will push the salesperson to get specific. So a conversation with a Go-Getter that is all about the vision and light on the details is likely to be over before it starts. At the same time, the seller must guard against letting the Go-Getter get too narrowly focused too fast. What was designed to be a big-picture conversation about a big, transformative idea can quickly devolve into a lesson in Six Sigma project planning if the seller isn't careful. Before you know it, your meeting is over, and the Go-Getter might have a clear sense for the project plan but won't be equipped to rally others with the emotional side of the proposed change.

Teachers are a very different animal—as we discussed earlier, sort of the polar opposite of the Go-Getter. So engaging with a Teacher, the seller is going to want to tailor his approach by appealing to the Teacher's desire for a grand, sweeping vision. Selling an idea with stories and metaphor is

FIG. 7.7. "The Teacher" Engagement Road Map

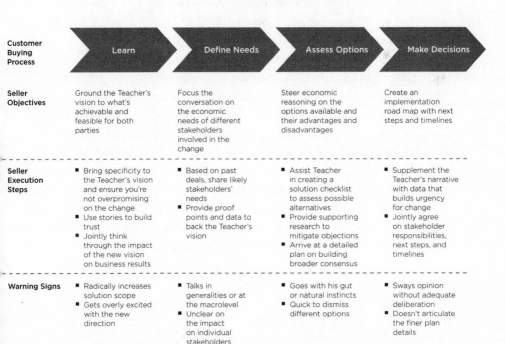

Customer Buying Process	Learn	Define Needs	Assess Options	Make Decisions
Seller Objectives	Ground the Teacher's vision to what's achievable and feasible for both parties	Focus the conversation on the economic needs of different stakeholders involved in the change	Steer economic reasoning on the options available and their advantages and disadvantages	Create an implementation road map with next steps and timelines
Seller Execution Steps	▪ Bring specificity to the Teacher's vision and ensure you're not overpromising on the change ▪ Use stories to build trust ▪ Jointly think through the impact of the new vision on business results	▪ Based on past deals, share likely stakeholders' needs ▪ Provide proof points and data to back the Teacher's vision	▪ Assist Teacher in creating a solution checklist to assess possible alternatives ▪ Provide supporting research to mitigate objections ▪ Arrive at a detailed plan on building broader consensus	▪ Supplement the Teacher's narrative with data that builds urgency for change ▪ Jointly agree on stakeholder responsibilities, next steps, and timelines
Warning Signs	▪ Radically increases solution scope ▪ Gets overly excited with the new direction	▪ Talks in generalities or at the macrolevel ▪ Unclear on the impact on individual stakeholders	▪ Goes with his gut or natural instincts ▪ Quick to dismiss different options	▪ Sways opinion without adequate deliberation ▪ Doesn't articulate the finer plan details

Source: CEB analysis.

going to get the Teacher excited about the opportunity that lies ahead. At the same time, if the Teacher is allowed to take an idea and run with it, there's a good chance that he may radically increase the scope of the proposal and get shot down when floating it by colleagues. So while sellers should appeal to what naturally makes Teachers tick, they'll want to be mindful to infuse the discussion with details on the economic benefits and expected payoff of the proposed change—otherwise, Teachers will anchor entirely on the vision, ignoring the important implementation details and potentially raising alarm bells with other stakeholders.

Finally, when dealing with a Skeptic, the seller will want to tailor his approach by encouraging questions and exploration—but at the same time remaining steadfast in terms of instilling confidence that the supplier is a reliable and credible partner when it comes to executing disruptive, large-scale change. Using data is a key tailoring point when engaging with Skeptics—they aren't persuaded by rhetoric or promises. Instead, they need to be convinced that risks are being controlled for and uncertainties are being run to ground. But like the Go-Getter, while it's important to tailor your approach with a Skeptic by meeting their challenges and questions head-on, the seller needs at some point to get off the witness stand and spend time emphasizing the story and the vision that will be required to get others on board.

Each Mobilizer's strengths demand a tailored engagement approach. Pulling the right levers can make all the difference in terms of getting that Mobilizer bought in and supportive of the proposed change. At the same time, while the seller wants to tailor to each Mobilizer's perspective, they must also guard against allowing those perspectives to overtake the message. A Mobilizer's strength, in other words, can also become a weakness when it comes to getting others on board, effectively grounding an idea before it ever has a chance to take flight.

So that's it, a few simple steps to determine not only whether we're talking to a Mobilizer, but also what kind of Mobilizer we've found and how a salesperson should tailor their approach. This is a simple, concrete road map for determining what otherwise feels more like art than science. It's a Mobilizer qualification and identification road map with three easy steps. It's the kind of thing star performers have hardwired into their brains, without even realizing it. In fact, after we built this tool, we went back and showed it to the high performers we had interviewed, and they said—yep, makes complete sense. They'd just never thought to write it down.

FIG. 7.8. "The Skeptic" Engagement Road Map

Customer Buying Process	Learn	Define Needs	Assess Options	Make Decisions
Seller Objectives	Focus on getting buy-in—encourage more questions and exploration	Arm Skeptic with a vision that appeals to the business more readily	Temper rational mind-set with a broader change story backed with key data points	Ensure the vision supersedes the change implications
Seller Execution Steps	■ Use a compelling teaching insight that drives urgency for change ■ Use both data and testimonials to build trust ■ Reduce ambiguity by detailing how other companies have taken similar action	■ Jointly assess how needs will vary across organization ■ Help articulate the common needs across the organization that will anchor the new vision for change	■ Sensitize Skeptic to the emotional needs of other stakeholders ■ Arm the Skeptic with emotionally oriented ways to handle objections while building consensus	■ Present a project plan that gives Skeptic more certainty around implementation steps ■ Break the implementation down to bite-size pieces with clear wins at each stage
Warning Signs	■ Struggles with change implications ■ Is unconvinced on the supplier's ability to partner	■ Gets lost in the implications ■ Focuses on stakeholder differences and exceptions, not big-picture needs	■ Gets bogged down on solution details ■ Loses sight of the broader vision	■ Stalls the change if absolute certainty doesn't exist ■ Looks for constant reassurances

Source: CEB analysis.

Now that we have an appreciation for how to identify and qualify Mobilizers more broadly—as well as how to adapt our approach to engaging with different flavors of Mobilizers, all through precise and purposeful tailoring—we've still made it to only Phase 2 of a typical customer purchase process—securing Individual Willingness to Explore Alternate Course of Action. We're still a long way off from an actual closed deal, as we have yet to cross that long second chasm spanning the "solutions graveyard" of stalled deals resulting from lowest-common-denominator thinking. So how do we think about tailoring here? Well, let's look at the answer conceptually first, and then we'll get after it more practically in our review of "taking control" across the following two chapters.

TAILORING FOR GROUP CONSENSUS

Having identified someone willing not only to consider an alternate course of action but also to mobilize for that action among their colleagues, we now need to transform that into group consensus. This is a tough row to hoe, moving from "me" to "we." Here we have to bring in other stakeholders and win them over as well. Procurement has to get involved. Finance has to approve. Legal has to look things over. As we noted in chapter 1, this is why the movement from Phase 2 to Phase 3 is so much longer than the move from Phase 1 to Phase 2.

It's exactly here that a supplier organization must modify its approach to tailoring if it's to have any chance at successfully connecting those stakeholders to each other. For it's safe to say, even for those organizations deeply familiar with our original Challenger work, the most logical approach to winning customers' collective buy-in would still be some application of the "track them all down, and win them all over" strategy we first saw in chapter 1.

So if we think back to our three-phase purchase process, imagine identifying each of the 5.4 stakeholders, conducting the necessary due diligence to identify their needs and priorities, carefully constructing an independent mental model for each, and then systematically breaking down each of those models and building up an alternate view designed to resonate directly with whatever that person cares about most. Essentially, it's breaking down 5.4 A's and building up 5.4 B's—collecting a "Yes" from each stakeholder until everyone is on board with the required change embedded in that supplier's Commercial Insight. Graphically speaking, this process would look like a series of parallel lines from left to right across the purchase process depicting 5.4 closely related, but nonetheless largely independent Commercial Insight interventions (see figure 7.9).

Now, not only would a process like that be extraordinarily time-consuming, it would be incredibly difficult to execute as well, as it would require the construction and deconstruction of 5.4 independent mental models in serial fashion.

But more to the point, even if an approach like this *were* practical, notice what would happen as those 5.4 stakeholders came together to consider a collective action. Insofar as the individual B's that they've bought into independently don't fully align, then those stakeholders will natu-

FIG. 7.9. Tailoring Commercial Insight for
Individual Stakeholder Action (illustrative)

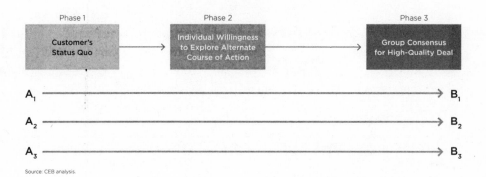

Source: CEB analysis.

rally downsize that deal until they do. That tells us, even when done well, in other words, a Challenger sale based on 5.4 different flavors of the same Commercial Insight can lead to just as much trouble as a sale based on no insight at all, as either way customers will be forced to do on their own what the supplier failed to do on their behalf, namely, establish clear alignment across a common B—a mutually agreed-upon alternate mental model.

So what's the alternative? As we'll see in greater detail in chapter 8, the alternative is to break down the A individually, but then build up the B collectively—effectively tailoring the delivery and consideration of the Commercial Insight in a manner that not only wins over a Mobilizer but *anticipates* the potential objections, concerns, and alternate perspectives of the other 4.4. So to be sure, individual stakeholder outreach must necessarily speak to each person's particular views and priorities, but it must be done in a way that simultaneously builds a mutually agreeable common vision and steers that person closer to a view shareable by their 4.4 other colleagues. In the world of the 5.4, tailoring isn't only about helping stakeholders see *themselves* in the supplier's insight, but just as importantly about helping them see *each other*. It's about creating *convergence*. Despite stakeholders' inevitable differences, suppliers must find a way to help members of the 5.4 converge on the same mental model—a mental model that leads them to collectively value the kind of support available only through that supplier's sustainably unique strengths (see figure 7.10).

**FIG. 7.10. Tailoring Commercial Insight for
Collective Customer Action (illustrative)**

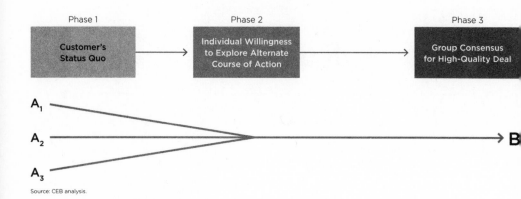

Source: CEB analysis.

Just to bring us full circle, this is why we find Commercial Insight so powerful. For it allows a supplier to create that kind of convergence not just around Supplier Selection, but—insofar as Commercial Insight teaches customers to address a problem or pursue an opportunity that they otherwise didn't realize they had—also around Solution Identification, and even Problem Definition. Commercial Insight, in other words, initiates customer contact at the very beginning of the purchase process. Or, put another way, done well, Commercial Insight has the power to initiate a *new* purchase process altogether, leading customers collectively on a journey across the "me to we" mountain. But only when that Commercial Insight is tailored to create convergence from the very beginning.

That said, Commercial Insight cannot carry the day for convergence on its own. Creating that kind of customer connection will take a significant amount of work on the part of the supplier well beyond building and deploying well-tailored Commercial Insight itself. In fact, our research has uncovered a way in which suppliers must take control of the customer's buying process to ensure not only that the 5.4 *can* converge around their Commercial Insight, but also that they *will*. So that's where we'll turn next.

CHAPTER EIGHT

TAKING CONTROL OF CONSENSUS CREATION

If dysfunctional groups are marked by diverging mental models, "functional" groups are characterized by *converging* mental models. Now, that doesn't mean the 5.4 must be in complete alignment on everything. But it does mean that we'd find significantly greater overlap of mental models in a functional group than in a dysfunctional one. That overlap is crucial, for it allows individual stakeholders to connect on shared priorities and problems, to address far broader challenges and pursue far greater opportunities than a basic common desire to save company money and avoid organizational risk. In fact, the data is dramatic on this point. On average, *functional* buying groups are 40 percent more likely to purchase a more ambitious offering than dysfunctional ones (see figure 8.1).

FIG. 8.1. Impact of Reducing Group Dysfunction on Likelihood of Purchasing More Ambitious Offering (indexed)

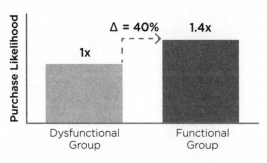

n = 946.
Source: CEB 2013 Sales Customer Panel.

If we think back to the Venn diagram we introduced in chapter 1, we can see why. As mental models converge, the area of agreement—or shared understanding at that central overlap—expands significantly (see figure 8.2).

FIG. 8.2. Illustration of Stakeholders' Convergent Mental Models

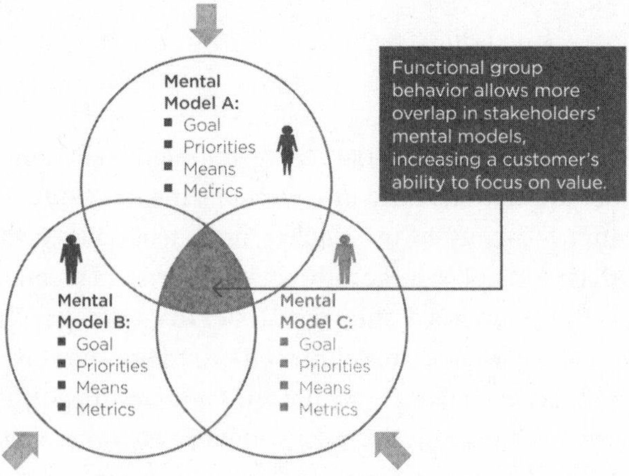

Mental
Model A:
- Goal
- Priorities
- Means
- Metrics

Functional group
behavior allows more
overlap in stakeholders'
mental models,
increasing a customer's
ability to focus on value.

Mental
Model B:
- Goal
- Priorities
- Means
- Metrics

Mental
Model C:
- Goal
- Priorities
- Means
- Metrics

Source: CEB analysis.

Ultimately, this is where deal quality is won or lost. The greater the overlap, the less likely that 1 + 1 + 1 is going to equal 0.

If we think about what might be necessary to encourage this kind of convergence, especially among otherwise diverse customer stakeholders, we begin to see hints of the types of things a supplier might do differently to encourage mental model alignment. The first might be to create a common language. After all, just as an example, much of the time IT has no idea what marketing is talking about, and vice versa. Just think of the CMO and CIO of your organization engaged in a typical conversation. How likely are they to use the same terms, or discuss the same business challenges—or, for that matter, even agree on what those challenges are in the first place? Second would be encouraging collective understanding of individual perspectives and goals—making sure everyone understands not only what each stakeholder wants, but why. Why does this decision matter for their function? How will it impact their work? What might it mean for their personal performance dashboard? Third is clarifying group objectives—ensuring that the buying group is working toward a single, agreed-upon business goal in the first place. Fourth is overcoming individual and group biases that might stand in the way of establishing higher-order agreement. Let's face it. Everyone comes to the table with a certain amount of baggage. That's normal. Probably even inescapable. But to what degree is the group aware of those biases and able to acknowledge them constructively as part of group deliberations?

If we step back and think about this, what we see here is the potentially dramatic impact of a powerful force that behavioral psychologists call "norming." Norming is the process of people learning from one another in order to establish common ground and collective expectations. At its best, it's driven by a collaborative exploration of problems, objections, and opportunities, all designed to find compromise and build upon points of agreement in order to establish a view far greater than the sum of individual ideas. So unlike the lowest-common-denominator agreement we saw in chapter 1, this kind of norming isn't about establishing common points of obvious agreement as an *ending* point, but rather taking those shared connections as a starting point and then asking: Where can we go from here? How can we expand on this?

That's what suppliers need customers to do if they're going to escape the otherwise seemingly unavoidable commodity trap of lowest-common-denominator collective consensus. Quality wins aren't the result of getting each individual on board with the supplier's solution, but rather getting the entire group *collectively* on board with a broader vision of what they should even be doing in the first place, *irrespective* of supplier. Remember the "me to we" mountain? This is the real challenge of customer dysfunction—establishing collective agreement at every step of the way across that mountain that organizational change is even necessary in the first place. It's a Collective Yes around Problem Definition, Solution Identification, *and* Supplier Selection, not just a collection of yeses around the value of that supplier's particular offering.

So how is this kind of connection supposed to happen? One head of sales told us it sort of sounds like some kind of dark magic: "Poof! Then a miracle occurs and everyone agrees!" Of course, one option is to simply qualify deals according to the level of connectedness already present in a group of otherwise diverse customer stakeholders. So one might imagine, for example, adding a "group functionality" score to an existing customer qualification scorecard as a nice way to better predict deal quality much further in advance of an actual sale. But at the same time, as both the number and the diversity of customer stakeholders increase over time, given the very tight connection between diversity and dysfunction we saw earlier, our research tells us that finding groups that *already* score high on the "functional meter" is going to become harder and harder over time. So far beyond *finding* functional groups of customer stakeholders, suppliers are going to have to find a way to *make* functional groups of customer stakeholders. This is largely what we mean by "taking control" of consensus creation.

But how is that possible? Let's return to the data for an answer.

A BETTER WAY FORWARD

Earlier, we looked at the statistically significant drivers of winning a "high-quality sale" and found something rather surprising: a minimal impact from greater access and an unexpectedly *negative* impact from better individual positioning. As our focus has now shifted to consensus creation, we can add a third and final finding that provides incredibly valuable insight into how suppliers might think very differently about driving commercial success in a 5.4 world. For it turns out, there is indeed a statistically significant driver of deal quality that has a measurably meaningful impact—and that's something we've come to call Collective Learning (see figure 8.3).

In fact, this one finding dramatically dwarfed everything else in our analysis of high-quality deals. What it tells us is: if the customer goes from below-average performance to above-average performance on Collective Learning, then the likelihood of a supplier closing a high-quality deal goes up by 20 percent. It is by far the single biggest driver of deal quality we found in all of our data.

So what *is* Collective Learning? At a high level, Collective Learning is:

An *interaction* where stakeholders explore and socially norm by debating and building on each other's perspectives, finding points of unrecognized agreement, and arriving at a shared decision.

In other words, it's the ability of a group of customer stakeholders to overcome their natural disconnects and *learn* together. To identify, debate,

FIG. 8.3. Comparison of Drivers on Likelihood
of Supplier Winning a High-Quality Deal

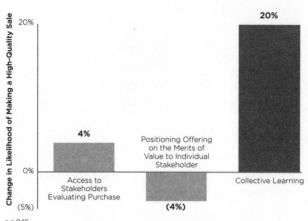

n = 946.

Source: CEB 2013 Sales Customer Panel.

ᵃ Change in likelihood of making a high-quality sale is defined as the increase in chance of being selected as a winning supplier and the customer (1) did not settle for a less ambitious solution or (2) purchased a premium offering relative to the base offering.

and decide on a common course of collective action. If we think about everything we just reviewed, this finding makes a lot of sense. The primary challenge suppliers must address in winning quality deals isn't so much overcoming each stakeholder's limited understanding of them, it's helping those stakeholders bridge the gap in their limited understanding of each other. Their lack of any real common connection other than a collective desire to avoid unnecessary risk and reduce organizational expense. That's why Collective Learning is such a powerful driver of deal quality, because it dramatically drives down group dysfunction. The data tells us that when customer stakeholders *learn* together, overall dysfunction goes down by nearly a third (see figure 8.4).

Why? Because of the types of activities customers demonstrate while engaged in Collective Learning. If we were to build a list of behaviors that would serve as a good indication that Collective Learning is happening, that list would look something like this:

1. Thoroughly Exploring Concerns and Uncertainties Across the 5.4
Customer stakeholders are asking themselves things like "What are we worried about?" "What do we not know but should?" "What are we missing?" "What *haven't* we discussed thus far?"

FIG. 8.4. Impact of Collective Learning on Dysfunction (indexed)

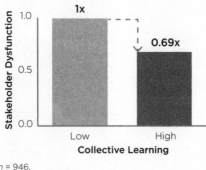

n = 946.
Source: CEB 2013 Sales Customer Panel.

2. Honestly Surfacing Disconnects and Competing Ideas

Here, rather than running away from points of disagreement or generally avoiding debate as "too hard" or "too stressful" or "unhelpful," customers run directly at potential problems and disagreements, purposefully putting them on the table and actively discussing them.

3. Mutual Willingness to Explore Problems and Consider Alternate Views

This one is more about "posture" than behavior, but either way, stakeholders actively seek out alternate viewpoints, examining options from multiple angles until they've thoroughly considered alternate views. Rather than impatiently hurrying to "get things done," group participants are deliberatively looking to "get things right."

4. Active Probing for Potentially Overlooked Interdependencies

Stakeholders cast a wide net in exploring alternate courses of action, seeking to uncover and understand the more subtle or unexpected implications of their decisions on various parts of the organization.

5. Establishing Joint Resolution

Like any good deliberative body, stakeholders ensure that objections and concerns aren't left hanging, but are thoroughly addressed in a way that all participants stand by and publicly support the output of the group's deliberative process.

These five characteristic behaviors of effective Collective Learning aren't simply hallmarks of an effective purchase process; they're indicative of effective group-based decision making more broadly. In that respect, one might argue there's no real surprise here. That said, let's not lose sight of the underlying purpose of this analysis. The question we're asking here is not "What kind of behavior makes for effective decision making?" Rather, we're asking "What kind of behavior is most predictive of a supplier winning a high-quality sale?" That's a hugely important distinction, because it raises a tough *agency* question that suppliers are going to have to address if they hope to get paid.

If we look through the list of "optimal" Collective Learning behaviors one more time, we'd likely all agree that every single one of those behaviors—while absolutely admirable—isn't particularly easy. While that list may indeed represent the *most desirable* customer buying behaviors, for many customers it simultaneously represents the list of behaviors *least likely* to actually occur. After all, there's no guarantee that customers will do any of this on their own—or, for that matter, even *want* to do any of this on their own. So if suppliers need to make Collective Learning happen to drive deal quality, and customers may or may not be either willing or able to do it on their own, then that means suppliers are going to have to do everything in *their* power to help them get this done. To be sure, Collective Learning is much less about the supplier than it is about the customer. But if suppliers don't find a way to intervene and own this process, there's absolutely no guarantee that their customers will either. Bottom line, if suppliers hope to close high-quality deals in a 5.4 world, they're going to have to *make* functional buying groups, not just find them, by taking control of the purchase process and ensuring Collective Learning happens.

Of course, the natural next question would be, "How in the world is a supplier supposed to do *that*?" On that point there's good news. It turns out there are a wide number of ways in which suppliers can influence the likelihood and quality of customer Collective Learning—both indirectly, or "by proxy," through a Mobilizer. Or more directly through very specific kinds of sales and marketing intervention. So across much of the balance of this chapter, we'll examine the former approach—supporting Mobilizers' efforts to create customer consensus through (largely asynchronous) Collective Learning interventions. And in chapter 9, we'll step back and look at the latter, with a wide-ranging review of a variety of tools and approaches sales and marketing leaders might deploy to support and expand on those Mobilizers' efforts to encourage Collective Learning.

Before we do, however, let's first ensure all of this effort is even worth it in the first place.

THE IMPACT OF COLLECTIVE LEARNING

Having established the broad importance of Collective Learning for driving overall deal quality, we wanted to understand just how big an impact improved Collective Learning might have on actual commercial outcomes. So the first thing we looked at was the impact of Collective Learning on the likelihood of a higher-cost supplier winning the deal. Essentially, we can think of this as the likelihood of a customer to pay a supplier a premium, rather than demand a discount. And what we found is dramatic. By bringing diverse customer groups together to learn before they buy, suppliers can boost customer willingness to pay a premium by over two-thirds—nearly 70 percent (see figure 8.5).

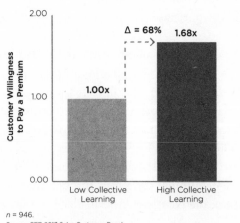

FIG. 8.5. Impact of Collective Learning on Likelihood of Higher-Cost Supplier Winning a Deal (indexed)

n = 946.
Source: CEB 2013 Sales Customer Panel.

That's pretty incredible, given the price pressure suppliers are feeling today on even their most complex solutions and unique offerings.

But not only does Collective Learning boost customers' willingness to pay more now, it also has a direct impact on their willingness to buy more later, boosting a customer's willingness to purchase additional future offerings by 23 percent (see figure 8.6).

FIG. 8.6. Impact of Collective Learning on Group's Willingness to Purchase Additional Future Offerings (indexed)

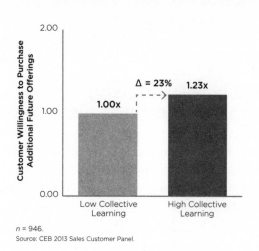

n = 946.
Source: CEB 2013 Sales Customer Panel.

Why is that? Largely because Collective Learning effectively establishes a vision not just for a near-term purchase, but for a longer-term direction. Remember, as customers climb the "me to we" mountain together, they're not just debating what to *buy*, they're deliberating what to *do*. It stands to reason that effective Collective Learning will lead to a "long tail" of future decisions—and purchases—that all follow naturally from the common mental model established by the Collective Learning exercise in the first place. Now imagine a world where that learning journey was initiated in the first place by a Commercial Insight carefully crafted to lead back to that supplier's unique strengths. In that case Collective Learning has the potential, at least, to lock the customer into a long-term purchase path where the customer's strategic priorities and the supplier's unique capabilities are aligned across multiple months or even years. Indeed, as we'll soon see, the combination of Commercial Insight and Collective Learning can be incredibly powerful when the one is initiated and supported by the other.

That said, to realize these kinds of benefits, commercial organizations will have to think very differently about how, when, and why they currently interact with their customers. To show you what we mean, let's examine three different aspects of sales rep behavior best designed to ensure customers collectively learn, and then consider just how different those behaviors are from what most reps do right now. As we go, we'll rely on both deep quantitative analysis and extensive qualitative research to establish a set of three "key operating principles" defining world-class supplier-led Collective Learning.

PRINCIPLE 1: SUPPLIER-LED COLLECTIVE LEARNING REQUIRES FACILITATION, NOT JUST PRESENTATION

If we return to the data, we can find a very practical answer to the question "What exactly does a sales rep need to *do* in order to increase the chances of customers engaging in Collective Learning in the first place?" But that answer isn't necessarily what one might initially expect (see figure 8.7).

When we tested the relative impact of a range of rep behaviors on increasing the likelihood of customers engaging in Collective Learning, the first thing we found—perhaps not surprisingly—is that actively pointing out to individual stakeholders the personal risks of pursuing a particular solution will dramatically decrease the probability that Collective Learning will ever get off the ground at all. While it's a pretty straightforward finding, it's an interesting one nonetheless insofar as 29 percent of the nearly 900 customer stakeholders we surveyed as part of this work told us that the sales reps calling on them actually *demonstrated* this very behavior. While it is unclear from the data alone whether that was the intent of the rep or an accidental by-product of how he or she positioned the conversation, it's nonetheless troubling to find that some sales reps may indeed be actively *reducing* the likelihood of Collective Learning by articulating concerns—inadvertently at least—at far too personal a level rather than at a more appropriate organizational level.

FIG. 8.7. Impact of Rep Actions on Collective Learning

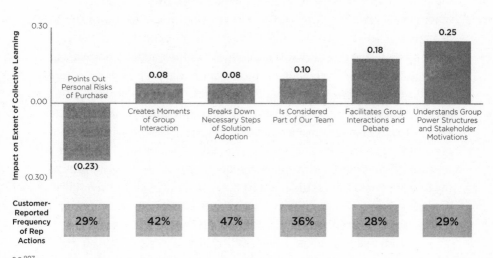

n = 897.
Source: CEB 2013 Sales Customer Panel Survey; CEB analysis.

More surprising, however, was the second finding from our analysis. It turns out that creating moments of group interaction does indeed drive up the likelihood of Collective Learning—as one might expect—but only marginally at best. And that's strange. After all, one might naturally think the best way to prompt Collective Learning is to get everyone together in the first place. That kind of gathering may not even be necessary at all. Collective Learning isn't about putting stakeholders together in a room and hoping for the best. It's about getting them to interact with one another in a very specific way *irrespective* of whether they're assembled in a room or not. If we think about it, there are *all sorts* of ways in which a rep might win on this behavior, but still lose on Collective Learning. Getting customers together, for example, for a product demo, or possibly presenting a response to an RFP, are both great examples of collective stakeholder meetings, but they're also designed to connect customers to *suppliers*, not to each other—so are poor examples of Collective Learning.

So what *does* promote Collective Learning? Two things. First, it's the rep's ability to understand stakeholder power structures and individual motivations. Not surprisingly, if sales reps are going to more effectively connect stakeholders to *each other*, then they need to understand the unspoken dynamics of power and influence among those stakeholders.

Second is effective *facilitation* of group interaction, including managing productive debate. This turns out to be especially important if for no other reason than how different it is from what most reps do today. To demonstrate, let's focus on two words in particular: "facilitate" and "debate." Particularly in the case of "facilitation," we're talking about a behavior or skill most reps have likely found unnecessary in the past. Indeed, it's rare to find any sales organization that formally trains facilitation skills. However, in a 5.4 world, if sales reps hope to effectively connect stakeholders to each other, much of that work will likely constitute *facilitating* a conversation, rather than conducting a presentation. One senior sales trainer at a Fortune 50 company saw this data and declared, "I need to stop training my reps in *presentation* skills and start training them in *facilitation* skills." And in a 5.4 world, she's probably right. In chapter 9, we'll lay out a step-by-step framework for that training to follow.

That said, this may not be just a "skill" challenge. There's likely a "will" challenge here as well. Take another look at the second key element of this behavioral attribute—what the rep is facilitating in the first place: customer *debate*. That's not something most reps—particularly core-performing reps—would *ever* consider to be a good idea. Indeed, only 28 percent of customers report ever seeing reps engage in this kind of behavior. One of the two rep behaviors most important to driving Collective Learning is also among one of the behaviors least likely to happen. Not because of a lack of training, but rather because of a general belief that facilitating customer debate would just be a bad idea in the first place. How many sales leaders have gone on a "ride-along" at some point in their career with a sales rep who told them prior to the sales call, "Now, we're going to go see these two people, and *whatever* you do, don't bring up this one topic, because the two just don't see eye to eye at all on that issue." The general belief is: Debate is bad. Disagreement is something to be avoided: "If customer stakeholders can't agree with one another, well, that's *their* problem, not *ours*. The *last* thing we should do in that kind of dysfunctional environment is go in and stir things up even more!" But as we saw earlier in laying out a definition of Collective Learning in the first place, that kind of debate is not only important, it's *desirable* as it's part of the natural process necessary to align otherwise divergent mental models.

If open, productive debate is one of the primary means for buying groups to reduce dysfunction, the fact that sales reps are not only failing to promote it, but quite possibly consciously *avoiding* it, speaks volumes as to why suppliers are struggling with lowest-common-denominator buying in the first place. So in chapter 9 we'll examine a wide range of activities sales and marketing teams can take to better facilitate these kinds of customer interactions.

PRINCIPLE 2: SUPPLIER-LED COLLECTIVE LEARNING REQUIRES BOUNDING, NOT JUST PROMPTING

Our second principle for promoting effective Collective Learning has to do with the actual mechanics of conducting Collective Learning itself.

As a reminder, Collective Learning is: an interaction where stakeholders explore and socially norm by debating and building on each other's perspectives, finding points of unrecognized agreement, and arriving at a shared decision.

You'll notice there's nothing in that definition that necessarily requires Collective Learning to happen in a single place or even at a single time. At the end of the day, Collective Learning can be either synchronous or asynchronous. Colocated or dispersed. In-person or over the Internet. As long as it's about helping stakeholders learn collaboratively.

Now, what *does* matter are two attributes we would append to that definition: "prompting" and "bounding." These are two important—and proven—ways in which a facilitator (including a seller or a Mobilizer) can direct Collective Learning to maximize its impact.

Prompting is all about getting stakeholders to disclose concerns they might otherwise fail to reveal on their own—whether because they're afraid to bring them up, they can't be bothered to bring them up, or it hasn't even occurred to them to bring them up. The point here is to prompt stakeholders to *share*, so the group can recognize and deal with disconnects and explore alternative options and solutions. So get it all on the table.

This matters—not surprisingly—because researchers have found that groups naturally gravitate to shared information. Psychologists speak of "social sharedness," the idea that information and perspectives shared among group members tend to have a disproportionately large impact on the group's deliberations. Simply put, groups focus on and discuss shared information at the expense of unshared information. So if it's not on the table, it's not in the discussion and not accounted for in the shared mental model. So prompting ideas to be explored, problems to be addressed, and misunderstandings to be overcome really matters.

That said, these discussions have to have some kind of boundary. Otherwise, they become pretty unproductive pretty quickly. That's where bounding comes in. Because if a facilitator were to prompt everything, but bound nothing, then that group would quickly become overwhelmed and easily revert back to the lowest common denominator as the only means to cut through information overload and find common ground. By scoping the conversation to a specific challenge and a specific objective, a group is significantly more likely to coalesce around a more expansive mental model.

At the same time the supplier's going to have to ensure they bound Collective Learning in a way that uniquely allows them to win. This can be a delicate balance, as Collective Learning must focus on helping customers *learn* something and not just buy something. First and foremost, Collective Learning is about Problem Definition and Solution Identification, not Supplier Selection. This is why Commercial Insight is so important, for it allows suppliers to bound the conversation in a way that allows customers to learn, but still leads them back to the ways that supplier can help better than anyone else. We'll show you exactly what that might look like and how to make it happen with a number of examples in chapter 9.

PRINCIPLE 3: SUPPLIER-LED COLLECTIVE LEARNING REQUIRES COACHING, NOT JUST LISTENING

We do a lot of interviews with the highest-performing salespeople among our 700+ sales organization membership base. We also interview a lot of average performers. Invariably, when speaking with average performers about relying upon Mobilizers, we hear comments such as "I'd never trust a customer to explain *my* point of view" or "They are important because they tell me how to position *my* offering" and finally "I just need them to recommend *my* product—internal references are hugely powerful." The average-performing rep is trying to get *their* product endorsed while simultaneously pumping that customer stakeholder for as much information as possible that might help in that positioning. Indeed, these average performers embrace the conventional view that sellers need customers to coach them through the sale. The goal here is for the customer to tip the seller off to all things that might affect how they position their product and, ultimately, ensure their point of contact provides the ever important endorsement.

On the other hand, when we speak with high-performing sellers, we hear a completely different perspective altogether. "My job is to make sure that the customer is making the right decision for *their* business" is a common refrain. Similarly, we hear things like "I've got to support my customer through *their* purchase experience" or "I don't see my job as selling at all. I see it as *helping my customers*." In many ways, the most common perspective we observe among top sellers isn't so much the customer *coaching them through the sale* but, rather, *they coach the customer through the purchase.* Indeed, we saw this difference in an analysis we conducted examining dominant behaviors of average-performing and high-performing sellers (figure 8.8).

The implication here is that the best sellers entrust their Mobilizers far more than average sellers. After all, Mobilizers have privileged access to the customer's decision makers and their decision-making processes. Sellers rarely do. They have a voice at the table. Sellers don't. They can better establish a point of view in a much more objectively perceived way as compared to a salesperson. But entrusting a Mobilizer at this level is inherently risky. Does the Mobilizer *really* know what to do? After all, it's not like Mobilizers lead purchase efforts on a daily basis. Do they know how to answer likely questions they will get? Do they know what next steps to take in the decision-making process? Do they understand various other stakeholders' functional roles and how those roles will influence their decision? Can they effectively *speak* the language of IT, HR, marketing, procurement, operations, or any of the other functional areas that are likely to be involved in the purchase? For all the access, exposure, and action that Mobilizers bring to a purchase, there is clearly some downside risk that needs to be managed.

High-performing sellers recognize the limits of Mobilizers. Additionally, and perhaps more importantly, high performers understand that over

FIG. 8.8. Comparison of Approaches to Working with Mobilizers
(by seller performance level)

Distinctive Core Performer Behaviors
From Quantitative Survey

Core Performer
n = 699 of 987

- **Understand** what people are looking to achieve personally
- **Determine** make-or-break criteria for purchase
- **Understand** stakeholders' relation to each other

Distinctive High Performer Behaviors
From Quantitative Survey

High Performer
n = 288 of 987

- **Arm** the customer to convey the message
- **Help** buyers negotiate requirements with each other
- **Help** customers understand what needs to happen

"You've gotta be in a **discovery mode.** The customer organization is constantly moving—I can't keep up unless I'm always **asking questions** and **using my coach.**"

Core Rep, Health Care Company

"I see my job as **helping the customer,** not the other way around. It doesn't mean I'm not learning, but I'm always trying to share what I know to **make their job easier.**"

Hi-Per Rep, Energy Company

▼

Customer Coaches the Rep

▼

Rep Coaches the Customer

Source: CEB analysis.

the course of hundreds of sales interactions, they *better* know what it takes to successfully purchase their products than customers do. Taking advantage of the information they've amassed, they quite literally take control by coaching Mobilizers through the purchase. We call this Commercial Coaching (figure 8.9). Commercial Coaching is just that—de-risking the Mobilizer's job by coaching him or her through the twists and turns of building consensus and productively moving forward with a purchase. It's meant to be a highly collaborative dialogue with the Mobilizer, laying out guardrails for them to follow as they drive action. At its core, Commercial Coaching is an empowering force for a Mobilizer, helping them assess the obstacles they will need to overcome to generate the business outcomes they are seeking. It provides them with added confidence to move forward and alleviates much of the planning and thought work they would normally have to do (typically off the side of their desk) to manage the consensus-building process. We call this *Commercial* Coaching since it inherently reinforces your Commercial Insight and arms the Mobilizer to share that insight within their organization, ensuring that you are positioned as the best supplier. All this is done in the spirit of enabling the Mobilizer to build consensus in the easiest and most productive way possible.

FIG. 8.9. Commercial Coaching Requirements

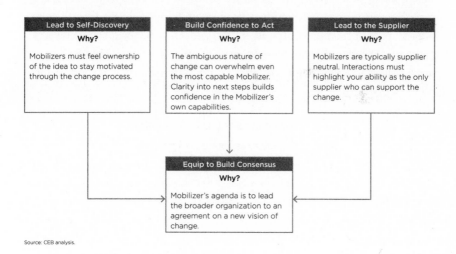

A series of **collaborative** interactions designed to **actively lead** Mobilizers to **identify and resolve** obstacles in the consensus-driving process.

Lead to Self-Discovery	Build Confidence to Act	Lead to the Supplier
Why?	**Why?**	**Why?**
Mobilizers must feel ownership of the idea to stay motivated through the change process.	The ambiguous nature of change can overwhelm even the most capable Mobilizer. Clarity into next steps builds confidence in the Mobilizer's own capabilities.	Mobilizers are typically supplier neutral. Interactions must highlight your ability as the only supplier who can support the change.

Equip to Build Consensus
Why?
Mobilizer's agenda is to lead the broader organization to an agreement on a new vision of change.

Source: CEB analysis.

There are a variety of aspects for which Mobilizers can be commercially coached, and we will discuss these briefly in the remainder of this chapter. However, among the most important aspects is coaching the Mobilizer to engage their team in Collective Learning interactions (figure 8.10).

FIG. 8.10. Illustration of Mobilizer Facilitating Collective Learning

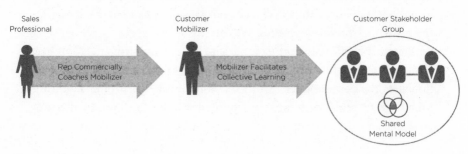

Source: CEB analysis.

In an analysis we conducted, we looked at what Mobilizer actions supported Collective Learning outcomes (figure 8.11). These actions included preparing the broader stakeholder group for Collective Learning moments as well as facilitating these moments. By better understanding various stakeholders' points of view, engaging in informal dialogue with colleagues regarding the purchase, teaching colleagues about new perspectives to consider as part of the purchase, and setting expectations for discussions and meetings related to the purchase, Mobilizers effectively prepared for Collective Learning interactions. We also found Mobilizers facilitating group

FIG. 8.11. Selected Mobilizer Activities That
Support Collective Learning for Customers

1. **Helps colleagues understand** the benefits/disadvantages of various courses of action

2. **Initiates informal conversations** with other stakeholders about this purchase

3. **Sets up group discussions** about this purchase

4. **Facilitates group discussions** about this purchase

5. Helps stakeholders in the buying group **realize they share needs/goals**

6. **Teaches colleagues something new** about business needs that supplier's solution should address

7. **Resolves disagreements** between colleagues about buying from supplier

n = 367.
Source: CEB B2B Value Survey.

deliberation, resolving disagreements among colleagues, and highlighting where diverging views exist and urging the group to find more commonalities, not surprisingly, as highly supportive of Collective Learning outcomes.

So how should Mobilizers be commercially coached to build consensus? While there are naturally a variety of ways to work with your Mobilizer, our research has highlighted a fairly clear approach that creates a starting point for nearly any seller to commercially coach their Mobilizer through the consensus-building process.

THE CONTOURS OF BUILDING CONSENSUS

Similar to most sales enablement tools we design, our Commercial Coaching guidance is derived from extensive interviews with some of the highest-performing sellers from our vast member network. This guidance helps sellers create a more structured approach for their Mobilizer to amass consensus. This guidance is not meant to become a massive checklist to hand off to a Mobilizer but, rather, to help sellers communicate tips and tricks to help the Mobilizer productively move their purchase forward. As such, this guidance is aligned to the consensus-building stages that nearly any customer purchase will inherently follow (figure 8.12).

In the first stage, the seller helps the Mobilizer construct a plan for building consensus. Now, this *isn't* sitting down and overwhelming the Mobilizer with a Gantt chart noting precise stages and project owners. On

FIG. 8.12. Commercial Coaching Process Steps

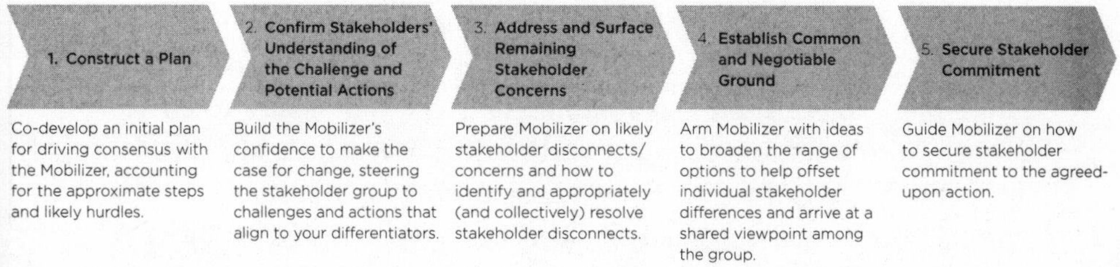

1. Construct a Plan	2. Confirm Stakeholders' Understanding of the Challenge and Potential Actions	3. Address and Surface Remaining Stakeholder Concerns	4. Establish Common and Negotiable Ground	5. Secure Stakeholder Commitment
Co-develop an initial plan for driving consensus with the Mobilizer, accounting for the approximate steps and likely hurdles.	Build the Mobilizer's confidence to make the case for change, steering the stakeholder group to challenges and actions that align to your differentiators.	Prepare Mobilizer on likely stakeholder disconnects/concerns and how to identify and appropriately (and collectively) resolve stakeholder disconnects.	Arm Mobilizer with ideas to broaden the range of options to help offset individual stakeholder differences and arrive at a shared viewpoint among the group.	Guide Mobilizer on how to secure stakeholder commitment to the agreed-upon action.

Source: CEB analysis.

the contrary, remember that you are helping the Mobilizer feel confident in moving forward and, in particular, making it easy for the Mobilizer to take action. This is more of a general overview of what is likely to happen throughout the purchase process and taking account of what *should* happen. Here you want to note likely stall points based on similar-in-kind deals with other customers—stories can be powerful at this stage. "In a similar organization we worked with last year, some unexpected challenges arose with their CFO . . . ," you might explain. At this point, you want to listen to the Mobilizer explain their organization's circumstances—and each stakeholder's interests and personalities—and take those into consideration. This is an appropriate time to obtain a copy of the org chart and work through the key players with your Mobilizer, noting likely disconnects and common views related to the purchase. Your objective at this stage is attuning the Mobilizer to the likely points of view they will encounter as they move forward with building consensus: "In all likelihood, HR will get involved, and that's fine—we need them involved—but here's what resistance I've usually seen from HR teams. We can handle that as it arises." Again, this is not meant to be an exercise in overwhelming the Mobilizer. This is laying out the path, giving them confidence in your ability to take control of the situation and help support their efforts.

In the first stage, be mindful of tailoring to your Mobilizer strengths and weaknesses. Mobilizers who are natural Go-Getters or Skeptics tend to have stronger project management and process orientation, and therefore may need less guidance at this stage. However, Teachers will need greater coaching to help them create a timeline of sorts and think through how to best sequence their consensus-building efforts.

You will want to avoid moving to the next Commercial Coaching stage if you (and your Mobilizer) have little understanding of the other stakeholders involved, find yourself (and your Mobilizer) continually speculating without actual evidence, or find your insight is not resonating with anyone beyond your Mobilizer. Those are indicators that the Mobilizer is not yet ready to move forward with building consensus. Continue to take control of the customer purchase by urging your Mobilizer to gather more information and continue to gauge stakeholder reactions. You may also want to reconsider whether you *truly* have a Mobilizer at this point, however. Ideally, what you are looking for at this first stage is your Mobilizer expressing their confidence in next steps, and taking stock of the likely decision makers and influencers in the purchase. Think of those as your verifiers—the way that you'll know that you and your Mobilizer are ready to move to the next stage.

The second stage helps the Mobilizer confirm their organization understands its true problem and the best course of action. Remember, these are the points where consensus efforts will most frequently derail, so we treat this as a very important stage in the Commercial Coaching process. This stage largely depends upon you getting your Commercial Insight *confidently* into the hands of your Mobilizer. Just because you've initially shared your insight with your Mobilizer, and they are excited, does not mean they are necessarily ready to share that insight broadly. You will want to help your Mobilizer refine the Commercial Insight for their organization's various stakeholders. Obviously, force fitting your Commercial Insight into the customer's organizational context would be a huge mistake. So in this stage, partner with your Mobilizer to determine how they can effectively tailor the insight to the various roles represented in their stakeholder group. This is about capturing the *nuances* of each stakeholder's current mental model and leading the group to have a collective and shared view of the desired mental model (which leads to your solution).

At this stage, it's vital to ensure your Mobilizer understands the cost of *inaction* on their organization's part. They *must* be able to convey this. As one head of sales operations coined, "Remember, the pain of *same* must be greater than the pain of *change*." That can't be underscored enough. This is the stage where you will want to arm your Mobilizer with data points and "cost of pain" calculators to help them communicate the cost of inaction. Invariably, the Mobilizer will encounter a variety of reactions and disconnects to the Commercial Insight. This is to be expected, but it's important that the Mobilizer share those reactions with you at this stage, as those disconnects become the basis of the Collective Learning interactions that you'll support them in conducting soon. The entire stage is geared toward gauging the customer organization's reaction to you and your Mobilizer's newly proposed direction, and assessing next steps based upon that reaction. You will undoubtedly see a mixed reaction. Some stakeholders will love the new direction. Others will be skeptical. Some will distance themselves. All this is important context to understand and take into account for the next stage, which is where stakeholder alignment will either succeed or fail.

Similar to the first stage, in this second stage you will want to account for your Mobilizer's strengths and weaknesses. Mobilizers who are natural Teachers are great storytellers and can articulate a vision extremely well—leverage that strength. Allow them to tell their story and convey your insight in a way they feel most comfortable doing. However, for Go-Getters and Skeptics, you'll want to coach them on sharing the insight in compelling and engaging ways, as these profiles can get overly focused on the details and lose sight of the bigger picture.

You will want to avoid moving to the next Commercial Coaching stage if you (and your Mobilizer) realize that the other stakeholders do not believe they are facing a challenge. Without some degree of organizational commitment to explore a challenge—let alone consider a new direction—consensus will never be forged for a purchase. The reaction you want at this stage is for your Mobilizer to have a strong opinion on how their colleagues view their problem, even how they perceive potential solutions to the problem. It should also be clear how the problem is impacting various stakeholders' KPIs and broader organizational metrics. Once you've attained these progress verifiers, attention can be shifted to the third stage of Commercial Coaching.

In this third Commercial Coaching stage, you'll support your Mobilizer in surfacing and addressing any remaining stakeholder concerns. Partnering with your Mobilizer, you will help highlight objections and stakeholder disconnects that may not be obvious at this point. Such disconnects are based on your experience—typically not the Mobilizer's. While you sell these types of solutions every day, it's highly unlikely your Mobilizer buys them every day! This is the stage where the bulk of Collective Learning occurs. You will want to help your Mobilizer think through opportunities to get their purchase stakeholders to convene—whether virtually or live. To make these sessions as productive as possible, arming the Mobilizer with a workshop or a diagnostic can be extremely helpful (in the next chapter, we'll explore some great examples of this). A good seller will naturally seek to involve themselves even more so at this stage, perhaps even leading a workshop where stakeholder disconnects can be discussed (we will also see an example of this in the next chapter). Providing your Mobilizer with proof points, stories, or other evidence to help overcome stakeholder objections is also a good idea.

The excitement a Mobilizer has for a solution may translate into more telling than listening. Be mindful of how your Mobilizer is engaging their colleagues at this stage in their purchase. Remind your Mobilizer to listen and relay stakeholder disconnects and concerns, so you can mutually determine the right course of action. Encourage Mobilizers, particularly Go-Getters, to not prematurely push a deal forward or compel action. Instead, coach them to involve the broader stakeholder group in Collective Learning moments to resolve points of conflict.

Blockers often exercise their influence on a purchase at this point in the sale. Do not prematurely move to the next stage of Commercial Coaching without accounting for and neutralizing Blockers (more on this in chapter 10). Further, pay close attention to the level of stakeholder alignment regarding the customer problem and the perceived course of action the customer believes they should be taking. You want to ensure that there is strong alignment across both the problem and the action being taken— specifically for the problem and action that lead to your differentiators. The verifiers of customer progress at this stage include at least one Collective Learning interaction having occurred among stakeholders, and customer stakeholders expressing agreement on the problem and the course of action they believe is right.

Once those verifiers are obtained, you can move to the fourth stage of Commercial Coaching, which establishes negotiable points related to the purchase. This is where you and your Mobilizer will take control of the purchase process by helping the customer actively make trade-offs related to the purchase. Arm your Mobilizer with options to help offset stakeholder differences and arrive at a shared viewpoint among the group. The best options are *negotiable* options, meaning attributes of the purchase that can be conceded in order to satisfy any remaining stakeholder concerns *without materially impacting your differentiated solution*. What's most important in this stage is ensuring that the customer is able to agree on the B state—the new and desired business approach—that your organization can best support. The reason this is so important is that this B state forms the basis of the *non*-negotiable aspects of the purchase. If the customer is committed to the B state as their new direction, it becomes harder and harder for the customer to then marginalize your solution by negotiating out certain aspects of your offering. The negotiable aspects, therefore, are attributes of little consequence to the B state. This is why it's imperative to ensure the customer's stakeholders are *still* aligned around their business problem and the action they need to take at this stake in the purchase. As the customer begins to rally around this purchase, and it suddenly becomes more a reality, their natural instinct is to attempt to commoditize your solution at this stage in an effort to gain pricing leverage. Coaching your Mobilizer to *ensure* that their colleagues are still committed to the problem and the new direction you've taught them to take is vital at this point. Beyond that, working with your Mobilizer to highlight the non-negotiable aspects of the purchase and encouraging them to convey those aspects to their colleagues should be happening at this stage.

In terms of how to coach your Mobilizers, it's worth noting that Teachers are more inclined to propose creative options to secure apprehensive stakeholder commitment. Be sure to help Teachers understand the implications of these more creative options. In some cases, their creativity may endanger your solution. Help Go-Getters and Skeptics avoid the urge to concede *something* to keep progress moving along. Also, help these more rational thinkers to consider less obvious and more creative ways to get apprehensive stakeholders committed to the deal.

Use extreme caution if all Blockers have not been neutralized at this point in the deal. Use particular caution in looking for silent Blockers, who commonly abstain from having any opinion until late. If there is a seeming influencer who has yet to fully express their views, assume they are a Blocker until proven otherwise. The last thing you want is for a Blocker to raise a significant (and late) objection as you enter into closing stages. It's common at this stage to see some degree of fractionalization among stakeholders. This too is a warning sign, and you and your Mobilizer should assess what's causing slightly differing views to form among the stakeholders. Differing views this late in the purchase process can quickly lead to inaction or the dreaded "we need to further evaluate" answer. The verifiers of customer progress at this fourth stage include all Blockers being neutralized and a clear sense among stakeholders that they grasp the inherent trade-offs of tweaking or limiting the solution. Once those verifiers have been obtained, you can then proceed to the fifth stage of Commercial Coaching.

This fifth (and final) stage of Commercial Coaching is predicated on securing stakeholder commitment to move forward. This is about ensuring there are no surprises late in the purchase. Coach your Mobilizer to reiterate the right course of action—and the fact that your company is best positioned to support that approach. This is the stage where getting a bit more commercially aggressive becomes acceptable from the customer's vantage point, so arming your Mobilizer with comparisons of your capabilities relative to the competition's is fair game. Coach your Mobilizer to monitor any remaining stakeholders (and identify any additional stakeholders that may insert themselves into the purchase) that may still balk late in the purchase and discuss their views with you.

This step is very detail oriented. Seemingly minor, overlooked concerns can become significant challenges. Pay particularly close attention to Go-Getters and Skeptics to make sure they are not overly focused on implementation planning, overlooking any outstanding concerns or new objections. Teachers will often prematurely start the celebrating at this point, assuming everything is in order for the purchase to move forward, and start to shift their attention to the next idea. Encourage them to remain diligently focused on this particular business initiative.

Be mindful of other competing priorities that may arise for your customer. Use caution in moving forward if other priorities have arisen. The ideal customer verifiers of progress at this stage include the customer committing resources and support to implementation of your solution, stakeholders being aware of broad support for your solution, and of course, broad stakeholder agreement that your solution is best positioned to support their business.

The clearest takeaway here is that Mobilizers are hugely valuable assets that allow you to take control of the customer's purchase behavior in remarkable ways. Given this, how you manage the Mobilizer relationship matters. Providing them with the support and guidance they need to navigate the daunting task of forging consensus is indeed best practice. Not only does this ensure the Mobilizer is supported, but it also ensures they engage in the most productive customer buying behavior they can, helping you achieve customer consensus *on your terms*.

The importance of Collective Learning can't be understated. In today's consensus-driven purchase, where divergent views and dysfunction reign supreme, and deals get compressed to the lowest common denominator, it's the clearest means by which customers can agree on high-quality purchases. Taking control of the customer's purchase by helping the customer engage in Collective Learning, supported by Commercially Coaching your Mobilizer, matters tremendously to overcome the challenges of today's consensus purchase.

In the coming chapter, we will bring the idea of Collective Learning to life through concrete examples of sales and marketing organizations from leading companies creating opportunities for greater stakeholder alignment, by better arming Mobilizers to better and more easily build consensus and drive change. We'll also look at a very different set of activities sales reps can pursue when that work with Mobilizers proves not to be enough on its own.

CHAPTER NINE

MAKING COLLECTIVE LEARNING HAPPEN

Creating collective learning starts with finding common ground. We'll still run up against a language barrier of sorts, as each function and each silo across an organization speaks its own language (even when they speak the *same* language!).

So half the time, different buying group stakeholders may want the same thing, but you'd never know it, because they're articulating that very similar need in very different ways. We need to find a common language to use in messages that bridges that apparent disconnect.

Marketing can attempt to get at this common language through classic customer-understanding activities—through customer observation and interviews. But we'd like to highlight an elegant and incredibly effective approach that Cisco uses, involving social listening and in-market message testing. As we dive into the example, notice how this approach from Cisco is all about identifying *shared* interests and language, not individual interests and language.

We all know Cisco, supplier of networking products and services. As Cisco's solutions continue to evolve, they're finding they need to engage—and ultimately win over—a new, diverse set of customer stakeholders. As marketing functions continue to spend more on technology, one of the key new stakeholders is the chief marketing officer. But on the face of it, the views of CMOs diverge from those of Cisco's traditional primary decision maker, the chief information officer (or chief technology officer). Superficially, at least, there's little common ground to bring these two groups together on decisions that they eventually have to make together.

So Cisco developed a technique to bridge that gap. By listening carefully to social conversations—specifically for the *building blocks* of a common language that might bring these two otherwise disparate groups together—Cisco is able to create messages purposefully built to demonstrate to CMOs and CIOs that they have much more in common than they ever realized.

If we think about how most B2B commercial teams engage in social listening, it's pretty basic. Typically, we're listening for one of two things. First, we listen for perceptions of us as a supplier. So we scan for mentions of our company, or our brand, maybe our products. Second, we listen for common search terms or discussion threads to improve our search optimization efforts. We'll pay some attention to *who*'s saying whatever it is we're listening to, but by and large we're more interested in what's being said.

But at Cisco it's the *who* that matters most. For example, given their new, important role in a typical Cisco purchase, Cisco needs to understand CMOs far better than ever before. What are they talking about? How are they thinking about technology? What issues are important? What language is common?

To do that, Cisco mines social media and digital publications to isolate content generated by or targeted to CMOs. While not all CMOs may be tweeting and posting, there's a huge amount of content out there produced and published on the things CMOs care about most.

Cisco taps into all of it—content produced by CMOs and content produced for CMOs. As illustrated in the graphic opposite, it's a very targeted search around a single stakeholder. But the key is what they're listening for here. It isn't what CMOs are saying about Cisco; rather, they want to know what CMOs are saying, period.

In the illustrative example shown in figure 9.1, Cisco finds that many CMO conversations revolve in some fashion or another around device connectivity. Marketers are talking a lot about what it means to live and work in a world where devices don't just connect with people, but increasingly connect with each other as well.

That's important to know, because we can use that information in just a bit to build a bridge to IT professionals—who Cisco knows (through the exact same process) are talking about the same thing. But before we build that bridge, we need to find the building blocks for a common language. In addition to finding the *topics* that matter most, the team then steps back from the terms themselves and analyzes the strings of words *around* those terms. The goal here is to better understand the broader context within which the topic "device connectivity" resonates for marketers.

FIG. 9.1. Cisco's Stakeholder Interest and Language Tracking

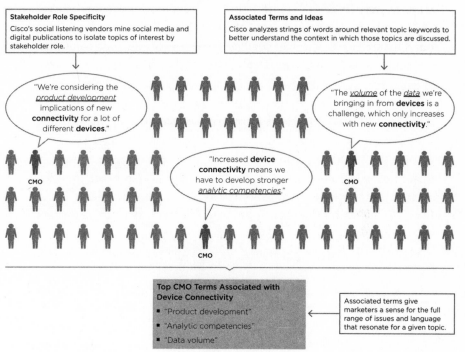

Stakeholder Role Specificity
Cisco's social listening vendors mine social media and digital publications to isolate topics of interest by stakeholder role.

Associated Terms and Ideas
Cisco analyzes strings of words around relevant topic keywords to better understand the context in which those topics are discussed.

"We're considering the *product development* implications of new **connectivity** for a lot of different **devices**."

"The *volume* of the *data* we're bringing in from **devices** is a challenge, which only increases with new **connectivity**."

"Increased **device connectivity** means we have to develop stronger *analytic competencies*."

CMO

CMO

CMO

Top CMO Terms Associated with Device Connectivity
- "Product development"
- "Analytic competencies"
- "Data volume"

Associated terms give marketers a sense for the full range of issues and language that resonate for a given topic.

Source: Cisco Systems, CEB analysis.

That allows Cisco to figure out not just *what* marketers are talking about . . . but *why* those things are important to them.

And it's the *combination* of these two things—*what* they say and *how* they say it—that allows the Cisco team to figure out a full range of both issues and language that resonate strongly for a particular stakeholder group.

If we stop and think about what they've done here, it's really powerful. This isn't what CMOs say about *us* as a supplier; rather, it's what they talk about *unprompted*, when we're not the focus of the conversation. But even more important, it gives us the raw material we need to establish a common ground. Remember, the ultimate goal here is to drive consensus.

Cisco can now take that information about how CMOs are talking about device connectivity and map it to how CIOs are talking about device connectivity. Here, Cisco is looking for the overlap. You see that represented by the two circles laid out in figure 9.2. In this case, for example, when it came to device connectivity, Cisco found an overlap between CMOs and CIOs around the issue of data volume. More specifically, they found the overlap in the huge *untapped potential* of all the data out there that could result from a more deeply connected world.

FIG. 9.2. Cisco's Stakeholder Language Tree

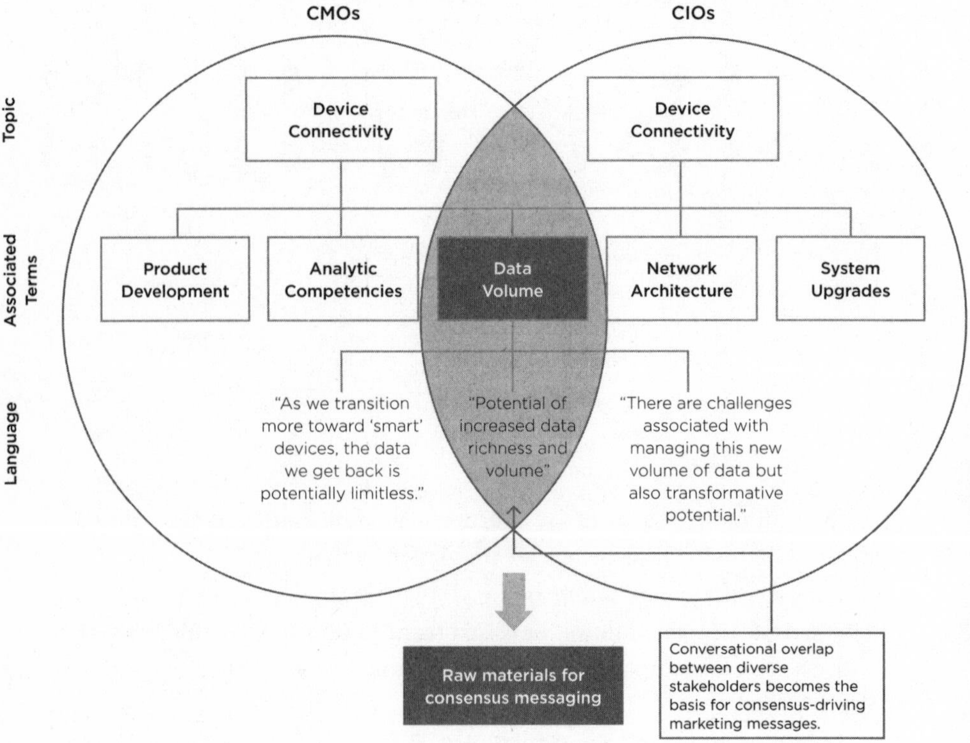

Source: Cisco Systems, CEB analysis.

This is the conversational overlap Cisco was looking for, which will enable Cisco to help connect these stakeholders together. That overlap can become the basis for messages engineered to speak to both groups *simultaneously* around an issue they both care about.

It would be easy to look at this diagram and see *five* different ways to talk about connectivity. But Cisco sees one, because their goal is to build the bridges between stakeholders in the buying group before sales reps ever get in and have a chance to roll up their sleeves.

The other piece to this we like is how Cisco then identifies the language that will resonate best with these stakeholder groups *simultaneously.*

You can see that happening in the process shown in figure 9.3. In Step 1, Cisco develops message prototypes. In this case, Cisco seeks to dial up the huge potential for greater connectivity—the common topic we identified from before. Cisco might try messaging like "Connectivity isn't as high as you think" or "Only 1 percent of the world's devices are connected."

FIG. 9.3. Cisco's Approach to Creating Shareable Messages

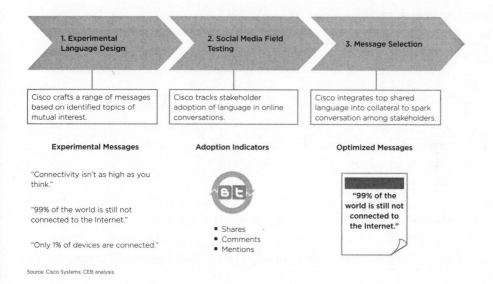

1. Experimental Language Design	2. Social Media Field Testing	3. Message Selection
Cisco crafts a range of messages based on identified topics of mutual interest.	Cisco tracks stakeholder adoption of language in online conversations.	Cisco integrates top shared language into collateral to spark conversation among stakeholders.

Experimental Messages

"Connectivity isn't as high as you think."

"99% of the world is still not connected to the Internet."

"Only 1% of devices are connected."

Adoption Indicators

- Shares
- Comments
- Mentions

Optimized Messages

"99% of the world is still not connected to the Internet."

Source: Cisco Systems; CEB analysis.

In Step 2, Cisco tests the messages. It embeds them in social conversations through LinkedIn, Twitter, marketing technology discussion boards, and common blogs. Cisco monitors which messages take off—not just that they get read or retweeted, but that the language in the messages begins to get adopted. Which language gets picked up and used more broadly.

Because once Cisco has found those turns of phrase, trending across multiple stakeholder groups, then they'll know they have their lingua franca, their common language, so necessary for building stakeholder bridges.

Those phrases—the ones most widely adopted by diverse target stakeholder audiences—then get built into more formal campaigns, which is Step 3. In this case, the phrasing "99 percent of the world is still not connected to the Internet" is what gets built into larger campaigns.

So it's a hugely important process of iterative testing and close observation, but always with an eye toward connecting stakeholders together, not just breaking through to each stakeholder individually. That's because these messages then become the groundwork—the backdrop of the social conversation as it were—that allows for CIOs and CMOs to find common ground on an issue they may have otherwise never realized they had in common.

On the face of it, this Cisco example could feel like rocket science, applicable only in the high-tech industry where there's a rich weave of conversations happening that involve potential customers. But remember, Cisco's approach doesn't just listen for our stakeholders' *social* conversations, it also mines *content directed at stakeholders*. There's a far larger set of stakeholders—from a broader set of industries than just high tech—for whom digital content is being created.

So at this point you've identified common ground and common language that can prime disparate stakeholders for consensus. Ideally, that common ground and language are going to be anchored in a Commercial Insight that reframes the way stakeholders can, *as a group*, start to think differently about their business.

But suppliers don't want to leave this to chance. If you can't have a sales rep on the ground, engaging the stakeholders of that buying center, you want your Mobilizers doing that for you. So the other thing we need to do as marketers at this stage is to *equip* Mobilizers to bring those stakeholders together.

EQUIP MOBILIZERS TO BRING STAKEHOLDERS TOGETHER

The key question here is, how do we equip Mobilizers to persuade other stakeholders? We'll show you how two companies, Marketo and Skillsoft, have done it. Let's start with Marketo.

As many readers will know, Marketo plays in the marketing automation space. It's a relatively new technology that allows marketing teams to automate many aspects of demand generation, as well as provide tracking and dashboarding to help optimize those efforts. What's interesting for the Mobilizer story is that, because this is a technology purchase, there are almost always multiple disparate stakeholders involved beyond marketing itself. You have IT involved. Sales. Finance. Procurement. So truly a 5.4 kind of situation.

Moreover, because this is a new technology, many of those stakeholders don't know that much about it. So their perceptions about the technology are likely to be both off and misaligned. In other words, this is a "high degree of difficulty" situation for the Mobilizer.

So if I'm a marketer who wants to mobilize for marketing automation technology, I need to engage all of these different stakeholders. How does that go? Well, once I've got my marketing colleagues on board, I might say to the CIO, "We need a marketing automation system." Typical response? "Well, we already have a CRM system. That should be configurable to get what you need. We spent a pretty penny on it!" As a marketer, you're thinking, "No! No! It's not the same!" But you don't quite know how best to convey that to a tech leader who talks in, well, tech-nese. How do I convey to these people that these technologies are different?

I might also go to the head of sales, and there you know what you're going to get, right? "I don't know, seems like there's five other things we could spend our money on before this 'marketing automation' platform. We've got a long list just to get more mileage out of our CRM investment." And so on. The CFO probably says something similar.

That's deflating for a Mobilizer, to think about these conversations. Some probably give up before they even try to have the conversations. Others may try and get stonewalled or get only so far.

So for Marketo, the challenge is how do you get this one Mobilizer to go engage and effectively persuade the other 4.4 stakeholders? Again, this is not about getting those stakeholders to connect better to us as a supplier; rather, it's about getting those stakeholders to connect better to *each other*.

The nice part of Marketo's solution is they've taken something that most commercial teams have already—a whole set of sales enablement tools—and with a few simple tweaks turned it into a powerful set of resources for that Mobilizer.

Think about that—how many of us have tools we've collectively created in marketing or sales, for use by our sales teams or channel partners? Have you got scripting documents and talking points for your sales reps? Objection-handling docs? Sales pitch decks? ROI docs? Stories and anecdotes? Business and use cases?

Almost all commercial teams have at least some of these. In effect, Marketo has taken many of these kinds of tools and with a few minor tweaks repositioned them from sales tools to become tools that help Mobilizers go and mobilize. They become customer-facing tools. Marketo puts them all online in a resource kit, so they're easily accessible for Mobilizers.

Marketo's toolkit is called *The Definitive Guide to Marketing Automation*. It's a giant online document on Marketo's Web site, broken into chapters, and downloadable by anybody in return for giving up a little information about yourself. A simple Google search on marketing automation brings it up.

Right off the bat, notice that this is NOT *The Definitive Guide to Marketo*. Remember, the peak of group dysfunction and the consensus problems suppliers face happen in just getting a group to agree to the nature of the problem and the solution. Settling on a supplier comes much later. So you need these toolkits to equip that Mobilizer to have better conversations about marketing automation, not better conversations about Marketo.

This is one area where you'll probably need to tweak your existing sales tools to turn them into Mobilizer tools. Because your sales tools were likely created to focus on you as a supplier, you'll need to modify them to focus more broadly on the nature of the problem and solution.

For example, the toolkit includes a talking points guide. Marketo has identified what each stakeholder is likely to consider as the alternative to marketing automation as a solution. In other words, what do those stakeholders view as the opportunity cost of your solutions? That's really smart. It gives the Mobilizer a glimpse into the kinds of early, very practical objections they are likely to face.

In this case, one of the biggest alternative solutions is CRM. Not because CRM and marketing automation do the same thing, but because some of those other stakeholders *perceive* CRM to do essentially the same thing. Marketo equips Mobilizers to have the conversations about the differences and to do so in a way that each stakeholder is going to care about most. Marketo is putting it in the stakeholder's language.

FIG. 9.4. Excerpts from Marketo's "Definitive Guide to Marketing Automation"

PART THREE: HOW IS MARKETING AUTOMATION DIFFERENT FROM..?
RELATIONSHIP TO CRM

	CRM	Marketing Automation
Departmental Focus	Primarily sales and sales management, some marketing	Primarily marketing and marketing management, some sales
Architecture	Database-oriented, transactional queries	Workflow-oriented, highly detailed behavioral data queries

Toolkit contrasts supplier solutions with each function's likely alternative or work-arounds.

Source: Marketo; CEB analysis.

One tool in the kit is a stakeholder guide. Marketo outlines who the other 4.4 stakeholders are likely to be, what they care about, how they think, how they view the world, the metrics they use to measure their world, and the language they use to talk about their world. It's very similar information to what you'd find in a persona. It's really important because it may not have occurred to your Mobilizer that they need to go talk to the head of sales and IT and finance and procurement. Beyond that, Marketo is laying out what the Mobilizer needs to say in front of those stakeholders and how to connect the dots between the solution and metrics they use to measure their world.

FIG. 9.5. Excerpts from Marketo's "Definitive Guide to Marketing Automation"

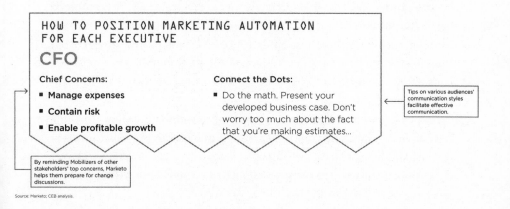

HOW TO POSITION MARKETING AUTOMATION
FOR EACH EXECUTIVE

CFO

Chief Concerns:
- Manage expenses
- Contain risk
- Enable profitable growth

Connect the Dots:
- Do the math. Present your developed business case. Don't worry too much about the fact that you're making estimates...

Tips on various audiences' communication styles facilitate effective communication.

By reminding Mobilizers of other stakeholders' top concerns, Marketo helps them prepare for change discussions.

Source: Marketo; CEB analysis.

Another tool is an objection-handling guide. Marketo has captured the likely objections the Mobilizer will hear from each stakeholder and has provided guidance on overcoming that objection, in terms that are going to be meaningful *to that stakeholder.*

As well, what you'll see throughout the toolkit are stories. These are very powerful ways of lighting the path for Mobilizers to go out and engage stakeholders. But note that these are not your typical customer stories, which tend to be very supplier specific, highlighting the value the customer got out of working that supplier. Rather, these are about companies that have gone on the marketing automation change journey, and what was in it for the company and the Mobilizers driving the change. These are absolutely stories that you want to put in the hands of your Mobilizers.

The other aspect of this Marketo toolkit we like is that it focuses on making it *easy* for the Mobilizer to go and mobilize. Mobilizing a group of disparate stakeholders feels hard and complicated. So the kinds of things they include are ready-made business case templates, in native Power-Point format. The Mobilizer can download a template, put a logo on it, make edits, add to it. This deck is the skeleton of the conversations that the Mobilizer needs to be having. It includes data points, talking points for presentations to different stakeholders, and guidance on which slides are key for which stakeholders. Again, it's all about making it as easy as possible for the Mobilizer to mobilize.

This is how to equip your most important customer, the Mobilizer. But remember, you'll need to tweak all of those existing sales tools, so they don't come across as supplier-centric. If you don't make the toolkit supplier-agnostic, you'll risk equipping your Mobilizers to be a shill for you as a supplier. That'll undermine their ability to persuade other stakeholders, and it may lead them to not want to mobilize at all. These toolkits should be built in the spirit of creating your Commercial Insight—because it's about the customer; it shouldn't lead *with* you as the supplier, but should lead uniquely back *to* you. Done well, these Mobilizer toolkits can have all the elements of chapter 6's Spark-Introduce-Confront content paths embedded in them.

Let's take a look at another example of a Mobilizer toolkit, this one from Skillsoft. It extends on the Marketo idea by centering on a Commercial Insight, using third-party thought leaders in a clever way, and layering customer engagement nicely to balance reach and depth of engagement.

SKILLSOFT'S MOBILIZER TOOLKIT

Skillsoft is a leading provider of cloud-based learning solutions, providing its products and services to over 6,000 large and small enterprises in the public, private, and education sectors around the globe. Skillsoft provides technology-enabled learning and talent management programs, platforms, and services to help learners build skills and knowledge across a wide range of technical and business subject areas.

Pam Boiros, VP of global corporate marketing for Skillsoft, saw the Marketo Mobilizer toolkit example at CEB's annual member summit in Las Vegas, and she immediately knew Skillsoft needed one. As Pam tells it, Skillsoft has 5.7 stakeholders in its typical purchase. As you'd expect, its primary stakeholders are in human resources, or more specifically, in the learning and development group. But for purchases of technology-based learning platforms like Skillsoft's, the stakeholder group also includes IT, procurement, finance, and legal.

Two additional challenges make the consensus purchase dynamic even more challenging for Skillsoft. Cloud-based learning solutions are a somewhat new technology, so even Skillsoft's primary stakeholders in HR often aren't deeply familiar with the ins and outs of what they might be buying. On top of that, Pam relates that HR personnel aren't cut in the classic Mobilizer mold. Their background, business experience, and position in the organization don't naturally put them in a spot to mobilize, or be Mobilizers. Pam told us, "A lot of times, there won't be a clear-cut Mobilizer for this kind of learning solution. So our view is, we have to *make* Mobilizers."

You can download the toolkit from Skillsoft's Web site. It's a great model for other marketers to follow. You'll see it feels similar to the Marketo toolkit. It is comprehensive—from educating Mobilizers to equipping them to build the business case. It is accessible—light on text, heavy on graphics, videos, and case examples. It makes mobilizing easy—it's loaded with practical guidance and downloadable tools and templates that reduce the effort that goes into mobilizing.

But Pam and her team made some key enhancements that are worth calling out.

COMMERCIAL INSIGHT-BASED REFRAMING: Pam and her team used a myth-busting structure to deliver key elements of Skillsoft's

FIG. 9.6. Skillsoft's Mobilizer Toolkit

Cloud-Based Learning Solutions: Making the Right Choice for Your Enterprise

Table of contents

Skillsoft

Source: Skillsoft; CEB analysis.

Commercial Insights around learning (see figure 9.7). The simple, one-page myths with evidence and stories begin to reframe how stakeholders think about learning in their organizations—these are great examples of chapter 6's Spark and Introduce content.

FIG. 9.7. Excerpt from Skillsoft's Mobilizer Toolkit

Section 1

Myth: Event-based learning is sufficient as a stand-alone learning program offering

Share On

Truth: Continuous learning heightens skill transfer to the job
Event-based learning programs are those that have a general start and end date or time such as instructor-led training (ILT) and workshops. More often than not, industry leaders question whether these event-based learning programs are sticking and creating desired behavior changes. Event-based programs certainly are not scalable. With the rapid need for skill development and transfer, organizations need learning solutions with enterprise-wide scalability.

We've all experienced it. We go to a great class or conference. We get a ton of incredible information. We get motivated and charged up about everything we learned. Then, we get back to our job,

get sidetracked with day-to-day responsibilities and don't take the necessary opportunity to reinforce what we learned while we were away. And because of that, we forget.

The Forgetting Curve (see page 10) shows us that most of what we learned is lost very quickly – that includes the investment we made when sending employees away for training events.

Because of this, learning should not be viewed as an independent event; rather, learning should be infused in the day-to-day and available anywhere and everywhere employees need it. Leading organizations embrace a continuous learning model where employees have access to a constant flow of succinct on-demand resources to support their development.

Companies can face obstacles by being too event-centric and by not addressing the skill gap challenges posed by the talent crisis. Learner expectations have shifted and most organizations have not adapted appropriately or with enough speed to accommodate the pace of change in the world around them.

Watch Now

Learn how an organization converted one ILT course to an elearning course and saved hundreds of thousands of dollars in doing so

www.skillsoft.com/Aniva

Skillsoft

Source: Skillsoft; CEB analysis.

THOUGHT-LEADER SNAPSHOTS: The Skillsoft team sprinkled five one-page thought-leader snapshots throughout the toolkit (see figure 9.8). Because these snapshots come from thought leaders outside of Skillsoft and don't endorse Skillsoft directly, they inject a huge dose of credibility to the toolkit. Remember, you need these toolkits to help Mobilizers drive consensus around the problem and solution, not around a supplier.

Pam and her team were surprised at how painless it was to get these thought leaders on board. Her team made it easy for them by drafting the page based on each thought leader's publicly available research and opinions. Skillsoft approached the thought leaders with the draft and the context on the toolkit. Pam tells us that all five of the thought leaders they approached agreed to have their material included. She says, "Choose thought leaders who are already well aligned to your company, including industry analysts, columnists, influencers, and others with name recognition. It's a win-win for them as they look to build their personal reach and brand."

FIG. 9.8. Excerpt from Skillsoft's Mobilizer Toolkit

Source: Skillsoft; CEB analysis.

LAYERED ENGAGEMENT AND SUPPORT: The toolkit itself is not protected by a download form you have to fill out before you can get to it—anybody can download it straight from the Skillsoft site or forward it to colleagues without filling out a form. But throughout, there are opportunities for the reader to download templates, tools, case studies, and white papers (see figure 9.9). These are gated, so Pam and her team can know who is engaging more deeply with the information and tools. The toolkit on its own, even without these downloads, is hugely valuable to a Mobilizer. But the downloads blow it out—they give the Mobilizer the deep detail and templates that make mobilizing *easier*.

FIG. 9.9. Excerpt from Skillsoft's Mobilizer Toolkit

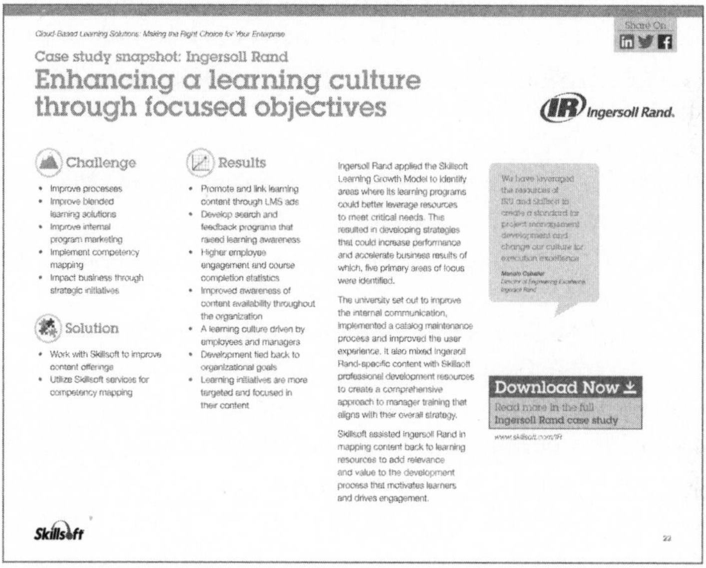

Source: Skillsoft; CEB analysis.

Notice how these downloads are great indicators of where a customer may be on the Spark-Introduce-Confront disruption path. Pam's team can tell when a Mobilizer has downloaded a detailed case study, which indicates the Mobilizer is somewhere in the Introduce stage. Or, if the Mobilizer downloads the RFP template, that Mobilizer is well into the Confront stage. These are powerful nurture indicators, informing Pam's team and the sales team on how best to engage that prospect next.

Putting this toolkit together required Pam, her team, and the broader Skillsoft organization to think and behave differently, to let go of some firmly held convictions about *how* marketing and sales should be done. For example, Pam tells us the decision not to gate the toolkit was a big one, and it was hard. Because as a marketer, if you have content that is this *great*, of course you'd want to gate it so you can know who is engaging with it, right? If a prospect downloads this huge piece of content, it'd be crazy not to have that lead go into your system! Let's start nurturing!

But the Skillsoft team reasoned that if the primary objective is to equip Mobilizers, who are themselves trying to drive consensus, then easy sharing was going to be critical. As soon as you put a gate up with a form to fill out, that's a huge speed bump in sharing.

Pam told us that it was also tough to stay true to building the toolkit in a vendor-neutral way. Every instinct in marketers is to want to paint the picture for *how you as a supplier are different*. You want to sharpen *your* value prop. But the Skillsoft team recognized that if the primary objective is to equip Mobilizers to drive consensus on the problem and the solution first, then it was going to be critical for the vast majority of the toolkit to be vendor neutral. Lead *to*, not lead *with*. That's exactly what the toolkit does—the first time you read about Skillsoft is in the last chapter, page 55 of a 60-page toolkit.

Finally, the Skillsoft team faced internal questions about sharing details on the contracting process. Some at Skillsoft viewed that as "secret sauce"—why would you want to equip your buyers with guidance that could help them during contracting, when negotiations are starting to take place? Pam's reaction was: "If we want to equip these Mobilizers to help us drive larger deals involving Skillsoft's full suite of services, they *have* to know how the contracting works." The only thing that's harder than *selling* solutions is *buying* them.

The toolkit has been in-market for a short time, but already the results are impressive. First off, Pam and the team did a great job of creating a toolkit that is "atom-izable"—chapters and even pages in the toolkit have great stand-alone value. The team has been able to seed and repurpose those content atoms in so many different ways. The team is getting extended mileage out of it, and it shows signs of having a long shelf life. For example, four months after launching it, Pam's team pulled out an infographic about the Top Two Myths of E-learning and uploaded it to SlideShare. Slide-Share chose it as a daily Top SlideShare, which drove 2,000 page views of the infographic within a single week, as well as awareness of the toolkit. In addition, blog posts, social "snacks," and other smaller derivatives have resulted from the content, and all are designed to drive awareness and downloads of the toolkit.

Skillsoft's sales force is loving the toolkit, as well. Pam and her team have gotten feedback from sales reps that the toolkit is influencing the shape of RFPs. One account team is using the business case section of the guide to chart a path to a larger e-learning solution, increasing an existing customer contract by a factor of ten.

Skillsoft and Marketo highlight how a Mobilizer can be enabled with great content and tools, whether a salesperson is involved or not. Let's transition into best practices where sellers are creating Collective Learning moments for their customers, with the support of their Mobilizers. These sales practices are highly complementary to the marketing best practices just described, and in tandem present a very powerful way to take control of the customer's purchase by encouraging and supporting Collective Learning.

ALPHA COMPANY'S STAKEHOLDER ALIGNMENT WORKSHOPS

Alpha Company has put a lot of thought behind this idea of Collective Learning and developed some great lessons based on customer workshops. The company (name is a pseudonym) is a division of a major financial information company, which sells software, data, research, and analytical tools for the financial services community.

As you can imagine, Alpha has a "5.4 stakeholders" story just like everyone else. Even a few years ago, their commercial teams traditionally engaged the head of the valuation desk and his or her immediate team. But over time, because of the scope, complexity, and regulatory implications of how financial valuation is conducted, Alpha found themselves speaking to compliance officers, regulators, various C-suite officers, and of course, general counsel. Traditionally, the team at Alpha could still effectively build resonance for their solutions with more traditional stakeholders. But as they engaged the other 4.4 stakeholders, they found deal support eroding very quickly. They had to find a way to get these diverse stakeholders to recognize and openly discuss disconnects much earlier in the purchase so that the various stakeholders could align around a common problem. This challenge is what led to their best practice—something they call "Stakeholder Alignment Workshops."

While this is very much a story of winning group consensus, the story starts with the individuals comprising the group. When we asked the team at Alpha how they manage to get customers to agree to attend a workshop in the first place, their answer was: "You need to do the hard work of getting each individual on board—not on board with your solution, but on board with the value of sitting down with their colleagues to discuss the potential value of an alternate course of action." In other words, they needed to create some buy-in for Collective Learning.

The best way to do that, they found, was to highlight the one thing that most sellers try to avoid: the fact that the various stakeholders are not nearly as aligned as they may have thought. Alpha found they needed to run directly at the disconnects among the customer stakeholders.

Securing stakeholder commitment for a workshop follows a four-step process at Alpha (see figure 9.10).

FIG. 9.10. Alpha Co.'s Stakeholder Commitment Process

	1. Assess and Convey Points of Disconnect	2. Create Urgency for Resolution of Disconnects	3. Confirm Support for Stakeholder Workshop	4. Set Expectation for Participation
Salesperson Actions	▪ Listen for stakeholder priorities/needs ▪ Express other stakeholders' views, highlighting points of disconnect or varying perspectives	▪ Illustrate possible consequences of existing disconnects in customer organization ▪ Share experiences from comparable customers with similar disconnects, illustrating potential costs (e.g., wasted time, resources, or suboptimal decisions)	▪ Clarify intent of the workshop—resolution of conflicts, not supplier presentation or demo ▪ Provide examples showcasing how a workshop can lead to resolution of disconnects and goal alignment	▪ Provide agenda and clarify intent of workshop, and rules for participation ▪ Attain explicit approval to share specific stakeholder concerns ▪ Confirm commitment to an open-minded discussion

Source: Alpha Company¹; CEB analysis.
¹ Pseudonym.

In the first step, their sales teams lay the groundwork for the workshop. First and foremost, their job here is to listen to the customer and try to get a sense for the goals and priorities of each stakeholder. While Alpha did not necessarily emphasize reliance for a Mobilizer, you can quickly appreciate how useful a Mobilizer is to understanding disconnects among the stakeholders in the first place. The idea here is to take those goals and priorities and then point out potential disconnects with colleagues. The Alpha sellers are trying to elicit a customer reaction of "Huh, I'd never thought of that before. Maybe we aren't as aligned as I thought we were . . ."

In the second step, Alpha encourages sellers to build some urgency around why the stakeholder disconnects matter so much. The idea here is to paint a picture of what happens if the disconnects go unresolved. At this point sellers are encouraged to share stories from similar companies, where their disconnects were left unresolved and caused all sorts of unforeseen pain, cost, and delay. Here Alpha is trying to get the customer to think, "We've got to do something about this. This whole effort is going to die on the vine, or blow up in bad way, if we don't get on the same page."

Once the customer is thinking like that, the seller moves to Step 3. Here, a facilitated workshop is offered. Now, this isn't the typical workshop that customers expect from suppliers—rather, this is positioned purely as an opportunity for the customer to work through their disconnects and reach a state of alignment before they proceed. Alpha sellers carefully position this workshop as a *resolution of conflicts* and not a demonstration of Alpha value. This is all about the customer, not Alpha. The goal here is to win each stakeholder's commitment to attending a workshop, to convince them that a collaborative session isn't just a good idea, it's urgently necessary.

There is an important aside related to this third stage—it stems from the old saying in sales "If you're gonna lose, lose early." When we asked the team at Alpha about what happens when customers fail to commit to a workshop, they told us it signals all they need to know about the customer's inclination to move forward. In this way, the workshops become an important verifier of customer intent to purchase and a smart way to qualify or disqualify the opportunity. Instead of gearing up for a slow-drip loss on a high-cost pursuit, Alpha is able to get out early or put the opportunity on hold.

Once stakeholders are committed to the workshop, the seller moves to the fourth step. This step is crucial. Here, Alpha sellers are encouraged to reach out and prepare each stakeholder for the workshop itself. They're looking to ensure that each stakeholder attends the workshop in the right frame of mind, with the right expectations for an open-minded discussion focusing on finding common ground despite differing views. In this step, the Alpha seller will attain explicit permission from everyone involved to lay out their different, even conflicting, views, in order to seek common agreement. That way, no stakeholder feels blindsided when their views are raised in the workshop.

This entire four-step conversation is very calculated. This is all about creating momentum, even enthusiasm, for a Collective Learning interaction among stakeholders. When the workshop happens, everyone knows why they are there, what is at stake, and how the event will play out. They have tapped into something the customer wants, and then they have very candidly shared with the customer how they are unlikely to achieve that goal unless they resolve their differences. These differences are typically unrecognized by customers, and they will get in the way. What Alpha is doing here is: *forward resolving the change management challenges* that the customer will invariably face.

As you think about this approach, ask yourself if this looks like the type of conversation that your sellers are having with their customers today. It probably doesn't. In fact, most of our average performers avoid conversations like this. "It's messy and tough to navigate. This isn't my problem, it's the customer's problem," they'll say. But *this is the crux of the seller's problem.* Conversely, when you discuss this approach with high-performing sellers, more often than not their reaction is "Yeah, that's similar to what I do too," as most stars have implicitly recognized the need to connect customer stakeholder to one another.

So what happens in the workshop itself? Alpha has learned some great lessons that apply to Collective Learning interaction (see figure 9.11). Some quick facts about the workshop itself: These are half-day workshops typically, though occasionally they will last a full day. On average, five or six customer stakeholders are involved (if there are more, Alpha warns that it can become difficult to manage the conversation and make progress). Alpha has at least two people facilitating the workshop—typically, the seller leads the session and a subject matter expert or a sales manager plays a support role. There is good reason to have more than one person run these. It's nearly impossible for one person to facilitate the session, take notes, monitor the customer's reaction, and track progress. Indeed, for a very significant deal or partnership, a senior Alpha leader may run point. But generally, their salespeople are tasked with running these types of sessions.

The typical flow of the workshop follows the prompting and bounding principles we highlighted in the last chapter. This is done through a three-step motion, which ensures that a broad but bounded range of issues are addressed and discussed. This motion involves prompting, exploring, and ultimately converging. Before any of this starts, however, one of the clear recommendations that the team at Alpha offered is to have the most senior leader from the customer organization set the expectation that conflict and disagreement are acceptable. This is important to ensure that attendees feel like they can offer their views in a safe environment and that disagreement is to be expected—even encouraged. This is a very different expectation than most senior leaders typically set.

FIG. 9.11. Alpha Co.'s Stakeholder Alignment Workshop Overview

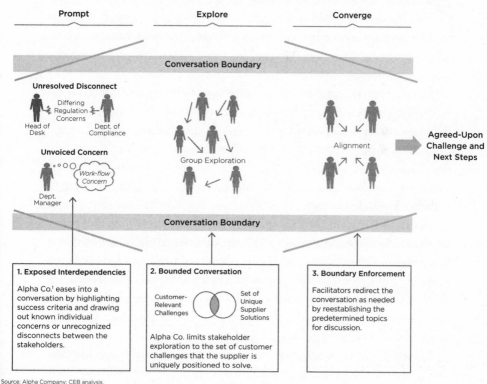

Source: Alpha Company; CEB analysis.

[1] Pseudonym.

After the senior leader sets the appropriate expectations, the workshop enters the initial prompting phase, and the first thing the Alpha seller does is lay out the set of goals that the participants articulated in advance. The idea here is to elicit stakeholders' views on those goals and ensure alignment first and foremost on a single goal. As the goal is solidified, the seller then prompts the participants to discuss their challenges and priorities in pursuing the goal. Alpha sellers draw out individual concerns regarding the pursuit of that goal, exposing any unspoken or underappreciated conflicts. For example, perhaps the head of the valuation desk and the compliance director disagree about the best way to handle new regulatory requirements. So the Alpha seller would encourage input and debate to help the two resolve the discrepancy. While the discrepancy may not get fully resolved (indeed, in many cases, Alpha leaves with some homework to provide the customer with a recommendation), the point is that the stakeholders leave more aligned and better understanding each other's perspective. This allows the customer to agree on something greater than the lowest common denominator. So this first motion of the workshop is all about expansion—putting conflicts on the table. The next motion encourages the customer to explore those perspectives in order to identify opportunities to think more collectively.

In this second motion, the principle of bounding the conversation starts to enter the picture. Alpha sellers are very careful to ensure the conversation remains bounded by the initially agreed-upon goal set at the beginning of the workshop, as well as keeping the customer focused on the challenges that Alpha can support. As the group slows their progress in the exploration stage, the Alpha seller then guides the group to begin to converge around next steps.

In this third motion of the workshop, it's important to note that this is not meant to drive the customer to "buy more from Alpha" (at least, not yet). Instead, in these early stages of the purchase process, Alpha is trying to win broad agreement that a specific challenge is worth addressing in the first place and that a specific course of action is the best way forward. The goal here is to get the stakeholders normed around a new perspective compared to when they entered the workshop.

Clearly, there are many different potential paths a workshop like this may go down, and for that reason Alpha takes planning very seriously. They have planning sessions, relying upon worksheets to help capture their ideal session plan, as well as a contingency plan should the stakeholders take the conversation in an unproductive direction.

FIG. 9.12. Alpha Co.'s Pre-Workshop Planning Samples

Disconnect Anticipation Worksheets

Potential Points of Disconnect to Surface	Strategy to Surface	Where Customers May Deviate from Objectives	Strategy to Mitigate	Who to "Reset" Conversation
Need for training staff on any new platform	Prompt stakeholders to discuss adoption rate of the current platform in use	Stakeholder proposes maintaining the status quo as a low-risk option	Provide examples of other customers who have experienced negative consequences of inaction; reinforce the potential value of an alternate course of action.	SME
Concern over additional source of data increasing variability in valuation model	Prompt stakeholders to discuss how current data sources affect bond valuation model	Stakeholder indicating that the real issue is lack of skilled talent	Educate them on the true root cause by illustrating how another customer tried resolving this challenge by hiring new talent but ultimately failed	Senior Manager

Source: Alpha Company¹; CEB analysis.
¹ Pseudonym.

One of their worksheets acts as the guide for the session (see figure 9.12). Here, Alpha sellers think through the sequence of disconnects to surface for the group—think of this as the *prompting* guide. This ensures that the critical conflicts get raised throughout the workshop in a calculated and controlled manner. The second worksheet acts as the *bounding* guide. It's the contingency plan should the workshop attendees take the conversation into territory where Alpha is less able to help. Importantly, the idea here is to note the areas, in advance, where customers are most likely to deviate from the workshop's central objectives and have a plan to get the conversation back on track. Of course, this plan is not comprehensive, but that is not necessary. By thinking through and planning for most of the areas where the conversation may derail, the seller has a good sense for what to watch out for and generally has some ideas on how to correct course. This planning ensures that bounding of the conversation occurs—but not just any bounding; this is making sure the conversation is managed to places where Alpha can help the customer.

Alpha also told us about some helpful practical tips for planning. When the stakes are particularly high, their teams will role-play the workshop. After all, for a conversation this nuanced, you would not want to be saying any of these things for the first time in front of the customer. Another tip is to be mindful that your customer does not consider these types of services often, yet you sell these types of solutions every day. As a result, your team is arguably in a better position than the customer to anticipate possible conflicts and disconnects. Use that knowledge and bring that experience to bear. It can help stakeholders recognize things they'd personally failed to consider.

Alpha realizes a significant payoff from this practice. Since the entire workshop is predicated on "front-loading" as many concerns as possible, they find that deals that progress through a workshop have much shorter cycle times and, therefore, lower cost of sale (see figure 9.13). That's because instead of stakeholder objections occurring throughout the purchase—without warning—Alpha works through these objections early. This allows the objections to be collectively handled by the customer stakeholders and also be dealt with in a far more controlled fashion.

FIG. 9.13. Workshop Impact on Sales Cycle

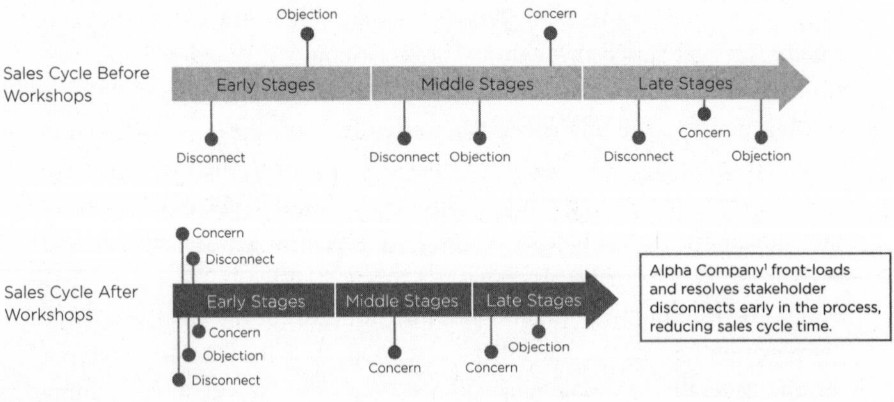

Source: Alpha Company; CEB analysis.
[1] Pseudonym.

As Alpha's head of sales strategy and operations explained to us, "Helping customers gain consensus in a managed environment reduces sales cycles and positively influences our commercial opportunity by identifying customer commitment early in the sale. Accordingly, we have also seen a related reduction in sales expense." Improved qualification, shortened deal cycle, and reduced cost of sale are all due to creating Collective Learning interactions.

CHAPTER TEN

SHIFTING TO A CHALLENGER COMMERCIAL MODEL:

Implications and Implementation Lessons

To win today, you need a Challenger *inside* the customer organization. That is the central premise of this entire book. It turns out, the far bigger story isn't about suppliers' struggle to *sell* solutions; it's the customer's struggle to *buy* them. Arming Mobilizers with world-class Commercial Insights and supporting their efforts to rally consensus *for that insight*, and inherently then for your solution, requires a new go-to-market strategy.

The implications of such a significant shift in commercial strategy are numerous. Sales and marketing must work together, bound by a new common language of disruption. Seller skills, something we covered in depth in *The Challenger Sale*, must be reconsidered. Marketing content must be atomized and lead customers to a clear narrative that discloses *what they've gotten wrong*. There are likely sales coverage and territory implications for many organizations, as more capable sales talent is aligned to prime growth markets. To say this shift happens overnight, or even within a single year, is not realistic. This shift takes time, it takes coordination among sales, marketing, and product teams, and above all else, it requires strong and continuous senior leadership support.

That being said, there are a handful of implications that our research has highlighted as particularly tricky to navigate. What follows is by no means an exhaustive summary of change management paces. Instead, these are a series of implications that many organizations "get wrong" from the outset. Left untreated, these implications can undermine your organization's efforts to make this shift entirely. We'd even argue that attempting to make this shift without properly accounting for these implications is downright dangerous. So what are these implications?

IMPLICATION #1—DEMAND GENERATION: Most marketing teams aim their demand generation efforts at developing leads that are "ready to buy." Traditional criteria of "BANT" (budget, authority, need, and timing) dominate demand generation efforts. True, while this approach delivers a ready-made customer to the sales team, it fails to do so on *your* terms. This approach does nothing to shape demand and create high-quality leads. We call that "mobilizing demand," and we'll explore it here.

IMPLICATION #2—MARKETING TALENT: Most marketing teams are disproportionately focusing their skill building in the digital space. While we agree that's necessary—to a degree—there are a set of skills related to the consensus purchase that are being overlooked. These skills are the ones that drive a marketer's ability to create and deploy Commercial Insight. These skills are more important than digital skills because *go-to-market strategy* rests upon them.

IMPLICATION #3—SOCIAL SELLING: While it's clear that sales reps ought to be using social media tools to engage customers, we observe many social selling efforts that amount to little more than broadcasting (or perhaps more accurately, noise). Yet there's a powerful role for social media in the Mobilizer purchase. It centers on challenging Mobilizer mental models in social media, where Mobilizers increasingly go to learn. We'll explore how marketing and sales need to collaborate to deliver social *teaching*, not social *selling*.

IMPLICATION #4—MANAGING BLOCKERS: Blockers can quickly demoralize your sales teams as they engage in consensus-building efforts. Sellers must confidently address Blockers and neutralize their influence for high-quality consensus to be forged. Far and away, the prevailing thought for managing Blockers, however, is to ignore them. Rarely do sales methods teach approaches for Blocker management. Even rarer are instances where sales managers ask who the Blocker for a deal might be and what should be done to minimize their influence. So it should come as no surprise that sellers do the same, hoping the Blocker goes away or relinquishes their objections. We'll explore several methods for actively managing Blockers in this section.

IMPLICATION #5—SALES PROCESS AND OPPORTUNITY PLANNING: The sales process has long centered on providing a clear frame of reference for seller actions, sequenced in order to maximize sales velocity, create a series of stages that dictate sales progress, as well as govern next steps with customers. Remember, much of the commoditization pressure suppliers face today isn't the result of customers' willingness to settle for "good enough," it's *their failure to agree on anything more.* Today's sales process must better reflect how sellers can enable the *right* customer purchase behaviors, rather than march a deal forward through the supplier's sales stages. Similarly, opportunity planning follows the same logic.

Let's dive into these implications.

IMPLICATION #1: DEMAND GENERATION

In this section, we'll take a look at how marketing needs to rethink its demand generation system as a result of the insights CEB research has uncovered about the consensus purchase and the role of Mobilizers. By "demand generation system," we mean the people, process, technology, and data that go into lead generation, lead scoring, and lead nurturing. Clearly, this is a large and growing area of investment for marketing organizations, and it's a key piece of achieving greater marketing accountability. The stakes for getting this right couldn't be higher.

Here's the risk, boiled down to its simplest: if marketers rely on a bad go-to-market strategy to drive what they put into their demand gen systems and how they tune those systems, out of the other side they're going to get "bad" demand (demand that leads to low-quality, commoditized deals, as described in chapter 1).

Unfortunately, as we've researched all that's been written about demand generation in the blogosphere, we believe much of the conventional wisdom is based on an outdated conception of B2B purchasing. Based on the consensus and Mobilizer dynamics uncovered by CEB research, we believe the conventional wisdom is taking marketers in the wrong direction.

If you pick up a white paper from most any marketing automation supplier or read a blog post from a content-marketing guru, the conventional wisdom goes something like this:

➤ It's an increasingly noisy world, so breaking through to B2B buyers is tough.

➤ To break through, you need GREAT content. Great content isn't about you, it's about the customer.

➤ In fact, it's not about the demo-firmographic customer (e.g., CIOs at companies larger than $100M in revenue), it's about buyer archetypes or personas, and their pain points and objectives. Businesses don't make purchase decisions, after all. People do.

➤ Personalize your content to these personas. Be present with your content in the spots they frequent. Say smart things, so they think of you first when they're ready to evaluate suppliers.

➤ Set up your marketing automation to drive engagement with these personas, to nurture them. Feed them content that further speaks to those persona pain points and objectives, and whatever they need at that stage of the purchase journey.

➤ Measure purchase readiness by level of engagement and signals of BANT (budget, authority, need, timing).

➤ Pass those nurtured leads to sales for closure.

➤ High fives all around. Open champagne to celebrate.

Sounds great, doesn't it? Much of this wisdom *feels* so right. How could this possibly be so wrong?

By now, having read the preceding chapters, chances are you can point to a few spots where this conventional wisdom might lead marketers astray. There are three main failure points:

1. Conventional wisdom **leads us down a path of creating ever more content, and content quantity quickly trumps content quality**. Coupled with the drive to generate leads and outbound marketing efforts, marketers risk turning off customers who are already bombarded with supplier messages.

2. Conventional wisdom is **mum on the absolute criticality of upending how customers think of their own business**, thereby changing the customer's direction when they are learning on their own. That means marketers will generate demand that commoditizes their own solution.

3. Conventional wisdom is about **better connecting individuals in a buying group to you as a supplier, not about connecting them to each other**. So marketers will fail to lay the groundwork for the early consensus that needs to happen about the problem and the solution (forget about the supplier!).

Let's unpack those, in turn.

The Failures of Demand Generation

The first failure point is very straightforward. Marketing creates all of that content in its drive to engage, engage, and engage! The thinking goes something like: "Be present, on a regular basis, for each of my major personas, in all the places they go for information. Since I've got all that content, go ahead and blast it out through e-mail campaigns and other outbound communications."

Deep down, marketers know what happens here, right? Customers get turned off, as the quality of content inexorably slips when marketing teams face the pressure of creating the quantity of content that conventional wisdom encourages. Customers inherently tune out suppliers. Or even worse, they bad-mouth suppliers in social forums or refuse to take visits from supplier sales reps.

FIG. 10.1. Customers' Response to Supplier E-mail and Other Communications

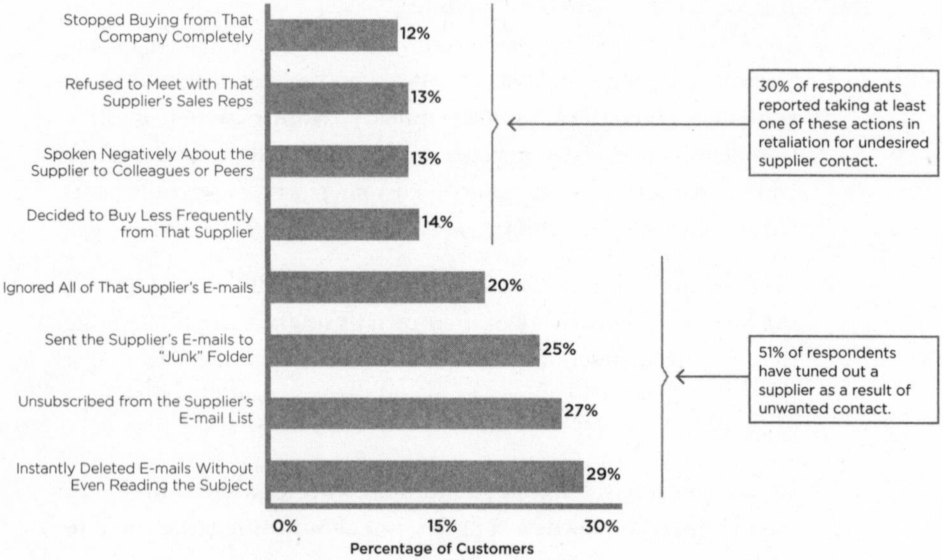

Response	Percentage
Stopped Buying from That Company Completely	12%
Refused to Meet with That Supplier's Sales Reps	13%
Spoken Negatively About the Supplier to Colleagues or Peers	13%
Decided to Buy Less Frequently from That Supplier	14%
Ignored All of That Supplier's E-mails	20%
Sent the Supplier's E-mails to "Junk" Folder	25%
Unsubscribed from the Supplier's E-mail List	27%
Instantly Deleted E-mails Without Even Reading the Subject	29%

30% of respondents reported taking at least one of these actions in retaliation for undesired supplier contact.

51% of respondents have tuned out a supplier as a result of unwanted contact.

Percentage of Customers

n = 545.
Source: CEB analysis.

We heard the following spooky anecdote from one prominent demand generation leader, who heads up regional marketing for a Fortune 100 tech provider. Over an eighteen-month period, fully 60 percent of this supplier's opt-in customer database has opted out. This supplier was no demand gen slouch, either. They have been a pioneer in demand gen. In a crazy, noisy world, something starts to give if we continue to operate by an outbound, engagement-obsessed demand gen model.

On the second failure path, the conventional wisdom approach will lead to smaller deals at lower margins by delivering what we call "established demand." Established demand is the exact opposite of high-quality deals that we discussed in chapter 1. Established demand comes from customers who learn on their own, norm around minimum thresholds, and then invite a supplier in to compete with two other suppliers in the price-based bake-off. It's the 1 of 3 Commoditization Problem in spades. These are customers who might have read some of your thought leadership as they went about the research process. But they *never had their perspective changed* about the way their business currently works. So their view of what they need to purchase is *established* by the time you engage this customer.

If you revisit the conventional wisdom above, nowhere are we explicitly confronting customer mental models. However, that's what suppliers need to do to knock the commoditization freight train off its tracks. That's the way to change the customer's direction when they wait until they are 57 percent of the way through their purchase experience before reaching out to a supplier. In the conventional wisdom above, all marketers are called on to do is create content that speaks to customer's known pain points, or that demonstrates how smart they are as a supplier. Recall from chapter 3, such approaches do not work, because they don't change the customer's direction.

The conventional wisdom *encourages* that freight train. BANT-based lead-scoring criteria detect customers who have budget, a clear need, and a set timeline for purchase. Leads that show all of these qualities garner more points in marketers' lead-scoring systems and get passed to sales. In effect, you will have passed sales a lead who has settled on buying criteria, "good enough" performance thresholds, and is ready to pit you against your two main competitors to extract the best price. What sales rep wants to waste time chasing that "opportunity"? This is one of the primary reasons our research shows that the highest-performing sellers deprioritize marketing qualified leads.

Let's touch on the third failure path, which has to do with consensus. The conventional wisdom would have marketers build stronger connections between their companies as suppliers and people in the customer organization. Marketing creates content that is tailored to personas, on the theory that if suppliers can engage those personas more deeply, they can boost customer willingness to buy from them and that will translate into more deals.

But by now we know that individual willingness to buy, in a consensus purchase, *means very little.* The conventional wisdom largely misses this consensus dynamic. Personalizing messaging and content to such an extreme leads to driving diverse buying group stakeholders further apart! Even in the best case, this approach will lead suppliers to get a collection of individual yeses, but we know that's insufficient too.

It's no wonder that, based on CEB demand gen benchmarking research, only 3 percent of marketing-qualified leads ever convert into deals—and that's on a good day! How many leads never have a chance to progress further because that stakeholder doesn't feel equipped to help drive consensus in her organization around the problem or solution, much less the supplier? Based on CEB research, that's likely happening to a large chunk of the 97 percent of marketing-qualified leads that don't ever progress.

Many of those prospect nibbles you get on your white papers, Webinars, infographics, and demand gen e-mails? Those are nibbles from solitary stakeholders, making their daily rounds of industry news sites or LinkedIn groups. They "engage" because you spoke to their pain points, but they don't come away feeling there's any chance to overcome inertia and create consensus in their large organizations. And that's where the lead dies.

Don't Generate Demand, Mobilize Demand

To fix these failure points, suppliers need a demand generation system that accounts for the critical role of Mobilizers in overcoming group dysfunction and stitching together consensus. It has to be one that accounts for the peak dysfunction of consensus happening 37 percent of the way through the purchase, long before sales reps meaningfully get involved.

Here's what that looks like, at a high level. We'll come back to unpack each one of these in more detail, but the themes will be familiar from what you've read so far.

1. Create Content Paths That Confront and Connect.

Recall from earlier chapters, we need Spark-Introduce-Confront content for several reasons. It attracts the Mobilizers we need. It forms the basis for Collective Learning at its most powerful and thereby helps drive consensus. The only way to change the customer's direction is by changing their mental models, not through thought leadership or content that is useful to target personas.

Moreover, if marketing has created those Spark-Introduce-Confront content paths for Mobilizers to encounter and get pulled into, they are mobilizing high-quality deals. Marketing is intercepting and changing the direction of Mobilizers before any kind of consensus on the nature of the problem or solution is starting to gel in the customer organization.

Through Spark-Introduce-Confront content, marketing has greatly improved the chances of shaping that early demand to favor the supplier's unique strengths.

2. Adjust Lead-Scoring Criteria to Reflect Confrontation and Connection.

Marketing should score leads in a way that gauges how much those leads have been "disrupted" by content and how well the supplier's content has connected buying group stakeholders within the same account *to one another.* To do that, marketing will need to tag content according to whether it (1) sparks, (2) introduces, or (3) confronts (see chapter 6 for more detail). That's well within the capabilities of content management and marketing automation technology today.

Marketing will also want to assign more points for engaging multiple customer stakeholders on the same idea. So as marketing automation systems detect individual stakeholders engaging with content that is more disruptive (either introducing or personalizing disruptive ideas), marketing should also program those systems to detect when that stakeholder has shared that content, or when peer stakeholders in the same customer organization have engaged with the same kinds of disruptive content. That kind of activity will indicate that groundwork is being laid for consensus in the customer organization. Marketing should assign more points to those leads.

Clever design of content, with sharing and targeted gating built in (as in the Skillsoft Mobilizer toolkit), enables marketing to do this kind of lead scoring. Think about how *powerful* it is to know if you've got a prospective customer who is engaging with content that reflects your Commercial Insight and who is sharing that with other stakeholders. That's the kind of demand our systems should prioritize!

See how *different* that is from typical BANT-based and engagement-based scoring criteria?

Instead of assigning points for purchase "readiness" (BANT), which tells you how close you are to capturing established demand that leads to commoditization, you are now gauging how *disrupted* the prospect is.

As well, instead of scoring leads on individual "engagement," where you assign progressively more points to content that requires more and more time from prospects, you are giving points for multistakeholder *consumption of counterintuitive content*, no matter what form it takes. Engagement for engagement's sake is meaningless. Marketers should focus on Spark-Introduce-Confront engagement that begins to rally the broader set of buying group stakeholders. Modest points for Spark content; more points for Introduce content; and lots of points for Confront content. Bonus points when any of this content is shared with or consumed by fellow account-level stakeholders.

3. Nurture Leads Explicitly for Commercial Insight and Collective Learning.

Now, when you have leads that aren't yet qualified to be passed to sales for closing, you'll know more precisely what to engage them with next. It will be driven by the likely state of mental disruption and stakeholder connectedness at a prospective account. For example, if you've generated a lead in which one stakeholder who has consumed Spark and Introduce content, and another lead from a stakeholder at the same account who has consumed only Spark content, you might want to put Confront content in front of the first stakeholder and invite her to bring in the other stakeholder. Maybe that's a pain calculator or a diagnostic that the stakeholders work on *together* so they can learn around a common rallying point. Or, perhaps this is where you'd suggest a Collective Learning workshop, bringing in the sales rep to help execute.

This is a very different approach to nurturing. The typical approach is oriented to feeding stakeholders with a predefined string of progressively more "engaging" content. Too often, "engaging" here means content that provides more detail and therefore takes more time to consume. "They engaged with our infographic? Let's send them a white paper!" or "They saw our white paper? Let's invite them to a Webinar!" Just because a piece of content provides more detail doesn't mean it's done anything at all to further overcome the customer's mental model or lay the groundwork for consensus.

Because nurturing paths are built on customers' most common purchase path—one where they learn on their own and commoditize suppliers—marketers may be unwittingly feeding them content that greases the tracks for the commoditization freight train!

How to Know If You're Mobilizing Demand

If you've taken these three steps to reorient your demand system so that it mobilizes demand, what should you expect? How will common demand metrics move?

In figure 10.2, we lay out the common demand indicators and how those are likely to change. This is important to understand, because you're going to want to set expectations in the broader commercial organization, and even the C-suite, on what will happen to demand as you reorient from generation to mobilization.

If you're doing this well, overall lead volume may initially dip because you should be producing less content than you're putting into the marketplace. However, that new content will begin to take on a life of its own as it is more likely to get shared and picked up in earned media. Based on our experience working with commercial teams here, this can take upwards of twelve to eighteen months, but you'll see lead volume increase.

More important, lead quality will improve, provided you've redefined lead quality to reflect emerging demand and not established demand. That's because you've engineered content to attract Mobilizers early on, when suppliers still have a chance to shape how the customer defines the problem and nature of the solution.

Now, over time, as your improved content finds its way through earned and shared channels into a broader part of the marketplace, you may find that you get inbound inquiries that don't qualify as leads. You can catch the attention of a variety of marketplace actors and industry players—from industry associations, to sole proprietors of small businesses, to academics. *Inquiries* will increase because these players want to learn more about what was under that surprising content. But those should not be interpreted as poor leads or included in any kind of lead dashboard. The key metric to pay attention to here is therefore *absolute* volume of *quality* leads.

Shifting from a generating demand to a mobilizing demand approach should also increase sales-generated leads. Marketing should be equipping sales with counterintuitive social sound bites to help reps engage customers early in their passive learning process, on LinkedIn and other social communities (see the implication on social selling later in this chapter). Because Spark-Introduce-Confront content is more likely to catch attention and get shared, it should boost sales reps' ability to source leads through their own social networks.

FIG. 10.2. Anticipated Metric Movement When Shifting
from Demand Generation to Demand Mobilization

Demand Gen Metric	Metric Shift	Explanation
Lead volume	⬅➡ ⬇ initially; ⬆ ultimately	Shift away from content quantity toward quality initially could reduce lead volume until earned media effect from higher-quality, provocative content kicks in twelve to eighteen months.
Lead quality	⬆⬆	Lead quality should increase dramatically, assuming lead-scoring system is updated to reflect customer exposure and adoption of disruptive ideas.
Sales-generated leads	⬆	With marketing-equipping sales to engage with customers in the prefunnel passive learning stage, sales-generated leads should increase.
Win rate	⬆⬆	Because disruptive marketing resets customer mental models to favor the supplier's buying criteria, win rate should increase significantly.
Sales cycle time	⬅➡	On the one hand, sales should be engaging customers earlier, which could lead to cycle time increasing, on top of which disruption can take some time to process. On the other hand, disruptive content done well can increase buying momentum. Overall, the result is probably flat sales cycle time.
Deal profitability	⬆⬆	Disruptive marketing should create less pricing pressure since competition happens on suppliers' differentiated buying criteria.

Source: CEB analysis.

Win rate and deal profitability should also increase. You should be able to get ahead of the RFP and influence not just buying criteria, but the minimum thresholds of performance for those criteria. That translates to higher win rate, larger deal size, and/or larger margins. Based on CEB research and our members' experiences, 15 to 20 percent price premiums are not unusual for demand that is mobilized and carried through to the sales interaction. It's the same effect that John Golitz, the Xerox account executive, described back in chapter 5 in using the "color drives student performance" insight. *"It's as if the door closes. I'm on the inside, and everyone else is on the outside."*

So far, so good. Higher volume of quality leads (after an initial downtick). Larger deals. Better margins. Higher close rates. But what about sales cycle time?

There are multiple forces driving cycle times in different directions here. It's very likely that prospective customers will encounter that Spark-Introduce-Confront content earlier in their purchase journey. They may encounter content in a passive learning stage, perhaps in earned media, *before* they even begin the journey. That can, in a way, start the purchase "clock" early, if you measure cycle time from the first moment that you have a "lead" through to deal close. All else equal, that might *extend* sales cycle time.

On the flip side, there are also forces shortening sales cycle time. By engaging Mobilizers early, and equipping them with content and tools that they use to drive consensus in the buying group and surface stakeholder objections *early*, you can more effectively build deal momentum much like Alpha Company accomplished in its Collective Learning workshops (from Chapter 9). That will enable those buying groups to agree on *more* (larger problems and more valuable solutions) and more *quickly* than if you aren't connecting them early to overcome group dysfunction.

Soft Indicators of Success

If you step back to look at the big picture on KPIs, you'll see that motivating this shift in content and demand generation strategy takes some courage. You're likely to face short-term pressure on lead quality and cycle time as you give the marketplace a chance to digest content. It has to work its way through sharing channels. It has to get noticed and picked up in earned media and by influencers. Mobilizers have to encounter that content, share it with fellow stakeholders, and rally around it.

As we've talked to CEB members who have been on this demand mobilization journey, they shared with us the "confidence-giving" softer indicators that let you know you're on the right track, especially in the face of some dashboard KPIs that may move (temporarily) in the "wrong" direction. Figure 10.3 arrays these examples around a simplified demand funnel.

In the "prefunnel" stage, you'll know you're on the right track if you experience these kinds of things:

➤ **PROPRIETARY TERM ADOPTION:** You'll begin to see terms that you've coined get used in social media, or maybe even adopted by the broader marketplace (see the Cisco example from chapter 9).

➤ **THIRD-PARTY REFERENCES:** Earned media outlets, notable bloggers, and other influencers will start to reference your Commercial Insight. They love surprising or counterintuitive information, after all.

FIG. 10.3. "Soft" Indicators That Demand Mobilization Is Working

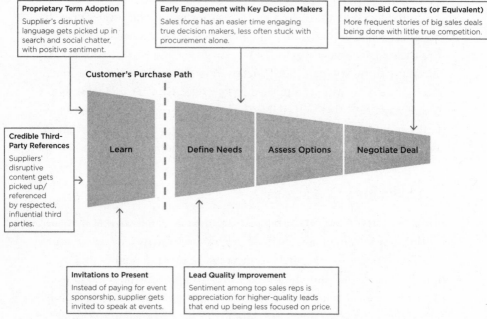

Source: CEB analysis.

> ➤ **INVITATIONS TO PRESENT YOUR INSIGHTS:** Rather than having to pay for event sponsorships, you'll start to get invited to present on your Commercial Insight. That's because your content is less likely to be about you as a supplier and more about the surprising things going on in your *customers'* businesses.

If you experience any of these kinds of events, you'll know you're on the right track. Likewise, you should start to see the following kinds of soft indicators in the demand funnel itself:

> ➤ **EARLY ENGAGEMENT WITH (NEW) KEY DECISION MAKERS:** Your content is winning early sales force engagement with decision makers, ones that you hadn't engaged before. Recall from chapters 5 and 6 how Xerox was able to engage with a new set of more senior decision makers outside of IT.

➤ **POSITIVE SALES FORCE SENTIMENT ON LEAD QUALITY:** You'll hear instances of very positive feedback from the sales force on the *different-in-kind* discussions that they are able to have with marketing-sourced leads, who are primed by your content to learn more about your Commercial Insight and how it applies to their business.

➤ **INSTANCES OF GETTING AHEAD OF THE RFP/NO-BID CONTRACTS:** You'll hear examples from your sales force of content helping to get ahead of the RFP, or spark no-bid contract situations. Recall from chapter 9 how Skillsoft's Mobilizer toolkit is enabling this.

When you experience these kinds of events, celebrate them! Share credit liberally with your team and your sales colleagues (if you've done this right, they were your copilots all along in designing a demand mobilization system). Above all, take courage to fight through the tough parts of the journey. Companies who have moved in this direction—like Xerox, SMART, Skillsoft, and others—tell us the prize is worth the fight.

IMPLICATION #2: MARKETING TALENT

The chief talent question marketing leaders should be interested in is "Have I got the right marketer talent to thrive in the world of the consensus purchase?" CEB has studied this question quantitatively, with special focus on marketers' abilities to generate and deploy Commercial Insight. After all, Commercial Insight is the key to engaging Mobilizers early. If you can get that right, you'll have set your commercial organization up for success against the consensus dynamic.

Here's the key takeaway: Commercial Insight skills and knowledge are in short supply. Moreover, it takes a special *blend* of those skills and knowledge, put into the right *operating environment*, to successfully build and deploy Commercial Insight. In other words, this can't be left to chance or to heroism on the marketing team. Marketing leaders need to step in to engineer the right kinds of working teams, and create a particular kind of environment that nurtures Commercial Insight creation.

Now, here are the details. To study this, we conducted survey-based quantitative research. We surveyed over 580 marketers in different roles and at different levels from twenty-nine different B2B suppliers around the world. In these surveys, we had marketers self-assess their performance across a wide range of attributes—skills, attitudes, knowledge, experience, and their work environment. We then had the heads of marketing from each of those companies assess each of their survey participants on their ability across four skills we consider crucial to Commercial Insight creation. Finally, we then used statistical analysis to determine, of all the things you could do well as a marketer, what matters most in building and deploying Commercial Insight.

Here's what we found.

First, let's look at the four skills we used as a proxy for Commercial Insight ability. These are the four skills that heads of marketing scored each of their people on, each represented by a bar in figure 10.4.

FIG. 10.4. Individual Marketer Ratings (by Managers) on Commercial Insight Effectiveness

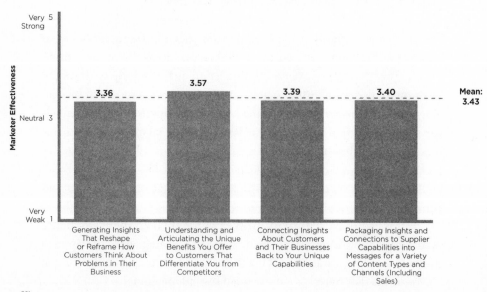

n = 581.
Source: CEB 2012 Commercial Insight Assessment.

We looked at marketers' ability to:

1. *Generate* insight that reshapes how customers think about their business.

2. *Understand* and *articulate* their company's differentiated capabilities and benefits.

3. *Connect* those insights about customers *back* to the supplier's unique capabilities.

4. *Package* all of that in compelling *messages* across a variety of content types, including sales collateral and other sales support.

These are the Commercial Insight indicators, or outcomes, we studied. In a moment, we'll take a look at the *drivers* of these indicators. But let's pause on these indicators for a moment. The first observation is: on a scale of 1 to 5, marketers are pretty average at these Commercial Insight indicators, as judged by their marketing leaders.

Not great, not horrible, just sort of "neutral." There's clearly room to run on improving marketers' performance on the skills that matter most for Commercial Insight. One thing worth noting—when we conducted the survey, we specifically asked participating heads of marketing to select *only* those members of their team who play a role in the creation of content and messaging. So this is an X-ray of the messaging and content engine itself.

When you look at the distribution of marketer performance underneath these bars, you'll find that only one out of four marketers averages above a four. Major deals arise from understanding the customer's business *better* than they understand it themselves (at least where your capabilities intersect the customer business). This is a high bar we're talking about here. When we think about the level of skill we need, it's troubling to see how few marketers excel at the skills required to counter customer's thinking.

It raises an interesting challenge for marketing leaders: "How do I get more of my team above that threshold? Can I shift them there or will I need to hire new people altogether?"

To answer that question, we need to better understand the drivers of our four Commercial Insight indicators. We included a wide variety of potential

FIG. 10.5. Drivers of Commercial Insight Effectiveness

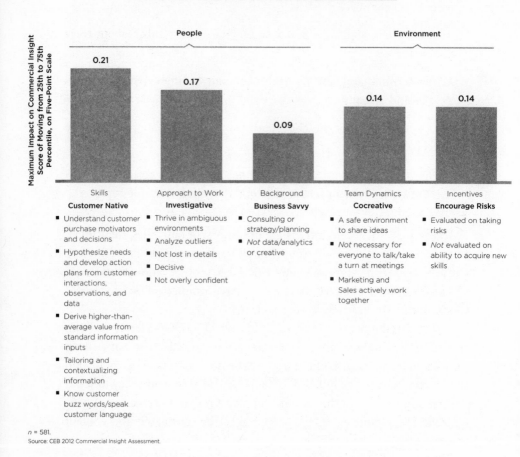

n = 581.
Source: CEB 2012 Commercial Insight Assessment.

drivers in our survey. What you see on the chart above are the factors that mattered most in driving marketers' Commercial Insight indicators.

They bundle into five statistically significant drivers—think of these as categories of attributes that naturally move together and drive those four Commercial Insight indicators mentioned above.

In case you're wondering about the scores, the number above each bar represents the increase in score on a five-point scale that we'd expect to see if we improved performance on that bar from *below* average to *above* average.

So, for example, that first bar, labeled "Customer Native," measures

0.21. That means improving from bottom-quartile to top-quartile performance on "Customer Native" attributes would increase a marketer's Commercial Insight performance on a five-point scale by 0.21 points.

Now, you're probably wondering, is 0.21 points a lot? Seems kind of small! But when you add all these bars together—which represents improvement on all these skills—you see a *very* dramatic impact on overall Commercial Insight performance. If you were to realize the full benefit of each of these bars combined, that would mean moving a marketer from *average* level of Commercial Insight performance to the top *15 percent*! That's a big deal, because it means moving into the zone of creating and deploying Commercial Insight that can lead to a quantum jump in commercial results.

Let's unpack what's in each of these bars. To understand what's underneath these findings, we have to transport ourselves into the actual meetings where these teams are trying to generate Commercial Insight in the first place.

They're looking for potential *hidden connections* in the customer's business that customers themselves fail to appreciate. They're hunting for *clues* to find these connections.

They're mapping customer mental models, depicting how that customer's business works and how they make money. They're looking for a place in that model where they can tell customers they're wrong. Then, they're finding creative ways to spark, introduce, and confront customers with those messages at arm's length.

That's not easy, so what does it take? Well, first things first, let's unpack the first driver, "Customer Native." What this driver captures is a world-class marketer's ability to *truly* understand the customer—their motivations, their decisions, how they speak, what they're thinking.

For example, within this driver you'll find activities like "hypothesize needs." The best Commercial Insight marketers can *anticipate* customer needs before the customers themselves. This goes way beyond *asking* customers what they need, or staring at backward-looking data about what customers have ordered. *This demands a knowledge of customers that lets you hypothesize what they don't yet even realize they need.*

That's the *key* to teaching—it's all about finding unrecognized customer needs.

That second-biggest driver is labeled "Investigative." This is more about the *posture* and *traits* of the folks you want on the Commercial Insight team. Think of this as a *detective* type of posture. Always asking "why." Sorting through mountains of ambiguous information. Testing assumptions. These marketers are looking for clues in their customer's business environment, in their own data about customers, in current market trends, and especially in unusual customer stories that might normally be dismissed. All with the aim of connecting information in new ways to show customers how their mental models are off base.

Also note the "not overly confident" subdriver under the Investigative heading. There's a type of marketer out there who runs *against* this investigative posture that you definitely do *not* want on your Commercial Insight team. That's the overconfident marketer who assumes he *already knows* what the customer needs and rationalizes away any evidence to the contrary.

The third-biggest driver is labeled "Business Savvy." This one is really interesting. Not just for what it *is*, but also for what it's *not*. It turns out, marketers with a consulting or strategic planning background perform well on our four Commercial Insight indicators, and people with a deep background in data/analytics or creative design don't.

Why? Well, the business savvy bring two things to the table. First, these folks are *already* good at building and tearing down mental models. That's essentially what consulting or strategic planning has trained them to do—work through complex and ambiguous problems. They *live* for that!

Second, they bring with them an extensive mental library of business and economic frameworks—how money is made and how business models work in a whole range of industries and situations. That's a critical ingredient for landing on Commercial Insight—finding the hidden connections that aren't just hidden but *economically meaningful*. Think about DENTSPLY and the modeling of absenteeism cost on the profitability of the dentist's practice. Those are the first three sets of drivers. They all fit under a "People" heading, because they're more about the attributes of the individual people who are building and deploying Commercial Insight. It's a special blend of skills, background, and knowledge.

The data tells us it's quite likely that you wouldn't find this blend in any single person. That's borne out in our experience working with organizations on Commercial Insight too. Building and deploying Commercial Insight is more of a *team sport*. Commercial leaders will probably have to look beyond marketing—to product, strategy, sales, insights, maybe even R&D—to find the right people mix here.

The crucial implication is: staffing for Commercial Insight can't be left to chance. It's not to be taken on by a casual mix of frontline marketers or volunteers. Commercial leaders need to deliberately engineer the right blend of people. Now, commercial leaders also need to set the right operating conditions for these people to work in. That's what the last two drivers speak to and why we've put them under an "Environment" heading.

The first one of these two drivers is "Cocreative Teams." Coming up with Commercial Insight is an organic, iterative, synthetic exercise. As a result, commercial leaders have to foster an environment where sharing and building on one another's ideas is not just encouraged but expected. Remember, Commercial Insight by definition is disruptive. Some of the *best* ideas are going to seem pretty far-fetched at first glance. They'll run *counter* to how customers currently view their world.

Under this driver, we observed that the best-performing teams have marketing and sales working together on this, collaborating to build on each other's experience and synthesize different ideas, and willing to accept when their ideas may not win out. Also under this Cocreative Teams driver, we observed an interesting dynamic about the high-performing teams *not* feeling like it was necessary to take turns to talk. We think this one showed up because commercial organizations often bring together teams that are *too large* to generate Commercial Insight. Four to five people is the ideal size. If you've got seven, eight, or more, chances are pretty good you've already made some sacrifices on the people skills and traits we've discussed. Then, whenever you get groups that large, the team feels compelled to include everyone's thinking, and that dilutes your keen insights.

It's the one-pizza rule: if you have to order two pizzas to feed the team for late-night work sessions, the team is too big.

The second of the Environment drivers is "Encourage Risks." By now, this one should come as no surprise. Generating Commercial Insight is fundamentally a creative task, and if you don't encourage risk taking, you're not going to get the lateral thinking and outlier ideas that end up being the richest kernels of Commercial Insight.

If you are to get breakthrough Commercial Insight, this is the kind of people mix and environment you need to engineer as marketing leaders. This responsibility extends to sales and product leaders as well, given the mix of talent that is required to generate Commercial Insight.

IMPLICATION #3: SOCIAL SELLING

In chapter 5, we focused on using content to challenge Mobilizers' mental models early. It's absolutely critical for marketing to do this, but that doesn't mean commercial organizations should give up on getting sales reps to engage with Mobilizers to begin "breaking down the A" as early as possible. The rise of social media gives occasion for marketing and sales to work together to create these early teaching opportunities. It looks very different from the typical "broadcast" approach we see commercial organizations taking to do social selling.

One of the key questions that our research highlighting that customers are 57 percent of the way through a purchase surfaced is: "If customers are delaying contact with supplier sales reps, how is it that some sales reps are still managing to 'get in early'?" What are they doing differently? So we studied sales rep behavior to find out.

That question led us to study sales rep behavior on engaging customers early—bringing both quantitative and qualitative research methods to bear—and unearthed an important set of insights.

We fielded a survey to over 1,000 sales reps from twenty-three B2B companies across all kinds of industries. We tested over ninety sales rep attributes and behaviors, all related to "getting in early" with customers. Then we conducted over 100 structured interviews with sales reps, managers, and leaders, all with an eye to understanding what separates high performers from average performers when it comes to getting in early.

The single most powerful behavior separating high performers from core performers is *using social media as a critical channel to engage customers and generate leads.*

What exactly does it mean to use social media in the context of getting in early? Well, when you unpack the data, it comes down to three things:

1. Connecting with potential customers

2. Using social networks like LinkedIn and Twitter to share points of view valuable to customers

3. Using social media for lead generation

FIG. 10.6. Drivers of Sales Rep Performance by Sales Activities for Engaging Customers Early

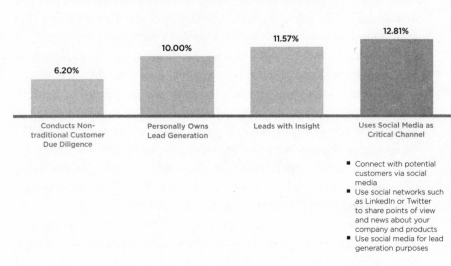

Change in Probability Going from 25th-Percentile to 75th-Percentile Performer

- Conducts Non-traditional Customer Due Diligence — 6.20%
- Personally Owns Lead Generation — 10.00%
- Leads with Insight — 11.57%
- Uses Social Media as Critical Channel — 12.81%

- Connect with potential customers via social media
- Use social networks such as LinkedIn or Twitter to share points of view and news about your company and products
- Use social media for lead generation purposes

n = 1,078.
Source: CEB analysis.

When we talked to a number of sales reps having huge success with this approach, what we found is this all adds up to *positioning oneself as a key influencer within social networks.*

To do that, we found the best reps work very hard to tap into a large social network, extending far beyond personal contacts and current customers. These reps are accessing the entire ecosystem of the marketplace that that rep sells into. So not just existing customers, but potential customers. Even people who might never be your customer but could potentially buy your product in another territory, through a different channel, or through another supplier altogether.

But that's just the beginning. Then there are channel partners, industry experts, market influencers, complementary suppliers, influencers from similar or adjacent industries—you name it. Basically, it's anyone and everyone who might be interested in engaging in a conversation around the broadest set of issues your products and services potentially touch.

So the best reps find the "watering holes" or those online communities where people in their industry gather and *learn*. In advanced cases, the very best reps will serve as *teaching connectors*—serving as a hub, bringing this group of people together in order to engage in a learning conversation around a common interest. Done well, sales reps who play this role as teaching connector are much more likely to attract Mobilizers into their orbit.

Now, there are clearly ways that rep use of social media can go wrong. The best reps who are involved in social media are very careful how they use it. The last thing star performers would do with this powerful network they've tapped into is use it to broadcast messages with no interaction or teaching—in other words, using it purely as an advertising channel. Yet we see far too much of social selling happening in exactly this way.

No one has any patience for posts like: "Just wanted to let you know our new XP9-100 is out next month! Preorder today!" We've all been on the receiving end of this kind of message on LinkedIn.

That's not what this channel is for. Rather, it's about actively engaging in a productive, interesting conversation. Ideally, conversation that *teaches*. It fits right into the Spark-Introduce-Confront model from chapter 6. Social watering holes are the ideal place to spark a target audience into exploring your ideas by sharing surprising data, insights, and provocative viewpoints. Because Commercial Insights are by definition not about you as a supplier but about customers, they are much less likely to be rejected on the grounds of being commercially slanted.

One star-performing sales rep we talked to in the health care space summed it up nicely. She told us, "You've got to weave yourself into the *knowledge fabric* where your customers learn. But you've got to *earn* that right. You've got to help the customer think differently than they would have otherwise."

Now, in some industries, there are more social watering holes and opportunities for our customers and ecosystem partners to learn and engage in conversations. There are some regulated spaces, like health care and financial services, where social media growth has been stunted. But we've been consistently surprised at how far and wide social watering holes are extending to some B2B categories where you'd never expect it. Chemistry? Check. Materials science? Yep. Auto dealership finance and insurance? Uh-huh.

We're seeing leading marketing and sales functions tag team to get this right. Suppliers like IBM, Cisco, National Instruments, and others are blazing the trail here. When it comes to social media, marketers complain that it's difficult to scale efforts there because social media is so time and labor intensive. Well, these organizations realize that, in sales, they have *multiple times* the people power that marketing can bring to bear.

We view this kind of social enablement as a critical part of the larger commercial strategy to teach Mobilizers and disrupt their mental models *early*, ideally when they are passively learning, but certainly before the 57 percent point when they are picking up the phone to talk to a sales rep. Teach where and when customers learn.

IMPLICATION #4: MANAGING BLOCKERS

There are times and situations where a purchase bogs down, where a stakeholder is so incredibly entrenched in their own views and won't budge. As we covered earlier in this book, we affectionately call these fine folks Blockers, though chances are good your sales teams use far more colorful language to describe them. Blockers readily derail consensus building and Collective Learning efforts, spoiling any chance of a new view emerging. When we've interviewed sellers on how to best engage a Blocker, a litany of hilarious responses usually ensued: "get 'em fired" or "football tickets" or "humiliate them" are among our favorites. *Perhaps* there is a time and place for any of those actions, but invariably the number one response we heard is "ignore 'em." For years, the conventional wisdom has been to avoid Blockers altogether. Like an ostrich burying its head in the sand, hoping they will somehow disappear. However, there is one problem with that strategy: Blockers don't go away or stay on the sidelines. They are present, either knowingly or unknowingly, in virtually every deal. Depending on their influence, Blockers have a powerful ability to stall and derail the most promising of deals. Fortunately, across the course of our research, we've identified a number of proven, proactive strategies to address and neutralize deal Blockers.

As a reminder, a Blocker is a customer stakeholder who tries to prevent a supplier from closing a deal, whether because they dislike the supplier, prefer a competing supplier, or want to maintain the status quo. Like the Mobilizer, Blockers don't fall into any pattern of seniority, buying role, or functional role. Unfortunately, they come in all shapes and sizes with different influencing levels. Making matters worse, the Blocker isn't necessarily even *known* to the supplier. They could be known, unknown, or even what we would call "stealth Blockers"—those who vocalize support to the salesperson but then turn around and torpedo the deal behind the scenes.

FIG. 10.7. Blocker Impact on High-Quality Deal Closure (indexed)

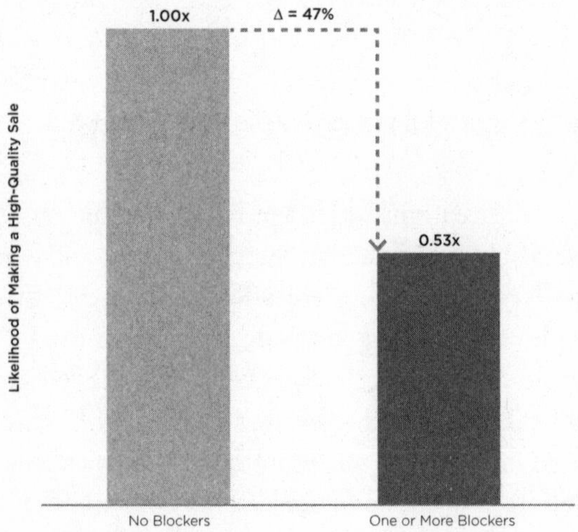

Source: CEB analysis.

With the inclusion of one or more Blockers in any given deal, a supplier's chances of making a high-quality sale decrease by 47 percent. As you well know, Blockers are present in virtually every deal. Therefore, logic would say that from the get-go for most deals, you have only a 53 percent chance of making a high-quality sale. Scary stuff.

As most sales managers will attest, salespeople rarely engage Blockers effectively. Most salespeople ignore the Blockers who are lying in wait to undermine their deals—hoping that they can rally enough support to overrule a Blocker's objections. We've observed the best sales managers quite literally force discussion of Blockers among their sales teams. These sales managers are taught to ask questions like "If I told you we were overlooking a Blocker to this deal, who would you guess it would be and why?" The wording alone is smart—the question doesn't allow the seller to say that there are no Blockers. They can't default to their natural tendency, in other words. Another powerful question used by managers is "What types of stakeholders typically block deals like this?"—a great question for prompting the seller to think about similar deals and where there might be common Blocker tendencies.

Blockers are tricky stakeholders and they will state objections that they *think* will align with other stakeholders' objections, as they don't want to be seen as explicitly rocking the boat. This makes it hard to uncover a Blocker's true concerns. Good managers will ask more straightforward questions like "Has the Blocker had any negative interactions with us in the past?"; but he or she will also layer in questions that dig at potential underlying concerns, like "How could this purchase make the Blocker's work more difficult?"

Finally, good sales managers will commit to a plan for managing the Blocker—the goal here is to address the salesperson's tendency to delay interactions with Blockers. "What is our strategy for dealing with the Blocker?" prompts action from the sales team.

OK, so how do you *manage* Blockers? The first question sellers should ask themselves is "Can the Blocker be persuaded by the supporters in the stakeholder group?" In other words, can social pressure be applied to *neutralize* the Blocker? Can they be influenced by Mobilizers and other supporters within the stakeholder group? If the answer is yes, you want to apply social pressure through Collective Learning. As we discussed earlier in this book, Collective Learning involves the exploration of objections, concerns, and uncertainties among stakeholders, surfacing disconnects and competing viewpoints—each of these actions is designed to get everyone on the same page, including the Blocker. You're hoping to turn the Blocker into a supporter or at the very least mitigate or decrease their influence on the collective group.

In addition to creating a Collective Learning interaction, these social pressures can be used to counteract a Blocker:

> ➤ Conducting a workshop or other event where stakeholders can exchange views with the Blocker

> ➤ Identifying influencers that the Blocker respects and having your Mobilizer broker an interaction

➤ Arming your Mobilizer or other influencers with information to convince the Blocker to support the deal

➤ Encouraging influencers to share why others are supporting the deal

In our research, we found that Collective Learning decreases likelihood of encountering a Blocker by 20 percent. Further, there is a 35 percent increase in the likelihood of making a high-quality sale when Collective Learning occurs within a stakeholder group that has a Blocker (see figure 10.8). That's an extremely significant jump and underscores the importance of Collective Learning. The reason we try this tactic first is that it is not only hugely effective, but it is also the lowest risk of all the tactics. Social pressure doesn't carry terribly high stakes. Sure, the Blocker might get annoyed if colleagues want them to stand down, but that's about the worst outcome.

FIG. 10.8. Impact of Collective Learning on Blocker Influence

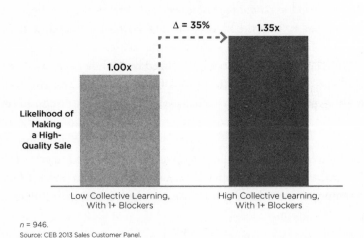

n = 946.
Source: CEB 2013 Sales Customer Panel.

What explains this impact? Engaging in Collective Learning creates a larger proportion of "supporters" in the stakeholder group, reducing the proportion of both Neutrals and Blockers, in turn reducing the impact of the remaining Blockers (see figure 10.9).

FIG. 10.9. Impact of Collective Learning on Stakeholder Preference

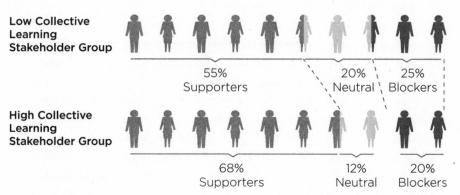

Low Collective
Learning
Stakeholder Group

55%
Supporters

20%
Neutral

25%
Blockers

High Collective
Learning
Stakeholder Group

68%
Supporters

12%
Neutral

20%
Blockers

n = 946.
Source: CEB 2013 Sales Customer Panel.

Blockers may still exist despite high Collective Learning. So if applying social pressure through Collective Learning does not turn or minimize the influence of the Blocker, what do we do next?

The second question that the seller should ask themselves is "Does the Blocker seem reasonable and approachable?" If yes, then the seller should attempt to communicate through tailored dialogue to persuade the Blocker to allow the deal to move forward. Note that we are *not yet* at the stage where we want to be making concessions—we will get to that in a moment. Different motivating factors drive different types of Blocker behaviors. Some want to avoid change, some want the competition to win the business, and some simply want to see you lose the business.

One of the Blocker types—the "Pro–Status Quo" Blocker—is best engaged by listening to and empathizing with their concerns regarding change. First, show that you understand their concerns, but also later reinforce the risks of not changing, creating urgency for the offering. You can also offer to connect them to previous or existing customers who had similar concerns. For the "Pro-competitor" Blocker type, you should engage them in discussing the main motivation for making a purchase in general, agnostic of supplier. Then explain how you can help them achieve their goals in a way that other suppliers cannot. For the "Anti-supplier" Blocker type, you should engage by asking them to lay out their honest thoughts about you as a supplier, no matter how brutal. Acknowledge the truth in their perspective, and share how you are committed to addressing and making up for your past mistakes.

Take note that direct engagement tactics carry greater risk. The chances of the Blocker taking a personal disliking toward you increase, and that's baggage no one wants to carry within a deal. But if social pressure failed to work, you may need to resort to this tactic.

So what do you do if your Blockers are not reasonable or approachable, or if your efforts to communicate fall short? At this point, it's now time to think about making a concession. The third question that the seller should ask as part of the progression is "Does the Blocker have concerns about a specific aspect of the offering?" If the answer is yes, consider making a targeted concession. Alter the deal to make it appealing but not entirely commercially damaging to your organization. Now, concessions are tricky and by no means does this approach provide an exhaustive set of guidance for concessions or negotiation, but we can provide some general guidelines to follow when considering and developing concessions:

➤ First, thoroughly plan ahead and identify negotiable and nonnegotiable aspects of the deal. This knowledge is crucial for how you formulate your concession strategy.

➤ Second, take those negotiable aspects and hypothesize which aspects the Blocker will react positively to and be more inclined to accept.

➤ Third, when developing the concession, you obviously want to concede as little as possible for your own benefit, but furthermore want to ensure that you do not endanger your support from other stakeholders because of a now watered-down or no longer worthwhile solution.

➤ Fourth, to the point above, you need to get explicit support for this new vision of the deal from our set of supportive stakeholders.

➤ Fifth, practicing good negotiating hygiene, secure a guarantee from the Blocker and other supporters that the deal will go through based on the new vision, preventing further concessions and further delays. You want to ensure that all the work that went in the concession leads to results; otherwise you have wasted time and money.

Again, you've stepped up the level of risk by altering the deal. It's possible that collateral damage is now done, and chances are good that you've had to remove something (versus making the deal bigger). Active trade-offs are now being made, and that's definitely more risky for your commercial outcomes.

If you get to the point where making a concession does not work, you then need to go to the final and last option, *escalate*. The question your sellers should ask themselves at this point is "Do senior leaders at the customer organization have an interest in this deal closing?" If yes, you want to leverage someone more senior than the Blocker to help grease the wheels and encourage the Blocker to allow the deal to push forward. This is clearly the riskiest option and carries significant political ramifications for the Blocker (it may potentially endanger their job or career path). Going over top of the Blocker and escalating is certainly a "last-resort" type of option. To that end, let's take a look at some of the action steps and guidelines for the "escalation strategy":

- ➤ First, contact one of the Blocker's leaders and explain the situation. But pick carefully. You'll want to pick a leader who you think can professionally manage the situation and would be receptive to escalation—someone who can be trusted with mitigating the potential awkwardness of the situation.

- ➤ Second, ensure the leader understands the Blocker's motivations. Don't just approach them and say "Johnny is not playing nice." You want to avoid making this an attack on the Blocker. Provide the leader with a balanced perspective, so they can judge and take action accordingly and professionally.

- ➤ Third—and this is contingent on Steps 1 and 2 above—if the Blocker continues to stall the deal, you can ask the leader to overrule the Blocker's influence. Now, this has the greatest potential for some "scorched earth," and we would certainly view this as a last-resort tactic. You obviously have to take into account the Blocker's influence for future deals and account growth.

In parallel with all of the steps above, it is paramount that you keep our supporters at the customer organization informed and in the loop to avoid concern around the deal but also to continue the collective pressure that they might be able to exert on the Blocker, either explicitly or implicitly.

What happens if this strategy fails? At this point you then have to seriously consider whether you want to actively pursue this opportunity any longer. Is it worth it? Does it still make business sense? That decision is going to depend on the nuances of your business and the type of deal. But in general, our view is that if a deal gets to this point, it's best to put it on the back burner, passively pursue, and focus elsewhere.

Just to recap, remember:

➤ Blockers cannot and should not be ignored, their impact is immense, and as we state here: Blockers reduce the likelihood of making a high-quality deal by 47 percent.

➤ Managers play a critical role—they can help lessen the likelihood of a Blocker obstructing a deal by forcing sellers to identify Blockers and conceive engagement strategies early on.

➤ You can minimize a Blocker's impact and influence, but you can't necessarily eliminate it altogether. Collective Learning minimizes a Blocker's impact, but more aggressive engagement strategies may still be needed.

The importance of Collective Learning can't be understated. In today's consensus-driven purchase, where divergent views and dysfunction reign supreme, and deals get compressed and compressed to the lowest common denominator, it's the means by which we can help our Mobilizers forge a purchase decision. It brings diverse stakeholders, including Blockers and procurement, together to make a meaningful decision.

IMPLICATION #5: SALES PROCESS AND OPPORTUNITY PLANNING

Buying Made Easy

The challenges of today's customer purchase experience have been highlighted throughout this book. If there is one takeaway you should have from all the research and best practices shared to this point, it's this: commercial organizations need to place far greater emphasis on supporting the customer's purchase process. One of our all-time classic best practices comes from an organization that has done just that and shifted their entire *sales* process to more of a *purchase enablement* process. The company is ADP, the global payroll and human capital management firm, and this is their "Buying Made Easy" Purchase Process (figure 10.10).

At first glance, ADP's approach might look a lot like your run-of-the-mill sales process. On closer examination, however, you'll realize this is very different. The first thing you'll notice is that ADP doesn't have a sales process at all. This is actually a very structured approach to moving deals through a customer's buying process. This is precisely why ADP refers to this approach as "Buying Made Easy." This entire approach is designed to support the customer through a series of *customer outcomes* throughout a typical purchase experience.

How most companies design a sales process, of course, is by mapping out the activities known to drive commercial success. Sellers are then expected to execute those activities as effectively (and efficiently) as possible. The idea being that if sellers do *these* things, in *this* order, the chances of the customer purchasing are maximized.

But what ADP is doing is different. From their perspective, the real question isn't "How do we help our reps better *sell*?" but rather, "How can our sales teams help our customer better *buy*?"

This process is predicated upon the major decision stages that nearly any customer will undergo, including:

1. Recognizing a need—This is where the customer initially determines a reason to explore a potential purchase, whether based upon an opportunity, a risk, or a problem. In this stage, the customer will frequently make excuses to maintain the status quo. The customer may preliminarily research suppliers and even conduct an initial supplier outreach.

2. Exploring options—Here, suppliers start to get initially compared. More extensive supplier research happens, including differing capabilities and pricing. Customers often request more detailed information at this stage.

3. Defining purchase criteria—Here, customers evaluate the efficacy of their current business processes, assessing precise areas where

improved performance is necessary, along with minimum thresholds for that performance. Customers undergo some form of risk/reward analysis. Buying groups convene and stakeholders are tapped to help evaluate the purchase. Purchase criteria are initially proposed.

4. Evaluating options—Here, customers present a clear business case to senior leadership. Solution providers are formally evaluated and a short list of preferred suppliers is created.

5. Validating options and selecting a favored supplier—Supplier return on investment is evaluated. Formal requirements are finalized. Funding is secured and a go/no-go decision is made.

6. Negotiating the purchase—Procurement is formally involved as terms are negotiated. A final round of executive sign-off occurs, legal reviews occur, and finally the contract is signed.

7. Implementing the solution—A project team is assigned. Old processes are retired and new processes are implemented.

8. Evaluating impact—Various service levels and other agreed-upon performance standards are evaluated relative to expectation.

This is the buying process that forms the basis of ADP's approach. The natural reaction that most companies have when they see this buying process defined is "interesting idea, but I couldn't do something similar because my customers buy in so many different ways . . ." The conventional thought is there are as many buying processes as there are customers. But take a look at that customer buying process again. In talking to ADP and in working with companies around the world to implement this best practice, what we've found is this isn't nearly as difficult as you might think. True, customers are all different, but the motion of buying is not nearly as different as you might initially think. (If you're not sure, go ask your customers and best sellers and see how truly different each purchase experience is. What you'll likely find is that you can abstract customer purchase experiences to a very scalable and valuable level just as ADP has done.) Indeed, many CEB member organizations, with our help, have adapted some variant of ADP's model with only some minor tweaks.

While very few organizations truly have implemented a customer purchase process to help manage their sales efforts, it would be unfair to lay claim to just *that* aspect of the ADP story as best practice. Increasingly, many organizations are shifting toward a customer buying process to manage sales efforts. The reason is simple: it encourages sellers to account for the dynamics happening inside the customer business, be more sensitive to those dynamics, and increase sales productivity by selling the way customers buy.

But where the ADP best practice starts to differentiate itself is in the details of how sellers are encouraged to *support* customers through the sale. ADP has created a series of actions that salespeople can take to support the customer purchase—these are referred to as the "Seller Leads" column within their process overview (figure 10.10). The Seller Leads actions capture the activities a rep can do to move the deal forward. For each stage of the customer buying process, ADP has also included a series of expected customer actions, which are referred to as "Buyer Signals." The Buyer Signals column notes a series of *customer verifiers* that indicate the customer is committed to and ready for the next stage in their purchase. This is a dance between the seller and customer, where the seller leads and customer responds, seller leads, customer responds. If the customer, for whatever reason, fails to respond, the seller immediately takes stock of what is happening inside the customer's purchase process. Perhaps new stakeholders have entered the picture. Perhaps the competition is encroaching on the deal. Or maybe a new debate is happening about the purchase criteria or required performance thresholds.

But consider for a moment if you had to choose whether seller actions or buyer signals are more impactful? Which matters most? After some thought, you'd likely land on buyer signals, because they are the outcome. That's the thing you are trying to achieve as you progress through the sale. These customer actions are what moves the *purchase* forward—not just the *sale*. Now, here's a different (perhaps more troubling) question:

Are seller actions or buyer signals the thing that is being tracked, right now, in your CRM to monitor pipeline health and forecast? For most organizations, it's the seller actions.

The traditional belief has been that seller actions naturally lead to a progression of the sale. So tracking seller actions is thought of as tracking customer purchase progress. So in a way, it's kind of the same thing, right? But as we've established across the balance of this book, given all the

FIG. 10.10. ADP's Buying Made Easy Purchase Process

	Buying Process	Seller Leads
Recognize Need	■ Recognize opportunity, risk, or needs ■ Make excuses to keep status quo ■ Research vendors; conduct initial meeting	■ Provide insight on opportunity ■ Make a case for change
Explore Options	■ Compare vendors ■ Compare and benchmark costs ■ Request additional information	■ Ask thought-provoking questions highlighting our strengths ■ Share case study for a similar company ■ Offer references
Define Criteria and Process	■ Evaluate current business processes against those proposed ■ Perform risk/reward analysis ■ ID and educate stakeholders ■ Define buying criteria	■ Conduct analysis to support value of proposed change ■ Show negative impact of status quo ■ Address stakeholder concerns ■ Present high-level options and pricing
Evaluate Options	■ Create business case for change with key stakeholders ■ Evaluate provider solutions ■ Create short list of final vendors	■ Provide value analysis ■ Provide demos and meetings with industry experts ■ Provide client references
Validate and Select	■ Evaluate presented business case ■ Validate ROI ■ Define requirements ■ Decide to proceed (or not)	■ Present formal proposal ■ Present final terms ■ Coordinate appropriate resources to be present at client site visit
Negotiate	■ Negotiate terms/procurement process ■ Secure final executive approval ■ Arrange legal review ■ Sign contract	■ Justify pricing by connecting value to revenue growth/cost savings ■ Review client implementation resources ■ Engage our legal team
Implement	■ Assign project team ■ Implement new solution; retire old processes	■ Introduce implementation team ■ Check in on key milestones in the implementation process
Evaluate Impact	■ Evaluate results of the solution against expectations	■ Get feedback and ask for referrals ■ Continue to provide new perspectives on ways to improve their business

1 The customer's buying process serves as the fundamental basis of the tool.

2 To help ensure the salesperson maintains control and assertiveness, a set of recommended seller steps is provided.

Source: Automatic Data Processing; CEB analysis.

Buyer Signals	ADP Enables
■ Verbally expresses demand for change ■ Commits to further explore	■ Sales process planning sheet ■ Client success stories that illustrate seller advantage
■ Commits to analysis with us	■ Questioning guides ■ Industry-specific case studies ■ Collateral, references, etc.
■ Shares decision-making process ■ IDs ultimate decision maker ■ Commits to seller demo ■ Commits funds	■ Analysis guide ■ Impact-of-not-changing calculator ■ Implementation success stories ■ Stakeholder guide
■ Provides required inputs to build a thorough proposal	■ Value analysis presentation ■ Meetings with industry experts ■ Client references
■ States we are the preferred vendor ■ Understands proposal details, desired impact, and financial implications	■ Proposal ■ Pricing & ROI presentation ■ Implementation and change management guidelines
■ Provides required implementation paperwork ■ Contract is completed and signed	■ Total value/ROI analysis presentation ■ Implementation checklist
■ Solution is implemented	■ Meetings with our legal experts ■ Meetings with implementation experts ■ Implementation plan and status updates
■ Provides referrals and references ■ Shows interest in our additional solutions	■ Client success story interview ■ Sales process planning sheet

3 Buyer signals are meant to be tangible and easily surfaceable in conversations with the customer.

4 Provide tools to support the customer in achieving their goals throughout the purchase.

emerging purchase dynamics, the consensus requirements, and the variability of decision making, this is no longer the case.

At ADP, the "Seller Leads" column is no longer considered the one path to closure but a description of many different possible paths. As a result, don't think of the Seller Leads column as the set of rules but rather a set of principles. These are suggested actions that might help the starting point for reps to apply their judgment to do what they believe is necessary in a particular situation to achieve the Buyer Signals that indicate purchase progress is being made on the customer's side.

The fourth column in the ADP process overview, "ADP Enables," notes the various sales enablement and customer enablement tools, which align to the various "Buyer Actions" that ADP's sellers are trying to elicit throughout the customer's purchase experience. In this way, ADP has created a unified approach for engaging customers through their purchase, supporting the moments where customers most need that support, and tracking progress of far more telling indicators of whether the deal is likely to happen or not.

The whole approach is predicated upon the "Buyer Actions"—very specific customer verifiers, which unequivocally signal the customer is moving forward (figure 10.11).

FIG. 10.11. Progression of Customer Buying Verifiers

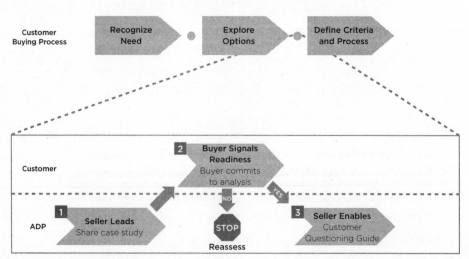

Source: Automatic Data Processing; CEB analysis.

For example, as the customer moves from exploring options to defining criteria, the expected customer verifier is for the customer to commit to an analysis to help refine their requirements. If the customer fails to commit to this analysis, the seller is instructed to stop all progress and reassess the situation. If, however, the customer commits to the analysis, the seller then provides the customer with a tool to support the next stage. In this case, ADP may provide a questioning guide that helps the customer determine what their purchase criteria *should* be. In this way, ADP's sellers are one step ahead (but only one step) of the customer, supporting the customer as they progress through their purchase experience.

For this approach to work, the customer verifiers have to be created in a special way (figure 10.12). First, they require active participation on the customer's part. In other words, a good verifier is not one where the customer could passively insinuate they're progressing. Instead, you want the customer to clearly state their intentions, take an action step, or otherwise signal their commitment to further explore a purchase. Second, good verifiers are clear, binary, and objective. In this way, they should leave little room for misinterpretation.

Otherwise you'll slip into a big debate about whether something is verified or not, and the power of a "customer-verified pipeline" will be lost. Finally, at least *some* of the verifiers (certainly not every single one) need

FIG. 10.12. Principles of Customer Verifiers

	What Does It Mean?	Why Is This Important?
1 Requires Active Participation	A discrete customer action at each stage of the customer buying process signals readiness to move forward.	Pushes customers to be upfront about deal status and demonstrates customer commitment to the purchase.
2 Binary and Tangible	A clear yes/no read on deal progress supported by the achievement of interim milestones.	Neutralizes risk of rep or manager biases skewing impressions and removes pressure-testing burden for managers.
3 Tests Willingness to Change	A clear signal, especially early in the sale, exhibiting customers' readiness and willingness to change.	Encourages demand creation, not simply response.

Source: CEB analysis.

to test the customer's willingness to change their current direction. These may include verifiers where the customer readily acknowledges the unnecessary costs their business is incurring, or commits resources to exploring the root causes of their business challenge. But in some way, shape, or form, you'll want to track the customer saying "we're currently doing this wrong and need help."

Shifting to a sales process that is governed by customer verifiers has a host of impressive results. ADP reported strong progress made on stalled deals initially run through this new "Buying Made Easy" process. These were deals that sales teams agreed were not moving prior to the program and then worked through this approach in the initial seller training. By assessing precisely where the customer was in their *purchase* process, ADP's teams were able to reassess what needed to happen to reinvigorate these opportunities. Managers were able to get a clear sense of where the customer was in their purchase process—not just where the rep reported the customer was in the sales funnel. For the first time it allowed managers to ask their reps two important questions during deal review sessions: (1) where is this deal? and (2) how do you know? Reps' ability to answer that second question changed tremendously with this practice. Other organizations that have relied upon this ADP best practice report significantly more accurate pipeline size and improved opportunity for deal coaching.

But there is an interesting and extremely important side benefit of tracking sales progress against customer verifiers. This practice allows for far greater seller judgment to be applied within the sale. By encouraging sellers to focus on the ends (the customer-verified outcomes that happen throughout the sale), not the means (the sales activities), sellers are better able to do what they need to do, naturally within ethical and moral boundaries, to help customers progress through the deal. In this way, sales managers and their sellers can exercise creativity without penalty. Adherence to a required set of sales activities gives way to creatively using insights to help customers recognize that they need to change and how they need to change.

Most sales organizations drive strict compliance to the recommended sales activities. There is a long-standing perception within sales that when marching opportunities through the funnel, despite naturally losing some along the way, a certain amount of business can be depended upon to make it through. The logic goes something like "as long as X number of opportunities are top of funnel, Y will ultimately find their way to conversion." So sales management focuses on driving compliance to a recommended set of sales activities. It's the sales machine, a pure volumetric approach to running sales. Sales activities, completed in sequence and in timely fashion, govern sales performance. The challenge with this approach is that in today's era of customer consensus, and all the variability of customer decision making that follows, the sales machine falls apart.

So what happens when you smash a sales process governed by strict compliance to recommended sales activities directly into the teeth of customer consensus? Customers working through difficult decisions are left by the wayside. "Good enough" customer decisions are accepted, even encouraged. Business nearing an RFP is prioritized over customers in a state of uncertainty. Invariably, commoditization ensues as there is little tolerance for helping customers get on the same page and make an ambitious decision for their business. Focusing your sales force on achieving customer verifiers of sales progress—the ends (even if they are interim ends), not the means—allows sellers to exercise greater judgment without sacrificing sales productivity and organizational visibility into the sales pipeline.

That leads to another significant benefit of tracking customer verifiers: namely, they're a heck of a lot more accurate for forecasting. Knowing precisely where a customer stands in their decision-making process, based upon their actions and commitments, is far more telling than a salesperson's estimate of when the deal is coming in. Again, ask yourself which you'd rather know about a given pursuit—which sales activities have occurred or which customer actions have occurred? One organization we worked closely with reported that by shifting away from sales activities to drive their forecasts and instead using customer verifiers, their forecasts became 70 percent more accurate. Initially, this was shocking to their leadership team and CFO, as the pipeline seemingly disappeared overnight. But this was merely overstated pipeline—most of which would never have come in anyway.

The Customer Verifiers for Today's Customer Purchase

We have partnered with numerous organizations to help them build their own version of the ADP best practice. In doing so, we've focused on accounting for the various principles we've explained throughout this book, ranging from shifts in sales behavior, to buying behavior, the role of the Mobilizer, and disruptive Commercial Insights. While the details of our Challenger sales process are too numerous for this book, following are some sample customer verifiers (figure 10.13) that will prove a great starting point for any organization interested in moving in this direction.

While a relatively simple five-stage customer purchase process is noted, feel free to adjust this as you and your organization see fit.

The first stage reflects customer learning. Customers are always in some state of passive learning. This includes reading articles, attending conferences, reading books, etc. The idea here is that customers are always

FIG. 10.13. Sample Customer Verifiers for the Challenger Sales Process

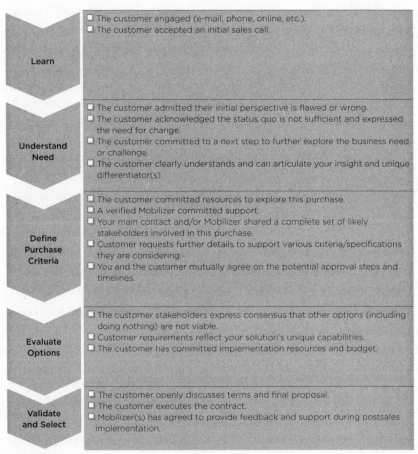

Learn	□ The customer engaged (e-mail, phone, online, etc.). □ The customer accepted an initial sales call.
Understand Need	□ The customer admitted their initial perspective is flawed or wrong. □ The customer acknowledged the status quo is not sufficient and expressed the need for change. □ The customer committed to a next step to further explore the business need or challenge. □ The customer clearly understands and can articulate your insight and unique differentiator(s).
Define Purchase Criteria	□ The customer committed resources to explore this purchase. □ A verified Mobilizer committed support. □ Your main contact and/or Mobilizer shared a complete set of likely stakeholders involved in this purchase. □ Customer requests further details to support various criteria/specifications they are considering. □ You and the customer mutually agree on the potential approval steps and timelines.
Evaluate Options	□ The customer stakeholders express consensus that other options (including doing nothing) are not viable. □ Customer requirements reflect your solution's unique capabilities. □ The customer has committed implementation resources and budget.
Validate and Select	□ The customer openly discusses terms and final proposal. □ The customer executes the contract. □ Mobilizer(s) has agreed to provide feedback and support during postsales implementation.

Source: CEB analysis.

looking for ways to improve their business and in search of new direction. This particular stage is relatively unique compared to the ADP best practice and incorporates a significant amount of marketing support and social selling to engage customers and "teach" them into the funnel (see Implication #3 in this chapter for more detail on social selling). The verifiers of this stage are merely customer willingness to take a live call—indeed, good verifiers don't need to be overly complex!

As customers progress through their purchase, they begin to better understand and refine their needs. The verifiers at this point largely center upon the customer acknowledging that their current beliefs, mental model, and state of practice are not sustainable or somehow flawed. Ideally, you are looking for your customer to show receptivity to your Commercial Insight and commit to exploring the implications for their business.

In the third stage, customers begin to define their purchase criteria. This is where a clear Mobilizer should be identified (preferably fairly early within this stage) and have committed their support to the purchase exploration. The customer committing resources to the exploration, as well as establishing some semblance of timelines, are important verifiers at this stage.

The fourth stage is where the customer evaluates their options. Stakeholders expressing consensus for a new direction becomes an important verifier for this stage. The customer's defined requirements should reflect your solution's unique capabilities as well.

In the final stage, the customer validates their selected supplier and enters into a signed deal. Gaining Mobilizer support to rally their colleagues for the implementation phase is a smart customer verifier at this point.

Tracking indicators such as these encourage the proper use of Mobilizers, Commercial Insights, Commercial Coaching, and a variety of other tactics we've discussed to this point. It ensures customers are well supported as they move through their purchase experience, while simultaneously understanding and acknowledging your company's unique capabilities.

Opportunity Planning

There are as many "flavors" of opportunity planning as there are sales consultancies. The best advice that we can lend is to use a method and use it consistently. We don't mean force march all sellers through a methodological opportunity-planning slog, but rather incorporate smart opportunity-planning principles into your sales process, your deal review sessions, your

CRM (via sales playbook software or by fields), etc. That being said, there are some important implications that today's consensus purchase highlights, which we think you should consider incorporating into your opportunity-planning approach.

You may be wondering why this brief opportunity-planning overview is seemingly relegated to the end of our review on sales process? Well, that precisely brings us to the first implication for opportunity planning. It should inextricably reflect the sales process and encourage sellers to consider the various ways and means by which they can obtain the customer verifiers we just discussed. It's remarkable how frequently opportunity-planning approaches encourage a completely different set—and sequence—of seller actions. Done well, it should be hard for your sales teams to distinguish between the process and the plan.

So what then *is* the difference between the two? Why have an opportunity plan at all? The answer is quite simple, though frequently overlooked: if the sales process captures the *what*, the opportunity plan captures the *how*. A sales process inherently is meant to capture what happened—particularly if it's based on customer-verified outcomes to track progress. As we just discussed, those are hugely important milestones that inform deal progress, forecasting, and resourcing, among other things. The opportunity plan, however, helps prompt sellers to critically assess how. How will they get to that next customer verifier and continue deal progression?

The notion of critically assessing how is why we think the best opportunity-planning approaches are based on questions. Forward-looking questions, which encourage a critical thinking mind-set based on whatever information (as limited as frequently is the case in a pursuit) is available. That brings us to the third principle of good opportunity planning, which is to base the plan on a series of such questions. Not just any questions, but a series of open-ended questions about the customer organization, the dynamics within that organization, the Mobilizer, and commercial opportunity itself. Here are some samples of the questions our Challenger Plan encourages sellers to consider as they prepare for each phase of pursuit. We share this not as a comprehensive overview but as a series of principles to incorporate into your opportunity-planning approach, your deal review session, and other coaching interactions that sellers and managers have.

LEARN STAGE: What need *should* this customer be learning about? What should be keeping this customer up at night? Here, sellers are encouraged to understand how the customer is currently mismanaging their business. In this stage, it's also important to understand whether or not the customer is aware of this need—that likely informs whether or not they've already conducted their own research. Will the seller have to initially shape or reshape the customer's demand? The thought process here encourages sellers to truly prepare for the initial sales calls with the customer.

UNDERSTAND NEEDS STAGE: How *should* the customer respond to this need? This is the stage where a disruptive insight challenges the customer's thinking—it's critical for sellers to plan for that conversation. Here, sellers are encouraged to consider a variety of ways to position their insight and tailor it for customer consumption. What might go wrong in that initial sales conversation? What reactions might the customer have? Good sales planning is just as much planning for the ideal as it is planning for the unexpected. Sellers also need to consider what the customer's reaction to the Commercial Insight meant and consider next steps based upon that initial sales call. Was healthy skepticism observed? Did potential Mobilizers reveal themselves? Did a potential Blocker tip her hand? If so, what does that mean as the sale progresses? This is key—it's not just *that* the customer responded, but is asking "What do I take from that? What should my next step be?"

DEFINE PURCHASE CRITERIA STAGE: How *should* the customer define the purchase criteria? Here, the opportunity planning heavily factors in the Mobilizer. Naturally, your Commercial Insight will have significant bearing on how the customer views the purchase criteria, but the Mobilizer will need to ensure that the nuanced details of the purchase criteria truly reflect that insight. Thinking through the best course of action for the Mobilizer's support here is critical. Sellers should be reflecting upon the purchase criteria that the competition will likely advocate and how the Mobilizer can then explain how that view is flawed or insufficient.

EVALUATE OPTIONS STAGE: How *should* the customer evaluate and reach consensus? Here, planning for Commercial Coaching interactions with your Mobilizer is the primary focus. Sellers should be considering what they'll commercially coach their Mobilizer on, how to tailor that coaching guidance, and how to arm the Mobilizer. This phase is all about considering how to get a "Collective Yes" from the customer stakeholders.

VALIDATE AND SELECT STAGE: How *should* the customer reach a final decision? Here, you'll want to consider how to arm the Mobilizer for any final objections he or she may encounter. In this final stage, as we already discussed, planning for the negotiable and non-negotiable aspects of the purchase must happen. Taking stock of how to achieve the ideal customer reaction is important, but almost always there will be a late objection or challenges in the negotiation. So taking stock of the negotiable aspects of the purchase well in advance matters tremendously.

Notice the key theme throughout these questions: how *should* the customer make their purchase. Each phase of planning encourages sellers to think through the ideal customer interactions, while realistically planning for the unexpected. These questions force sellers to think one step ahead. In this way, each customer interaction moves the deal forward—it's not merely an "information-gathering" interaction. Even in the face of limited information, the point is to critically assess what should happen and how to best make that action happen.

ACKNOWLEDGMENTS

PRINCIPAL CONTRIBUTORS

While this book has four authors on the cover, it is, like all CEB research, the product of an enormous team undertaking. At the top of the list of contributors are several individuals who, along with the authors, formed the core of the research team behind this work:

Eric Braun

Our longtime friend and colleague, Eric has been a driving force behind all our research on sales and marketing excellence for nearly the past decade. Eric serves as principal research leader for CEB Leadership Councils. In this role, Eric plays a critical thought partner, innovator, and steward to our teams through our lengthy research studies. His influence ranges from our initial research on Challenger Selling, to the Commercial Insight framework, to Mobilizers, to the content ecosystem, and the list goes on and on. Eric often serves in the thankless role behind the scenes, but, no doubt, Eric deserves significant credit for our research findings and holding the quality bar exceedingly high on our work.

Karl Schmidt

Kerstin, Liam, and Klara Schmidt

Karl serves as the practice leader overseeing the Marketing Leadership Council. Since joining the firm in 2012, Karl has quickly established himself as a thought leader in the B2B marketing space. He was the research team leader on the work detailing the consensus dynamic as faced by marketers, which is discussed at length in this book. Further, he's played a pivotal role in collaborating between our sales and marketing practice areas, specifically in areas related to consensus buying and demand generation. Karl has been a fantastic peer—ruthlessly focused on finding the right answer, challenging our teams to dig deeper, and producing fantastic research. Finally, when faced with a wealth of research, one of the most challenging decisions we face is determining the right angle to present all the work. We owe Karl a big thanks for helping frame this book around our main character—the Mobilizer.

Cristina Gomez

Isaac Liu

Cristina joined our team in 2012, just as *The Challenger Sale* started to gain traction in the market, and has masterfully picked up the torch. Cristina serves as the research director for the Sales Leadership Council, overseeing our sales research operations. Cristina's influence is marbled throughout this book, ranging from the challenges with customer consensus, to Collective Learning, to best practices for engaging Mobilizers and Blockers. Cristina embodies the spirit of collaboration across our sales and marketing research teams, serving as a valuable thought partner for all things B2B. She's penned our vast research surveys, analyzed the results hand in hand with our quantitative researchers, and surfaced best practices and tools to support the research. Cristina pushes our team to deliver the most cutting-edge sales research anywhere. A gifted coach, she's developed a tremendous research team and serves as a role model for others at CEB.

Anna Bird

Anna is the research director overseeing major research initiatives for the Marketing Leadership Council, having joined CEB in 2007. She led the study team that uncovered just how early and difficult consensus buying dynamics are for customer organizations. Moreover, Anna has been a key contributor in shaping how marketing teams need to work differently to address that early-consensus dynamic, in particular motivating and equipping Mobilizers to carry water on the supplier's behalf. Anna brings tremendous energy to our teams and continually pushes the creative boundaries of our work.

Shelley West

Shelley is currently a senior executive advisor with CEB's Marketing Leadership Council, spending her time advising members on the full range of marketing issues hitting CMO radar screens today, including Challenger and consensus purchase. Shelley also led the Marketing Leadership Council's research team on major studies of content marketing and the drivers of commoditization pressure discussed in this book, including customers' ability to learn on their own. Shelley is famously responsible for inserting the question into B2B buyer surveys that ultimately led CEB to the "57 percent" statistic—B2B buyers are, on average, 57 percent of the way through the purchase before they meaningfully engage supplier sales reps.

WITH SINCERE THANKS

Beyond the principal contributors to this research, there is also a long list of individuals and organizations without whose commitment and support this research and this book would have never seen the light of day.

First, we owe a tremendous debt of gratitude to the leadership of our firm, especially our chairman and CEO, Tom Monahan, our group presidents, Haniel Lynn and Warren Thune, and our group leader of CEB's sales, marketing, and communication practice, Molly Maycock, for their unwavering support of cutting-edge insights and this book itself.

Over the years, we've had the pleasure of working with many talented researchers, executive advisors, service delivery teams, and marketers, all of whom had a hand in producing, delivering, and productizing the research that went into this book. We wish to thank current team members Neha Ahuja, Dave Anderson, Mashhood Beg, Anthony Belloir, Anna Bird, Nathan Blain, Amber Bronder, Jessica Cash, Katie Castagna, Rufino Chiong, Scott Collins, Dave DeBuys, Evan de la Torre, Charlie Dorrier, Karen Freeman, Simon Frewer, Alex DF Gash, Peter Hawkins, Chad Hetrick, Matt Hoffman, Rick Karlton, Liam Kelly, Matt Kiel, Jonathan Kilroy, Jamie Kleinerman, Victoria Koval, Anja Leroy, Patrick Loftus, Martha Mathers, Matt McCance, Taylor Mitchell, Kelsey Nuttall, Peter Pickus, Lauren Schmidt, Andrew Schumacher, Courtney Schwartz, Zeke Sexauer, Stacey Smith, Jonathan Tabah, Alice Walmesley, Miranda Weigler, Jess Williams, and Spence Wixom for their contributions and support. We also wish to thank former team members Nicole Barbuto, Andrew Bastnagel, Chris Brown, Tim Bruno, Rory Channer, Alexandra Chiou, Jonathan Dietrich, Tom Disantis, Janet Dunne, Rob Hamshar, Timur Hicyilmaz, Michael Hubble, Wasim Kabir, Connie Kang, Andrew Kent, Alex Kloppenburg, Theresa Koerner, Rita Kokhanova, Ayesha Kumar-Flaherty, Lucia Litman, Aaron Lotton, Ted McKenna, Jasmine Sage, Max Schelper, Josh Setzer, Julia Shafer, Alex Tserelov, and Ian Walsh for their respective impact on our work over the past several years.

Outside of CEB, we of course owe tremendous thanks to a great many thought leaders in the sales and marketing space for influencing our thinking and serving as valuable sounding boards. While these individuals are too numerous to list (indeed, many don't fully realize their importance to us), the likes of Dave Brock, Dan Heath, Jill Konrath, Dan Pink, and Neil Rackham have been particularly influential and inspirational to our team.

At CEB, we are indebted to our members. Not only are they our customers, but they are our greatest source of inspiration and the very foundation of our product. They direct us to address their most pressing issues and give generously of their time so that we can learn how those issues impact their organizations. They allow us unrivaled access to their teams, customers, salespeople, marketers, managers, and peers, all in the spirit of understanding what drives commercial excellence in today's world. They push our thinking and challenge us to deliver breakout performance to their businesses. When called upon, these companies generously allow us to profile their best practices and tactics so that other members can avoid reinventing the wheel.

Within the global sales and marketing memberships, which number nearly 1,500 member organizations (and tens of thousands of sales and marketing leaders), we would like to specially thank a few of our current and former members for their above-and-beyond contributions to this research:

Kevin Hendrick, formerly of ADP, and his colleague Eddy South with ADP

Joanne Halle and Leah Quesada, and the sales training and marketing teams at Xerox

Jeff Lowe and the sales and marketing teams at SMART Technologies

Tom Cunningham and Pam Boiros and the sales enablement and marketing teams at Skillsoft

Charlie Treadwell and Bernadette Koscielniak and the marketing team at Cisco

Over 200 star-performing sales professionals and frontline managers who gave their time and shared their knowledge and expertise to inform this research

We would be remiss for not acknowledging the support of the many talented and dedicated professionals who helped guide this book through each phase of the journey: our agent, Jill Marsal of Marsal-Lyon; the energetic and supportive team at Portfolio, including our editor, Eric Nelson, who "challenged" our thinking on several occasions; head of marketing, Will Weisser, and publisher, Adrian Zackheim; our excellent design team led by Tim Brown; our PR and marketing teams at CEB, including Kelly Blum, Rob Chen, Laura Frisk, Yasaman Hekmat, Fletcher Jones, and Leslie Tullio; and last but not least, Gardiner Morse, senior editor at the *Harvard Business Review*, for his support in helping us to unveil several aspects of this work to the broader business community over the past few years.

The final thank-you is the most important one. This research and this book would never have been possible were it not for the support, sacrifice, and encouragement of our families. Brent would like to thank his wife,

Ute, for her boundless patience, love, and support; his parents, Joel and Annie, for imparting their passion for learning and keen powers of observation; and daughters, Allie and Kiera, for their endless hugs and limitless ability to keep all things in perspective. Wherever life takes you, may you grow up to embrace the single most powerful principle sitting at the core of this entire book, the power of empathy. But first . . . we're going back to Disney World.

Matt would like to thank Amy Dixon, his biggest fan, best friend, and loving wife for all of her encouragement and support. He'd also like to thank his four awesome kids—Aidan, Ethan, Norah, and Clara—who remind him that sometimes smiling and just going with the flow is more fun than challenging and taking control.

From Pat: For Melinda—my muse. For Gabriel, Kyrielle, Lyra, and Zoë—my pride. For Mom and Dad and Chris—my foundation.

Nick would like to thank his wife, Erika, for being the "Mobilizer" of the family, for her love, encouragement, and, most of all, keeping things fun; his son, Evan, for big squeezes, TTFs, and the gift that is watching a truly amazing person grow up. He'd also like to thank his parents, Cathy and Vern, and brothers, Jeremy and Mike, for their continued love, support, and wise counsel.

www.ChallengerCustomer.com

INDEX

Page numbers in *italics* refer to illustrations.